The Design, Implementation, and Audit of Occupational Health and Safety Management Systems

T0300311

Workplace Safety, Risk Management, and Industrial Hygiene

Series Editor

Ron C. McKinnon

McKinnon & Associates, Western Cape, South Africa

This new series will provide the reader with a comprehensive selection of publications covering all topics appertaining to the health and safety of people at work, at home, and during recreation. It will deal with the technical aspects of the profession, as well as the psychological ramifications of safe human behavior. This new series will include books covering the areas of accident prevention, loss control, physical risk management, safety management systems, occupational safety, industrial hygiene, occupational medicine, public safety, home safety, recreation safety, safety management, injury management, near miss incident management, school safety guidance, and other related areas within the Occupational Health and Safety discipline.

The Design, Implementation, and Audit of Occupational Health and Safety Management Systems
Ron C. McKinnon

For more information on this series, please visit: https://www.crcpress.com/Workplace-Safety-Risk-Management-and-Industrial-Hygiene/book-series/CRCWRPLSAFRK

The Design, Implementation, and Audit of Occupational Health and Safety Management Systems

Authored by
Ron C. McKinnon

CRC Press
Taylor & Francis Group
Boca Raton London New York

CRC Press is an imprint of the
Taylor & Francis Group, an **informa** business

CRC Press
Taylor & Francis Group
6000 Broken Sound Parkway NW, Suite 300
Boca Raton, FL 33487-2742

First issued in paperback 2023

© 2020 by Taylor & Francis Group, LLC
CRC Press is an imprint of Taylor & Francis Group, an Informa business

No claim to original U.S. Government works

ISBN: 978-1-03-257103-4 (pbk)
ISBN: 978-0-367-22690-9 (hbk)

DOI: 10.1201/9780429280740

Visit the Taylor & Francis Web site at
http://www.taylorandfrancis.com

and the CRC Press Web site at
http://www.crcpress.com

Contents

PART 2 Design, Implementation, and Audit of Occupational Health and Safety Management System, Safety Leadership and Organization Elements

PART 3 Design, Implementation, and Audit of Occupational Health and Safety Management System, Workplace Environment Conditions

PART 4   Design, Implementation, and Audit of Occupational Health and Safety Management System, Accident and Near Miss Incident Reporting and Investigation Elements and Processes

PART 5   Design, Implementation, and Audit of Occupational Health and Safety Management System, Emergency Preparedness and Fire Prevention and Protection Elements

PART 6   Design, Implementation, and Audit of Occupational Health and Safety Management System, Electrical, Mechanical, and Personal Safeguarding Elements

Preface

This book explains how to design, implement, and audit occupational health and safety management systems (SMS). These systems comprise a number of different activities and initiatives in the form of SMS elements, processes, and programs. More than 50 elements, processes, or programs are discussed in the chapters.

Rather than being seen as isolated activities, all these initiatives should be grouped and managed as a structured SMS. Each one of these SMS components should be driven by a written standard clearly indicating what should be done, how often it should be done, and who must do it. These standards should then be implemented as components, or elements, of a comprehensive SMS.

To monitor the achievement of health and safety goals and objectives prescribed in the standards, a system of internal and external SMS auditing is essential. This book gives practical guidelines on how to audit each of the elements discussed. It provides the reader with more than 50 example audit protocols to facilitate an audit.

With an international drive for organizations to achieve accreditation for health and safety management systems, this book is a useful tool to assist in the design, implementation, and auditing of a world's best practice SMS that will conform to national and international requirements.

Acknowledgments

This publication is based on 46 years of advising, guiding, implementing, and auditing safety management systems at many organizations in different countries. I thank those organizations and the people I have worked with for sharing their knowledge with me, and for the valuable lessons I learned from them. I also pay tribute to the safety pioneers who were my mentors.

For making this publication possible I thank my wife, Maureen McKinnon, who spent numerous weeks editing this manuscript. This support warrants my deep gratitude.

NOTE: Every effort has been made to trace rights holders of quoted passages and researched material, but if any have been inadvertently overlooked, the publishers would be pleased to make the necessary arrangements at the first opportunity.

Author

Ron C. McKinnon, CSP (1999–2016), is an internationally experienced and acknowledged safety professional, author, motivator, and presenter. He has been extensively involved in safety research concerning the cause, effect, and control of accidental loss, near miss incident reporting, accident investigation, safety promotion, and the implementation of health and safety management systems for the last 46 years.

Ron C. McKinnon obtained a National Diploma in Technical Teaching from the Pretoria College for Advanced Technical Education, a Diploma in Safety Management from the Technikon SA, South Africa, and a Management Development Diploma (MDP) from the University of South Africa in Pretoria. He received a Master's Degree in Safety and Health Engineering from the Columbia Southern University, Alabama.

From 1973 to 1994, Ron C. McKinnon worked at the National Occupational Safety Association of South Africa (NOSA) in various capacities, including General Manager of Operations and then Marketing. He is experienced in the implementation of health and safety management systems, auditing, and safety culture change interventions. During his tenure with NOSA, he gained valuable experience in the auditing of safety management systems in numerous countries.

From 1995 to 1999, Ron C. McKinnon was safety consultant and safety advisor to Magma Copper and BHP Copper North America, respectively.

In 2001 Ron spent two years in Zambia, introducing the world's best safety practices to the copper mining industry.

After spending two years in Hawaii at the Gemini Observatory, he returned to South Africa. He recently contracted as the principal consultant to Saudi Electricity Company (SEC), Riyadh, to implement a world's best practice safety management system (Aligned to OHSAS 18,001) throughout its operations across the Kingdom of Saudi Arabia, involving 33,000 employees, 27,000 contractors, 9 consultants, and 70 safety engineers.

Ron C. McKinnon is the author of *Cause, Effect and Control of Accidental Loss* (2000), *Safety Management, Near Miss Identification, Recognition and Investigation* (2012), *Changing the Workplace Safety Culture* (2014), and *Risk-based, Management-led, Audit-driven Safety Management Systems* (2016), all published by CRC Press, Taylor & Francis Group, Boca Raton, USA. He is also the author of *Changing Safety's Paradigms*, published in 2007 by Government Institutes, USA, with the second edition published in 2018.

Ron C. McKinnon is a retired professional member of the ASSP (American Society of Safety Professionals) and an honorary member of the Institute of Safety Management. He is currently a health and safety management system consultant, safety culture change agent, motivator, and trainer. He is often a keynote speaker at safety conferences and consults to international organizations.

Part 1

Introduction to Design, Implementation, and Audit of Occupational Health and Safety Management Systems

1 Introduction

OCCUPATIONAL HEALTH AND SAFETY MANAGEMENT SYSTEM

Modern workplaces call for a structured and sustained effort to reduce risk and consequent loss on an ongoing basis. Focusing on injury rates and reacting to safety losses is inadequate management control and does not contribute to making organizations safer places to work in. Implementing and maintaining a proactive structured occupational health and safety management system (SMS) is the only way to integrate health and safety into the day-to-day management of the organization. This will ensure ongoing processes and activities to identify and minimize risks taking place on an ongoing basis.

TERMINOLOGY

To understand the meaning of various terms and concepts used in this book, the following terms are explained:

OCCUPATIONAL SAFETY

Occupational safety is the identification and control of accidental loss before it occurs.

OCCUPATIONAL HEALTH

Occupational health refers to the identification and control of the risks arising from physical, chemical, environmental, and other workplace hazards in order to establish and maintain a safe and healthy work environment. Occupational health deals with all aspects of health and safety in the workplace and has a strong focus on primary prevention of hazards.

OCCUPATIONAL INJURY OR DISEASE

An injury is the bodily harm sustained as a result of an accidental contact. This includes any illness or disease arising out of normal employment.

LOSS

A loss is an unplanned, preventable waste of any resource, be it through injury, loss of time, damaged product or equipment, or loss of process.

DAMAGE

Damage is the physical harm to buildings, structures, equipment, product, process, and the environment normally caused as a result of an accident.

BUSINESS INTERRUPTION

A business interruption is a temporary delay in the work process as a result of an accident.

ACCIDENT (OFTEN CALLED AN INCIDENT)

An accident is an undesired event often caused by high risk acts and/or high risk conditions which results in physical harm, occupational illness, or disease to persons and/or damage to property and/or business interruption or a combination thereof.

NEAR MISS INCIDENT (NEAR MISS, CLOSE CALL, WARNING, OR NEAR HIT) (OFTEN CALLED AN INCIDENT)

A near miss incident is an undesired event which, under slightly different circumstances, could have resulted in harm to people, and/or property damage, and/or business disruption or a combination thereof.

OCCUPATIONAL HEALTH AND SAFETY MANAGEMENT SYSTEM (SMS)

An SMS is an ongoing activity and effort directed to control accidental losses by implementing and monitoring critical health and safety elements, processes, or programs on an ongoing basis.

SMS ELEMENTS

Elements of an SMS are components of the SMS that, when combined, constitute the complete SMS. Examples are risk assessment, inspections, hearing conservation, ladder safety, safety committees, and safety training.

ELEMENT STANDARDS (PROCESSES, PROGRAMS, STANDARDS)

Standards are written measurable management performances required by a structured SMS. They detail what must be done, how often it must be done, and who must do it.

SMS PROCESSES

An SMS process is a series of actions or steps taken in order to achieve a particular objective. Examples are the machine guarding process, risk assessment process, and safety orientation process. Processes are ongoing activities within the SMS and do not cease when the objective is achieved.

SMS Programs

SMS programs are a collection of planned activities and actions that constitute one element of the SMS and which have an objective. Examples are a hearing conservation program, safety training program, and off-the-job safety program.

2 The Philosophy of Safety

INTRODUCTION

Occupational health and safety (safety) is about the prevention of all forms of unintended or accidental losses. These losses could be in the form of fatal injuries, serious injuries, industrial diseases, or damage to property, products, and equipment.

Safety involves more than employees being injured as a result of undesired events, normally termed *accidents*. It also encompasses damage caused to equipment, installations, and the environment. Unfortunately *safety* and *injury* have become synonymous, and therefore the broader picture of the devastating results of accidental events are not always appreciated.

TIP OF THE ICEBERG

In safety, the serious injury only represents the tip of the iceberg. Below the waterline are numerous deficiencies and close calls that occur without consequence. Treating the tip of the iceberg is treating the symptom and not the cause. Often the cause is a weak control system caused by the absence of a structured safety management system (SMS), which should be integrated into the day-to-day management of the business.

Many misguided efforts have been directed toward employees in an effort to reduce accidental loss. These have proved ineffective, as the root cause of behavior, and of safety culture, lies in the organization's leadership and the systems and controls it puts in place to reduce total risk within the organization.

SAFETY PARADIGMS

Numerous safety paradigms also exist that hamper the progress of risk reduction by leading management down the wrong path. Internal company politics are also stirred by safety issues, and this too hampers positive action and acceptance of responsibility and accountability for safety.

The bottom line is that management at all levels are responsible for the health and safety of the organization, its employees, and its contractors, and can only fulfill that obligation by the implementation of a safety management system that is integrated into the existing management processes.

ACCIDENT CAUSATION

There are numerous loss causation theories, but one thing is agreed: accidents are normally a series of small blunders that result in some form of loss or disruption. They are caused and can therefore be prevented. This excludes acts of nature such as flashfloods, earthquakes, and other natural phenomena.

THE LUCK FACTORS

One factor that skews one's perception concerning accidents is that there are certain undefined factors that determine the outcomes of an undesired event. This means high risk behavior, or a high risk situation, may sometimes result in no loss. Nothing happens! Sometimes the consequence is of a minor nature. Sometimes the outcome is catastrophic. Many undesired events result in a close call, near hit, or near miss incident, where under slightly different circumstances a major loss may have been experienced. After many years of research into accidents and their outcomes, three Luck Factors have been proposed by McKinnon (2014).

> The high risk conditions and/or acts normally give rise to an exchange of energy and a contact which is the stage in the accident sequence where a person's body or a piece of equipment is subject to an external force greater than it can withstand, resulting in injury or damage, or both.
>
> A luck factor exists here because the high risk act or condition may only result in a near miss incident with no loss. A close call or close shave, as some would call it. There is no contact with the energy, no energy exchange, or the energy is insufficient to cause harm.
>
> Near Miss Incident Example
>
> Two employees working at an ore crushing mill were removing the heavy steel liners from the inside of the mill which stands about two storeys high. The common practice was to rotate the mill until the linings were at the bottom and once they were accessible at the bottom of the mill the retaining bolts were removed. Each lining weighed about 120 lbs. (260 kg). To free the linings, the mill was then rotated and gravity forced the linings to fall to the bottom of the mill where they could easily be removed. On this occasion a 3-foot long pry-bar was left in the bottom of the mill as it was rotated, and the lining fell to the bottom of the mill and struck the pry-bar causing it to shoot out of the mill like a missile. The flying bar missed the foreman by a few inches. He said he felt the wind on his cheek as it passed, narrowly missing him. Neither injury nor damage was recorded.
>
> This near miss incident explains the flow of energy which was the flying pry-bar. It missed the foreman, indicating that although there was a source of energy, there was no contact (with the foreman), and no exchange of energy, as there would have been, if it had hit the person. The reason it missed the foreman could be attributed to luck, or good fortune (p34).

RELYING ON LUCK

Once there is a contact and an exchange of energy, another luck factor determines the outcome of the exchange of energy. The result may be a serious injury, a minor injury, or simply property damage. In some cases the exchange of energy is below the threshold level of the recipient, and minor loss is experienced. It is far more beneficial to reduce risk by instigating controls via means of an occupational health and safety management system (SMS) than to rely on luck.

SAFETY MISUNDERSTOOD

Safety has been mostly associated with injury to employees, but contemporary research has shown that it affects more than employees in the workplace. It is a whole encompassing science that affects all of us at one time or another.

MANAGEMENT FUNCTION

Safety is a management science, a management function, and it is the responsibility of management. The key factor in health and safety management systems is management leadership and involvement. The safety management system must be initiated and supported by senior and line management. Only management have the authority and ability to create a safe and healthy workplace. This should be one of their prime concerns.

Health and safety systems that originate in and are maintained by the safety department will have little effect on the organization. It is estimated that about 10% of a company's problems can be controlled by employees, but 90% can be controlled by management. Most safety problems are therefore management problems. If managers can manage the intricate and difficult concept of safety, then they will be able to manage other aspects of management more easily, as managing safety enables them to be more effective. A management system is the framework of policies, processes, and procedures used to ensure that an organization can fulfill all tasks required to achieve its objectives.

THE PLAN, DO, CHECK, ACT METHODOLOGY

One process approach, based on the *Plan, Do, Check, Act* methodology, has six steps starting with the safety and health policy, followed by its planning, implementation, and operation, and after that, the checking and necessary corrective action. The last step is the management review of progress, and this cycle leads to a continual safety improvement process.

ISSMEC

The ISSMEC (*Identify, Set Standards of Accountability and Measurement, Measure, Evaluate,* and *Correct*) management technique is also often used as a framework for health and safety management systems. Setting standards refers to standards of measurement, as well as standards of authority, responsibility, and accountability. Corrective actions are called for once deviations are highlighted and commendation is given for compliance to standards.

SAFETY AUTHORITY, RESPONSIBILITY, AND ACCOUNTABILITY

Occupational health and safety starts at the top, is supported by the top, and is led by top management. The success or failure of the organization's safety efforts falls directly on the shoulders of the management team. The logical place to begin the SMS process is therefore by clearly defining each manager's level of safety authority, safety responsibility, and safety accountability. This is where positive safety leadership begins – with each manager being allocated safety authority, responsibility, and accountability for the SMS implementation in their area(s) of responsibility. This authority, responsibility, and accountability should also be clearly defined for all levels of employees as well as contractors, union officials, and other relevant parties.

Safety Authority

Authority in general is the right or power assigned to an executive or a manager in order to achieve certain organizational objectives. Safety authority is formal, specified authority which gives a manager the authority to act in the name of the sponsoring executive or on behalf of the organization.

These powers of authority are normally spelt out in the manager's, employee's, or contractor's position charter or job description. This is why it is vital to have updated and accurate position charters for all positions, as this is where safety authority is allocated. All SMS standards should include responsibility and accountability clauses.

Safety Responsibility

Safety responsibility is the obligation to carry forward an assigned task to a successful conclusion without accidental loss occurring. Safety responsibility is a heavy burden. With responsibility goes the authority to direct and take the necessary action to ensure success. Safety responsibility is also the obligation entrusted to the possessor, for the proper custody, care, and safekeeping of property or supervision of an individual or individuals.

Safety Accountability

Safety accountability is when a manager is under obligation to ensure that safety responsibility and authority are used to achieve safety and legal standards. It means being liable to be called on to render an account or be answerable for decisions made, actions taken, outcomes, and conduct.

Although these descriptions refer to management, they are applicable to all levels within the organization and also refer to executives, contractors, union members, and employees.

WHAT GETS MEASURED GETS DONE!

Traditionally, the only measurement of safety that is used as a key performance indicator is the workplace injury rate. This is a lagging indicator and only tells management where they have been. Risk assessment, on the other hand, is a predictive tool and tells management where they are going.

A formal SMS is comprised of a number of elements, actions, processes, and programs that all have a built-in performance indicator that can be measured by the audit process. What gets measured, gets done! By relying on audit results which examine and score the multitude of programs and processes within the SMS, management get a realistic measurement of its risk reduction opportunities and actions. This is far more reliable than relying on injury rates alone.

A STRUCTURED APPROACH

Designing and implementing a comprehensive SMS is a structured approach to safety management, and results in safety activities being integrated into the day-to-day management, rather than having it as a stand-alone component. As a stand-alone component safety only receives attention after an accident.

OCCUPATIONAL HEALTH AND SAFETY MANAGEMENT SYSTEM (SMS)

To guide management in controlling areas of potential loss and to set standards, an SMS provides an excellent framework. These are sometimes referred to as structured *safety programs*, but the preferable term is *occupational health and safety management system*, as it follows a system's approach to preventing loss. An SMS prescribes certain elements, processes, and programs that offer opportunity for risk reduction, and gives details of what should be done on an ongoing basis to maintain workplace risk as low as is reasonably practicable.

An SMS is a formalized approach to health and safety management through the use of a framework that aids the identification and control of health and safety risks. Through routine monitoring, management reviews, and audits, an organization checks compliance against its own documented SMS, as well as legislative and regulatory compliance. A well-designed and operated health and safety management system reduces accident potential and improves the overall management processes of an organization.

BASED ON RISK

The SMS must be a risk-based system. That means it must be aligned to the risks arising out of the workplace. Emphasis on certain SMS elements, processes, and programs will be different according to the hazards associated with the work and the processes used. There is unfortunately no one-size-fits-all SMS that will be ideal for all mines, industries, and other workplaces; therefore SMSs should be seen as a framework on which to build a risk-specific system for the industry. The main aim of any SMS is to reduce risk; therefore it must be aligned to those risks.

MANAGEMENT-LED

The SMS must be initiated, led, and supported by senior management as well as line, front line, and union management. The key factor in any SMS is management leadership.

DRIVEN BY AUDIT

Health and safety is an intangible concept and is traditionally measured after the fact – once a loss has occurred. The SMS must be an audit-driven system. This calls for ongoing measurements against the standards and quantification of the results via an auditing process. What gets measured usually gets done.

An SMS converts safety intended actions into proactive activities, and assigns responsibility and accountability for those actions in a way that is very similar to how a manager manages subordinates.

INTEGRATED SYSTEM

The most proactive, positive, and sustainable way to eliminate workplace risks and their devastating consequences is to integrate SMSs into the day-to-day management of the organization. Sometimes incorrectly referred to as *safety programs*, SMSs are a structured, management-led, and risk-based approach to risk reduction and accidental loss prevention.

INTEGRATED SMS SYSTEMS

Some organizations choose to integrate their SMS with the environmental management system, the quality control system, the reliability system, or a combination of all these. This results in an integrated safety and health, environment, quality, and reliability system (SHEQRS). While this may suit some organizations, many elect to keep occupational health and safety management as a separate system.

3 Designing an Occupational Health and Safety Management System (SMS)

THE DESIGN

An occupational health and safety management system (SMS) is the framework of policies, processes, programs, and procedures that are integrated, and which function as a whole, to ensure that an organization can fulfill all the tasks required to achieve its health and safety objectives.

It is an ongoing activity and effort directed to control accidental losses by monitoring critical health and safety elements on an ongoing basis. The monitoring includes the regular promotion, improvement, and auditing of the critical elements. An SMS identifies and treats accident causes, NOT symptoms.

A FORMALIZED APPROACH

An SMS is a formalized approach to health and safety management through use of a framework that aids the identification and control of safety and health risks. Through routine auditing, an organization checks compliance against its own documented SMS, as well as against legislative and regulatory compliance. A well-designed and operated SMS reduces accident potential and improves the overall management processes of an organization.

The design of the SMS is based on the risk of the processes within the organization, and the type of workplace in question. Many elements, processes, and programs of an SMS are common to many workplaces, but some are unique to certain industries or mines.

The design should include all planned and work-related activities, internal and external issues, the expectations of employees, legal requirements, and the needs and expectations of other interested parties.

ELEMENTS, COMPONENTS, PROCESSES, OR PROGRAMS

This book provides information on many SMS elements, components, processes, or programs, and offers guidance on which elements may be applicable to a specific workplace. Many are basic but are essential processes nevertheless, and cannot be ignored simply because lack of control over a specific safety element has never resulted in an accident. All basic processes must be in place to form a sound SMS. A rule of thumb is that if the element is applicable, it must be incorporated. If ladders are used at the workplace, for example, then a ladder safety program is needed as part of the SMS.

ENERGIES

During the design phase, management has to consider the risks and risk reduction opportunities appertaining to, for example:

- The energies involved in the process
- The raw materials used
- The inputs and outputs
- Chemicals manufactured, stored, or used
- Employees involved in processes
- Contractors deployed
- Off-site installations
- The environment in which the plant is located

SOURCES OF HAZARDS AND HAZARD BURDEN

Sources of hazards should be identified and documented in a risk register that is modified and updated regularly. This will direct the design and requirements of the SMS as the system must be focused around reducing risks arising from the workplace and its activities.

When measuring the hazard burden, the following questions should be asked:

- What are the hazards associated with our activities?
- What is the significance of the hazards (high/low)?
- How does the nature and significance of the hazards vary across the different parts of the organization?
- How does the nature and significance of the hazards vary with time?
- Is the organization succeeding in eliminating or reducing hazards?
- What impact are changes in the business having on the nature and significance of hazards?

HAZARD IDENTIFICATION AND RISK ASSESSMENT (HIRA)

Identifying hazards and the hazard burden within the organization is the first step in the Hazard Identification and Risk Assessment (HIRA) process. A number of hazard identification methods can be used, and, as with other safety processes, these are ongoing activities.

RISK ASSESSMENT

To help determine the potential probability, frequency, and severity of loss which could be caused by hazards, the technique of risk assessment is a major element in the health and safety management system.

The steps of risk assessment are:

- Hazard identification
- Risk analysis
- Risk evaluation
- Risk control
- Re-assessment

The risk management process is:

- To identify all the pure risks within the organization and which are connected to the operation (*hazard identification*).
- To do a thorough analysis of the risks, taking into consideration the frequency, probability, and severity of consequences (*risk analysis*).
- To implement the best techniques for risk reduction (*risk evaluation*).
- To deal with the risk where possible (*risk control*).
- To monitor and re-evaluate on an ongoing basis (*re-assessment*).

MANAGEMENT FUNCTIONS

The management functions of planning, leading, organizing, and controlling are all accomplished by the introduction and maintenance of an SMS which is integrated with the normal management of the organization.

THE PRINCIPLES OF SAFETY PLANNING

The design phase of the SMS is accomplished by management planning and its components.

THE MANAGEMENT FUNCTION OF SAFETY PLANNING

Safety planning is what takes place to schedule the implementation of an SMS by determining what must be done and when it must be done. It is the process of thinking about the activities required to achieve the desired goal of implementing a comprehensive SMS. Safety planning is the first and foremost activity to achieve desired results. It involves the creation and maintenance of a plan that includes timelines and milestones for SMS implementation.

SAFETY FORECASTING

Safety forecasting is a planning tool that helps management to cope with the uncertainty of the future, relying on data from the past and analysis of trends. Past safety trends could predict future safety performance, and by forecasting, management can form a picture of how the SMS will impact the opportunity for risk reduction in the future.

Safety forecasting is the predictive activity a manager carries out to estimate the probability, frequency, and severity of accidents that may occur in a future time span.

Good forecasting tools are risk assessment, critical task identification, and task risk assessment.

SAFETY BUDGETING

Safety budgeting is the allocation of financial and other resources necessary to achieve the safety objectives of the policy statement. A budget allocation may be required for repairs, machine guarding, and other upgrades. Training costs, the purchase of correct personal protective equipment (PPE), and other items must be budgeted for.

SETTING SAFETY OBJECTIVES

Setting safety objectives is when management determines what safety results they desire. This would include incorporating a formal, structured, and integrated SMS safety system into the organization.

Safety objectives should be upstream objectives and could include:

- Number of safety inspections to be done per week
- Employees trained in safety issues monthly
- Number of SMS element standards written per annum
- Degree of SMS standards implementation
- SMS audit scores
- Number of health and safety representatives trained and appointed
- Number and quality of contractor inspections
- Number of hazards eliminated
- Number of risk assessments completed

Time Related

The implementation of a fully-fledged SMS may take up to 5 years, depending on what systems and programs the organization has in place at the time of implementation. This means that many objectives set will be time related and will include complete implementation over a period of time, sometimes years.

Systems that have been in place for less than 6 months are not considered completely functional, and should not be considered for audit purposes. Bearing in mind the more than 70 programs, systems, and processes that constitute the SMS, it is clear that it must be introduced step-by-step to avoid the principle of resistance to change, that is, the faster the change is brought about, the more resistance it will face.

SETTING SAFETY POLICIES AND STANDARDS

Safety policies are a deliberate system of principles to guide decisions and achieve planned outcomes. They are statements of intent as they are implemented as a procedure, process, or protocol. The safety policy statement is the leading safety statement of intent that guides the activities of the SMS.

Setting safety policies is when a manager and his or her team develops standing safety decisions applicable to repetitive problems which may affect the safety of the organization. Policies, standards, and procedures for the SMS are drafted, circulated, and implemented with the objective of achieving the intent of the safety policy statement. Each SMS element calls for a written policy, standard, procedure, or program, and together these constitute the organization's SMS.

SAFETY PROGRAMMING

Safety programming is establishing the priority, and following the order, of the safety action steps that must be taken to reach the safety objective stated in the policy statement. This would call for a decision on which safety standards should be implemented first, and the order in which other standards are to be implemented.

SAFETY SCHEDULING

Safety scheduling is when time frames are established for the implementation of the elements of the SMS. This could include which elements are to be written first, and by when they are to be implemented. Many activities need to be scheduled, for example, safety inspection schedules and training dates.

ESTABLISHING SAFETY PROCEDURES

Establishing correct safety procedures is when certain tasks are risk ranked and analyzed, and safe work procedures (Job Safe Practices) (JSPs) are written for performing the work. Based on a risk assessment, the tasks can be risk ranked and the critical tasks identified. This will help prioritize the writing of procedures. There are numerous procedures within the SMS, and these need to be written. Training in the procedures must take place, and procedures should receive periodic review and update.

SUMMARY

The design of a SMS should be aligned to the risks of the organization and should consider employees, contractors, and other internal and external issues. Existing safety processes and standards must be incorporated into the system, and legal health and safety requirements should be the basic standard to achieve. SMS standards can exceed legal requirements but must not be less than such requirements. The design must be planned and scheduled, and an implementation roadmap developed.

4 Implementation of an Occupational Health and Safety Management System (SMS)

Before implementing an SMS, the organization should establish the status of existing health and safety controls and identify what standards, systems, and processes are in place and which are working, which need review, and which are non-existent. The implementation of an SMS is a challenging task and may take years to complete, depending on the existing controls.

BASELINE AUDIT

A baseline audit against a given standard, such as ANSI Z10.1 (American National Standards Institute) or ISO 4501:2018 (International Organization for Standardization) or similar guideline, will indicate where there are gaps in the existing SMS. A legal compliance audit will also indicate where the SMS should be improved.

Once the elements, processes, or programs needed have been identified, they need to be implemented into the organization. This is normally done by establishing written standards, policies, or procedures covering what must be done, who must do it, and how often the action must be done. These documents are referred to as health and safety management system standards (SMS standards).

SMS ELEMENT STANDARDS

All SMS element standards should have an objective and must set standards of performance, as well as a standard of responsibility, for the actions prescribed. All standards must be monitored, updated, and communicated to all interested parties.

Element standards must have a number and a title as well as a minimum standard and minimum standard details. The minimum standard is always the legal requirements. SMS standards can exceed the minimum requirements of safety laws but must never be lesser than that.

Example:

Element Number: Element # 41
Element Name: Machine guarding

Minimum Standard: Machines must be guarded

Minimum Standard Detail: rotating shafts, v-drives, pulleys, drive belts, conveyors, and fans must be guarded.

IMPLEMENTATION ORDER

The order in which the SMS elements are implemented will need to be decided. Many organizations believe that the highest risk elements should be implemented initially. Another school of thought is to start with the safety tangibles. This means implementing those elements that create a neat and tidy workplace first, which in turn helps to create business order. Creating a safe, neat, and orderly workplace is a short-term objective and one that is relatively inexpensive to achieve. The impact of business order, however, is great.

Training and coaching of employees may be a long-term process. Other elements may take more resources and time, and the benefits will not be seen in the short term. A good housekeeping program, for example, can change the workplace in a short period of time and has a positive effect on employees within that workplace. This is tangible safety. Employees can see safety changes being made. Cleaning up the workplace also cleans up the thought processes of people in the workplace. Once there is good business order, other less tangible elements can be introduced.

A plan for the implementation process should be compiled, indicating what will be done, who will be responsible, and what resources will be needed. Completion dates are essential. Methods of evaluating the progress and results should be included.

SAFETY PLAN

Some regulations call for safety plans to be available for the organization or specific aspects or elements of an SMS.

A safety plan is a written document that describes the health and safety intent of an organization. It could be specific to an organization or be customized for special projects. Based on a risk assessment process, it lists the hazards likely to be encountered and the SMS controls in place to reduce them. The written safety plan is a blueprint for keeping workers safe. The safety plan also lists health and safety responsibilities and could include emergency procedures, including steps to take when an accident occurs.

BASIC MANAGEMENT FUNCTIONS

It is generally accepted that a manager's main functions are:

- Planning
- Organizing
- Leading or directing
- Controlling

The four basic management functions are applied during the implementation of an SMS. These functions entail the management of employees, materials, machinery, and processes as well as the management of risk. As with daily management within an organization, the implementation and management of the SMS is facilitated by applying these functions.

THE FUNCTION OF SAFETY PLANNING

Safety planning, as discussed in the previous chapter, consists of:

- Setting health and safety objectives
- Safety forecasting
- Setting safety policies
- Safety programming
- Safety scheduling
- Safety budgeting
- Establishing safety procedures

THE FUNCTION OF SAFETY ORGANIZING

Safety organizing is what management do to arrange the work to be done to implement the SMS most effectively, by the right people. Setting up the SMS would also involve allocating persons to coordinate the SMS, to carry out inspections, to purchase safety equipment, to chair safety committees, to nominate health and safety representatives, first responders, accident investigators, and so on.

Integrating Safety into the Organization

Integrating safety into the organization means that safety activities, processes, and programs are integrated into the normal daily management processes of the organization. The SMS should not be regarded as a standalone system, divorced from normal operations. The more the SMS is integrated into the organization, the better the safety control becomes.

Safety Delegation

Safety delegation is what a manager does to entrust safety responsibility and give safety authority to his or her subordinates, while at the same time creating accountability for safety achievements. All employees will be given the authority to participate in the SMS processes and programs such as the reporting of hazards, participation in safety committees, and taking part in safety inspections.

Managers allocate safety work to be performed by the various levels of employees within the organizational structure, to implement and maintain the SMS. This includes writing safety duties and functions into the position charters of all levels of management and employees.

Creating Safety Relationships

Creating safety relationships is done to ensure that safety work is carried out by teams with utmost cooperation and interaction amongst team members. The SMS must be owned by all levels in the organization. The system requires participation, support, and action from all levels within the organization, contractors, and interested parties, and cannot be left as one person's or one department's or one manager's responsibility.

The Function of Safety Leading

Safety leading is what a manager does to encourage people to act and work in a safe manner. It entails taking the lead in safety matters, making safety decisions, and always setting a safety example. This is one of the most important management functions in implementing and maintaining an SMS. Safety leading involves visible felt management leadership by:

- Chairing health and safety committees
- Participating in inspections
- Attending safety presentations
- Visiting the shop floor
- Visible felt leadership

Making Safety Decisions

Decisions need to be taken when committing to a comprehensive SMS. These decisions may be based on the existing SMS status and the work and timelines required to improve the SMS. Decisions concerning resources, both financial and in terms of manpower, also need to be made.

Safety Communicating

Safety communicating is to give and get understanding of health and safety matters. Management and employees' expectations concerning participation in the SMS must be clearly communicated. Standards must be set and communicated to all concerning the requirements of their role in the SMS process.

Feedback on SMS activities can either make or break the momentum of the system and is an essential part of such a system. Employees will be skeptical of any new safety innovation and will constantly test the system. A formal communication system that ensures employees are constantly informed of the SMS progress is essential.

Many organizations have an internal intranet network which contains the SMS standards, the policy statement, and other pertinent information relating to the SMS. This keeps employees informed. Safety committees and other forums are also used to communicate information.

Motivating for Safety

Motivating for safety is the function a manager performs to lead, encourage, and enthuse employees to take action and partake in the SMS process. Acknowledgment of achieving certain milestones and objectives will ensure employees and contractors remain involved in the process.

Appointing Employees

Appointing employees is a function whereby management ensures that the correct employees are selected for certain positions. It further involves appointing employees to their roles as participants in the SMS.

Developing Employees

A manager develops employees by helping them improve their safety knowledge, skills, and attitudes. They should ensure that health and safety department staff are up to date with the latest trends in safety and risk management, and that there is an ongoing self-development program in place for them. Further studies, as well as membership in local, regional, and national safety associations, should also be encouraged.

Health and safety training would form an element of the SMS, and an objective should be set to ensure that all managers attend a basic program on safety management and that employees receive more than just the basic safety training required by legislation.

THE FUNCTION OF SAFETY CONTROLLING

The implementation of the SMS would be facilitated by the management safety control function. Safety controlling is the management process of identifying what must be done to implement the SMS, inspecting to verify completion of work, evaluating, and following up with safety action. The safety controlling function has seven steps:

Identification of the Risk and Safety Work to be Done to Implement an SMS

Based on risk assessments in his or her areas of responsibility, a manager lists and schedules the work that needs to be done to implement a suitable structured SMS, based on global best practice. This, in turn, will lead to a healthy and safe work environment and will help eliminate high risk acts and high risk work situations. The SMS should be based on the nature of the business as well as risk-based, management-led and audit-driven. Implementation strategies and timelines must be applied as per the SMS planning phase.

Set Standards of Performance Measurement

SMS standards are "measurable management performances." Standards are set for the level of work to be done to implement the system. Standards should be established in writing for all the SMS elements, processes, procedures, or programs. Performance levels are included in the standards document. Without standards, the SMS has no direction, nor are safety expectations established. (If you don't know where you're going, any road will take you there.)

Standards of performance could be, for example:

- The health and safety committee is to meet once a month.
- Safety inspections are to be carried out on a weekly basis.

- 80% of all employees must attend safety training per annum.
- Audit scores will be 50% in year one, 60% in year two, 70% in year three, and 100% in year four.
- Risk assessments must be done daily.
- Housekeeping (business order) to be maintained at 95% on a weekly basis.

Set Standards of Accountability

Management now sets standards of responsibility by delegating authority to certain positions for ongoing safety work to be done. This creates responsibility and subsequent accountability. Coordination and management of the SMS elements, processes, and programs needs to be allocated to certain departments and individuals, and these standards dictate who must do what, and by when, to implement and run the system. Each SMS element standard must include and indicate safety responsibility and accountability. This also entails allocating certain SMS elements to selected employees or departments, and making them responsible for the coordination of those elements. For example:

- Machine guarding (Engineering Department)
- Fire extinguisher maintenance (Fire Department)
- Employee selection (Human Resources Department)
- Ergonomic program (Industrial Hygienist)
- Cranes and lifting gear (Rigging Department)
- Monthly health and safety inspections (Health and Safety Representatives)

While workers at all levels of the organization should assume responsibility for those aspects of the SMS over which they have control, specific responsibility may be delegated as the example listed above.

Measure Against the Standard

By carrying out safety inspections, the actual condition of the workplace and the ongoing activities of employees are now measured against the accepted SMS standards. Physical inspection of the workplace offers a method of measuring the workplace conditions against the standards.

What gets measured gets done. If there is no formal system of measurement, then management does not know how well the SMS is performing, compared to its own standards and best practice. Conformance to standards set by management is a good indicator of a functioning SMS. For example, it can be determined if employees are doing monthly area inspections, critical task procedures are being followed, and so on.

Evaluation of Conformance

Depending on which measurement method is used, the results are now quantified in the form of a percentage allocated, marks given, or a ranking established. Safety audits, both internal and external, evaluate compliance with an organization's standards. Scores allocated indicate whether there is a deviation from the prescribed standards set, or whether compliance to standards has been achieved.

Periodic management reviews of the SMS also evaluate the degree of compliance to the standards.

Corrective Action

The amount of corrective action will be proportional to the amount of deviation from standards set. Corrective action may involve enforcing the safety standards and taking the necessary action to regulate and improve the methods used.

Once again, standards are established for these corrective actions and they state who must do what and by when, in order to get the situation rectified. Corrective action must be positive, time related, and assigned to responsible persons.

Corrective actions could include the better communication of goals, objectives, and standards to ensure they are understood. More effective training may be required, coupled with more feedback on safety performances so employees know where they stand. Procedures, standards, programs, and processes may have to be modified or improved.

Commendation

Managers commend by paying compliments to employees for adherence to an achievement of pre-set SMS standards or achievement of safety objectives. Employees enjoy being acknowledged for a job well done. Recognition for desired behaviors should be introduced. The awarding of a traveling trophy for good housekeeping, for example, creates a lot of enthusiasm and excitement. Since people are competitive by nature, introducing competition will help put some excitement into safety. Annual safety award presentations where certificates are awarded should be a part of the SMS process and can do more good than many other initiatives. Awards should not be based on injury-free criteria, but rather upstream achievements.

PLAN, DO, CHECK, ACT METHODOLOGY

Another management method that can be used to implement and monitor the progress of the SMS is the *Plan, Do, Check, Act* Methodology.

The Plan, Do, Check, Act (PDCA) cycle, also known as the Deming circle, is a four-step model for carrying out change and continuous improvement. Just as a circle has no end, the PDCA cycle can be repeated for continuous improvement. This repetitive management method is used in business for the control and continuous improvement of processes, and is also a recommended method for the implementation of safety management systems.

- *Plan* – involves determining the risks and opportunities concerning health and safety. Establish the objectives and the processes and actions necessary to deliver results in accordance with the expected outputs. Action plans are compiled and policies and critical safety performance indicators are established to meet the requirements of the health and safety policy statement. This is the SMS *design* stage.
- *Do* – the phase where information is collected, the plan is implemented, the SMS processes started, training commences, and SMS standards are set and implemented. This is the SMS *implementation*.

- *Check* – when inspections and measurements against the standard take place. This phase involves monitoring, inspection, audit, measurement, and review. This is the SMS *inspection*, *audit*, and *review* stage.
- *Act* – when corrective action is initiated to rectify deviations from planned achievements. Processes are amended, modified, and improved to create a system of continual improvement. This may entail reimplementation and modification of elements or training and application of processes. Action plans are compiled to rectify weaknesses in the SMS. Safety work is delegated and timelines for completion set. This is the SMS *action* stage.

IMPLEMENTING PROGRESS MONITORING

The progress of the SMS implementation must be plotted and recorded and progress measured on a simple 20%–100% scale, or similar. Possible criteria could be:

- Has the standard been written?
- Has it been approved by the Standards Committee?
- Has it been approved by the Executive Safety Committee?
- Has a checklist or other supporting documentation been written?
- Have employees been trained in the standard's contents?
- Have standard revision dates been set?
- Has the standard been made known to all via the intranet and other means?
- To what degree has the standard and its requirements been implemented in practice?

This tracking process should be applied to all the elements of the SMS, so that targets can be set for the writing, approval, and training in the standard and its implementation progress (Figure 4.1).

	NAME OF ELEMENT / STANDARD / PROCEDURE / PROGRAM (Element Number and Title)e.g. ELEMENT # 3.12 Ergonomics	20 %	40 %	60 %	80 %	100 %
1	Safety Management System Standard Written					
2	Approval by Standards Committee					
3	Standard Approved by Executive Safety Committee					
4	Checklist Compiled or Support Document Approved					
5	Training of Employees in the Standard / Procedure or Program					
6	Revision Dates Set					
7	Standard Posted on Intranet, Incorporated into SMS Documentation					
8	Degree of Implementation of the Standard (Rank 20% – 100%)					

FIGURE 4.1   Safety Management System Implementation Progress Report.

5 The Audit of Occupational Health and Safety Management Systems (SMS)

A safety audit is traditionally carried out by an outside team and examines all safety facilities and risk-reduction activities of an organization. The audit assesses the current level of risk reduction and loss prevention and subsequently helps in the preparation of an action plan to upgrade, modify, and improve health and safety inputs.

WHAT IS AN SMS AUDIT?

An SMS audit is a critical examination of all, or part, of a total health and safety management system (SMS), and is a management tool that measures the overall operating effectiveness of the SMS. An audit provides the means for a systematic examination and analysis of each element, process, procedure, and program of an SMS to determine the extent and quality of the controls. It confirms that management controls are in place to reduce risk, and that these controls are working. An audit measures the SMS effectiveness and highlights its strengths and weaknesses.

NOT A SAFETY INSPECTION

An SMS audit is not simply a safety inspection but rather a complete process of reviewing the SMS standards and their application and effectiveness in the workplace. The audit does include an inspection, which is the physical verification of the application of the standards in the workplace, and culminates in a review of the standards, policies, and programs during a formal documentation review session.

According to the Royal Society for the Prevention of Accidents (ROSPA) *Health and Safety Audits e-Book*:

> Safety audits are an essential part of a successful business. Effective health and safety auditing not only provides the legal framework for compliance, it also lays the foundations for continuous safety improvement to enhance competitive advantage. The main duty of any health and safety auditor is to look at your organization's safety management systems and assess them in line with the chosen criteria.

> Whilst an audit is used to assess Health and Safety management systems, it is important to view an audit as a positive – it's a chance to highlight company successes and an opportunity to praise staff for their excellent work. (p.5)

According to *Types of Safety Audit and Effectively Conducting Them* (2017):

> A health and safety audit is a planned, independent and documented examination of an Occupational Health and Safety Management System intended to evaluate the standard of controls and effectiveness of such system under evaluation. It is a proactive approach to measure health and safety performance of the organization. It helps in developing criteria for further improvements in organizational strengths along with the identification and control of organizational weaknesses. It provides a platform for taking effective planning decisions. (www.ask-ehs.com)

REACTIVE VERSUS PROACTIVE MEASUREMENT

Information on injury experience is reactive and is *not* control. Injury rates are lagging indicators and only measure the consequences of a weak or non-existent SMS. Since they are measurements of consequence, largely dependent on fortuity and integrity of reporting, they do not accurately reflect risk-reduction efforts. SMS audits measure both upstream and downstream indicators. They measure the amount of control an organization has over its risks. Since the majority of accidental events do not result in injuries, using their data as a sole safety gauge does not show the complete picture. More meaningful information is obtained from systematic inspection and auditing of physical safeguards, systems of work, rules and procedures, and training methods than from data about injury experience alone. Audits measure safety *effort*; injury rates measure safety *failure*.

SUBJECTIVE VERSUS OBJECTIVE

Audits of the SMS must not be subjective, which refers to personal perspectives, feelings, or opinions entering the decision-making process. This may be as a result of inexperience or some personal agenda with the organization being audited.

Audits should rather be objective, which is the elimination of subjective perspectives and a process that is purely based on hard facts. As with accident investigations, they should be fact-finding exercises and *not* fault-finding exercises.

BENEFITS OF SMS AUDITS

The concept of self-regulation is virtually accepted with the advent of the "performance standard" and "duty of care" approach. It is this obligation to self-regulate that reinforces the importance of an effective audit process as an essential management tool.

Well-structured and conscientiously conducted audits provide an objective view of the actual SMS status. They identify weaknesses, recognize successes, evaluate compliance, and determine the adequacy of standards, policy, and procedures against statutory requirements and organizational and world-class standards.

Further benefits of SMS audits include that they:

- Highlight the strengths, weaknesses, opportunities, and threats of the SMS.
- Measure the degree of conformance to regulatory requirement.

- Compare what is being done is against what was intended to be done.
- Help in the prioritization of corrective actions.
- Assist in the compilation of a detailed report on the SMS.
- Compare the organization's SMS with world's best practice.
- Facilitate a continuous improvement process.

A LEARNING OPPORTUNITY

SMS audits are a learning opportunity and should be viewed positively. Sometimes the word *audit* conjures up an image of a painful experience, and this should not be allowed to happen. The knowledge and experience of the auditors will be shared with the organization's staff, and they will make a positive contribution to the health and safety efforts. They also have the advantage of coming from the outside and may see deviations/problems/defects that employees in the workplace have become familiar with and have accepted as the norm (i.e. they can't see the wood for the trees).

TYPES OF SMS AUDITS

BASELINE AUDIT

This is more than likely the first formal and thorough audit an organization will experience. The audit of the existing health and safety system will be audited against world's best practice in health and safety. Regulatory requirements will be considered the minimum standard for this audit, and world's best practice health and safety standards will be the benchmark standard. Guidelines such as OHSA 18001, ISO 45001:2018, and ANSI Z-10 can also be used to reflect world class standards. Audit protocols are essential, and substantial work is required to compile audit protocols to measure and quantify compliance with these standards.

Records and Verification

The baseline audit can only be accurate if all pertinent documentation and records appertaining to health and safety systems in operation at the time of audit are available for scrutiny after the audit inspection. Employees who manage safety related issues should also be available to answer the auditor's questions.

Who Should Conduct the Baseline Audit?

The baseline audit should be carried out by a suitably experienced SMS auditor who has been exposed to world's best practice health and safety systems, and who has experience in auditing them. The auditor should ideally be accompanied by an assistant auditor who also has extensive knowledge of world's best practices in health and safety and the auditing thereof.

INTERNAL SMS AUDIT

Internal audits should take place every 6 months and be conducted by internal employees who have been trained in health and safety and in auditing techniques.

The organization must establish the impartiality and objectivity of the audit by ensuring that the audit role is separated from the employee's normal function. In some instances, health and safety staff from neighboring organizations or sister companies are invited to conduct these audits.

INDEPENDENT AUDIT (EXTERNAL THIRD PARTY)

Independent or external third party audits should take place annually. They should be conducted by expert agencies comprising well-trained, experienced lead auditors, technical safety experts, SMS audit specialists, and others. Organizations must give them full freedom to judge neutrally and independently without exercising any influence from any quarter. Objectivity becomes the key motto, and their disclosures are to be taken as bare facts, based on which further lines of correction and improvements are to follow.

COMPLIANCE AUDIT

A compliance audit is an audit to measure compliance with local regulatory requirements. The main question to be asked during a compliance audit is, "Does the organization comply with the requirements of the legal health and safety regulations?"

CENTRALIZED AND DECENTRALIZED SMS COORDINATION

In an organization with different departments that are physically decentralized from the head office, those departments would manage their own SMS on a decentralized basis. Head office would maintain a centralized version with elements that cover the entire organization. Together, both would comprise the company SMS.

Centralized elements would include:

- Health and safety policy
- Newsletters
- Employee pre-employment medicals
- Company safety goals
- Executive health and safety committee

Decentralized elements would include:

- Housekeeping
- Permit to work systems
- Appointment of health and safety representatives
- Safety inspections
- Motorized transport safety

AUDITABLE ORGANIZATION

Before any SMS audit, it should be determined if the organization represents an auditable unit. To qualify as such, the organization to be audited should be geographically, organizationally, and operationally together. The organization should be able to sustain and maintain a comprehensive safety system of 70 or more elements. Outlying offices, workplaces, depots, and other worksites are included in the audit and form part of the organization for audit purposes.

A comprehensive audit of a warehouse (as an example) that maintains only a few elements of the SMS, as they are the only elements applicable and are required due to the nature of the activities of the warehouse, is not feasible. The disadvantage of this is that if they are audited against fewer elements and the larger divisions are audited against the complete SMS, comparisons of scores are unrealistic and inaccurate. This unfair comparison could lead to upsets.

SOLUTION

A possible solution is to have different levels of audit protocols. For example:

- A main 70+ element audit protocol for the main organization.
- A 40 element audit protocol for smaller divisions such as an autonomous branch or division away from the main organization that maintains a smaller scale SMS.
- An office audit protocol for distant offices that are not geographically close to the main organization. The protocol is designed for offices and contains the relevant applicable elements.

These three levels of audit protocol will help enable each workplace to be audited against applicable standards. All workplaces should be audited using the elements that are applicable to them.

NON-AUDITABLE UNITS

Audits of small off-site depots or sub-stations which are unstaffed most of the time make it hard for them to be audited as separate units, as many elements of a safety management system are not applicable to these depots. These depots are therefore regarded as non-auditable units. Small depots with two or three employees are also regarded as non-auditable units, and while they need to be inspected and to conform to the SMS, they are not suitable for fully fledged audits. Where possible, should these smaller, outlying depots and warehouses form part of the larger organization, they should be inspected and included in the complete audit of the organization and not be audited separately.

PAST 12 MONTHS

The audit can only quantify the work done during the 12 months before the audit. The audit cannot measure future improvements, innovations, or amendments. It can only measure what was done and achieved during the last year. No recognition or score can be given for future intentions.

Elements, processes, and programs that have not been in operation for at least 6 months cannot be allocated a 100% score. These processes must have been in place, and operating, for at least a year to qualify for full marks.

REVIEW OF ELEMENT STANDARDS

A copy of each element standard should be available for the auditors to review. Element standards and their verification documents are normally kept in a file or folder which is opened for each element. This file could be in an electronic form. What is important is that all information pertaining to the element is stored in the folder or file, and updated as the SMS progresses.

DOCUMENT CONTROL SYSTEM

A document control system, which is an element of the SMS, must ensure that updated and revised documents replace the old, outdated documents as soon as possible, and that all employees are informed of the update or change.

INCOMPLETE VERIFICATION

Documents that are not signed where required will indicate a system breakdown. Incorrectly completed checklists or risk assessments should be identified as weaknesses in the system as well. The auditors must ensure that the verification matches what is happening in the workplace. If a system was followed during the inspection, the requested documentation should be requested and checked. The main question auditors should ask is, "Is there a process in place, and is it working?"

The audit protocol will guide the auditor as to what questions to ask and what verification to call for to verify that the actions are taking place.

AUDIT FREQUENCY

Both the frequency and extent of the audit will be based on the complexity and level of maturity of the SMS. Changes in the workplace, legal requirements, or an increase in work-related injuries and illnesses may call for more frequent audits. The following are guidelines on audit frequency under normal circumstances.

VERIFICATION

Audits establish the adequacy of the SMS and ascertain if it has been implemented appropriately in relation to the risk and nature of the business. Audits determine whether or not the controls being applied are suitable and how they fit the organization, its operations, and existing culture. Most importantly, the audits measure the effectiveness of the SMS and its contribution to the achievement of stated health and safety goals.

AUDIT PROTOCOL

An audit protocol is a vital audit tool. It guides SMS auditors and helps them audit against a specific standard. It facilitates comparing the company against its own standards. The audit protocol should be compiled to cover the company SMS standards. This means it summarizes the requirements of the standards into measurable and auditable elements, minimum standards, and minimum standard details. It also establishes an element risk ranking dependent on the degree of risks that elements, processes, or programs pose, or their contribution to risk reduction.

WHAT TO LOOK FOR

The protocol identifies what must be looked for during the inspection, what questions to be asked during the system verification meeting, and what documents, or verification, need to be reviewed. It indicates what elements must be followed through the system, and the processes that need to be examined. The protocol allocates a score for each minimum standard detail of each element and allocates a ranking, or score, to each element for scoring purposes. The audit protocol ensures that the auditors evaluate and measure each and every element of the SMS, and that each detail is scrutinized and each requirement ranked or scored.

WHO SHOULD CONDUCT AUDITS?

Experienced and qualified auditors are essential if the audit process is to be successful. Auditing a workplace and exposing its controls for evaluation is not an easy thing to do, and the process could lead to some supervisors being sensitive to criticism. The auditors must be professional at all times and ensure that the employees in the areas being audited see it as part of a learning experience. Compliments must be paid wherever possible. Leading questions should be asked, and the shop floor employee should be made to be a part of the audit, not a subject of the audit.

AUDITOR'S TRAINING

While it is difficult to prescribe exactly what training and experience an auditor should have, it is imperative that the person has a health and safety background and has been trained in auditing techniques. As a minimum, over and above the person's professional training, the following classes would be recommended:

- The Basics of Safety Management – 8 hours
- Practical Risk Management – 8 hours
- Accident and Near Miss Incident reporting and investigation – 8 hours
- Critical Task Identification and procedure writing – 8 hours
- Legal requirements – 6 hours
- Internal Accredited Auditor's Workshop – 40 hours

Once these classes have been attended, the aspiring auditor should accompany a qualified auditor on at least three audits. Depending on how the aspirant auditor performs during these audits, he or she could then be accepted as an internal accredited auditor.

GUIDELINES FOR AUDITORS

The audit should be regarded as a learning experience. Criticism should be avoided and a positive approach should be taken. Be factual and do not find fault. Professionalism is a must. The organization is exposing its workplaces and employees to scrutiny and the experience must result in a rewarding experience for them. Always pay compliments where possible. Offer positive advice and recommendations.

Auditor's Experience

While there are formal training programs for both internal and external auditors, years of experience is vital before an auditor can be fully effective. The auditor should know their subject thoroughly and be able to impart his or her knowledge in a professional way.

The auditor should have experience in implementing as well as auditing an SMS. Knowledge of the workings of SMS elements is important, as is knowledge and understanding of management principles and practices. Being an auditor, one would expect the auditor to be a professional member of a health and safety body and hold acceptable certifications.

Internal audits can be very political, and extra caution is required to select and train the correct people as auditors and to ensure they remain unbiased at all times.

Lead Auditor

The lead auditor is an auditor that leads the audit and is assisted by other auditors. The lead auditor should have extensive audit experience and must be able to conduct the audit in a professional manner.

Questioning Techniques

Questioning techniques are important to derive as much information as possible in the short time allocated. Questions should be asked during the inspection, and auditors should do most of the listening.

Compliment

To keep the audit on a positive note, auditors should complement adherence to standards where possible. Areas in the workplace that exhibit good housekeeping should receive praise.

6 The Safety Management System Audit Process

ALL SMS ELEMENTS

All elements of the safety management system (SMS) must be considered during the audit. The verification process should start with the first element of the SMS and proceed until all elements have been audited. Nothing should be assumed or taken for granted. If a particular item was not seen during the inspection, information on that item should be obtained during the documentation verification meeting. It is important for the auditor to endeavor to examine all items during the inspection, otherwise they must give the organization the benefit of the doubt when it comes to scoring the element.

For example: The storage of flammable substances was not examined during the inspection. The storage site and methods can be discussed during the review, but the organization cannot be penalized for what was not seen. Points cannot be subtracted for the storage if the storage area was not inspected.

AUDIT PROCESS

The external audit is a formal, scheduled event and includes the following:

AUDITORS

Once an audit is agreed upon, suitable auditors need to be appointed or selected. Careful selection of auditors is essential as in the past, so-called auditors have played down all the effort of the SMS implementation in order for their company to get the consultancy contract for the implementation of the SMS. Credible auditors who are qualified in health and safety should always be the first choice.

DATES AND TIME OF AUDIT

The dates and time of the audit should be agreed upon. The scope of the organization that is to be audited should be made known so that sufficient time can be allocated. A suitable boardroom or training room should also be made available for the opening and closing conferences. This venue should have suitable projection facilities to project the electronic verifications on a central screen for the auditors to view.

Audit Duration

There is no hard and fast rule for the amount of time which an audit takes. For large organizations, this could be up to five days. For example, this would be allocated as follows:

Day 1: Opening conference and inspection of the head office buildings
Day 2: Inspection of central manufacturing and operational areas
Day 3: Employee interviews, contractor sites, and outwork inspections
Day 4: Control document verification
Day 5: Close-out conference

Audits of small companies could use two days for the inspection and one day for the verification session and feedback meeting. Duration will differ from one organization to another depending on the size, nature of the business, and geographical location of the workplace.

Office Space

Office space should be provided for the auditors to store their equipment and for any administration work they need to do while on the premises. This would include the post-inspection meeting, note taking, and recording. They also need a private venue to discuss the feedback and score allocation after the verification session.

Pre-audit Documentation

At least two weeks before the audit, the organization should submit a docket of pre-audit documents to the auditors. This documentation should include an organization structure, a site plan of areas to be inspected, a brief description of the processes, an example of the safety policy and standards, loss statistics, examples of inspection reports, and a number of other documents needed to answer questions before the audit. This will save a lot of time during the audit.

The Audit Protocol Document

The auditors must be guided by an audit protocol. The protocol contains the same elements as the SMS and includes what to examine, what questions to ask, and what verification to scrutinize to ensure the intent of each element is fulfilled. Notes taken during the inspection are listed next to the element for discussion during the verification conference. The scores for each minimum standard of the element (as per the protocol) are not allocated during the inspection. They are only allocated when the element has been reviewed and all relevant verification documentation has been scrutinized.

A Guide for Auditors

The audit protocol is a guide for the auditors which helps them to audit against a specific standard. The audit protocol should be drawn up to cover the standards of the

SMS. This means that it summarizes the requirements of the SMS standards into measurable and auditable elements, identifies documents which need to be reviewed and
processes to be examined, and allocates a score to each element for scoring purposes.

Protocols can be written to cover all aspects of a company's SMS so that when
audited, the system is audited against its own standards.

An audit protocol document should contain the following:

- Name of standard and process
- Minimum requirements and minimum standard details
- What to look for during the inspection to measure conformance
- Instructions as to how to test the system
- The evidence required for the element details
- Questions to ask during the verification process
- The scoring scale for the minimum standard details

Audit Protocol Weighting

Each minimum standard detail is rated on a 1–5 scale. The total score of the element,
for example, could be 50 points. Each element of the SMS should have a weighting
dependent on the risk posed or risk-reduction opportunity offered. Due to the hazardous nature of unguarded machines, electrical terminals, machine guarding, fall
protection, confined space entry, and other high risk elements, these could possibly
rate 10 on a risk ranking scale of 1–10. For example, this means that the adjusted
maximum score would be 50 points (maximum) × 10 (risk ranking weighting) = 500
points for the element for scoring purposes.

Not Applicable Elements

Audit protocols should be in line with the SMS standards for the operation. In some
cases, certain elements, or minimum standard of an element, may not be applicable
to the operation being audited. Once the auditors agree that the specific requirement
is not applicable, either the allocated points for the item must be subtracted from the
total maximum score, or full points must be allocated for the non-applicable element
item. In practice, it is sometimes easier to allocate full marks to that particular item
if it is not applicable and cannot be scored.

For example, during the audit documentation review, a minimum standard detail
calls for an excavation permit system. There are 5 points allocated to this requirement. If the organization never has a need to excavate, has never excavated, and
never will excavate, then it is simpler to mark the requirement non-applicable and
allocate the full five points. It must be clearly established that an element is not applicable before allocating full points.

Opening Meeting

The opening meeting will include welcomes and introductions of the organization's
staff and of the auditors. This is normally followed by a presentation by the company

of their SMS achievements and highlights. Many organizations have a short video clip containing a snapshot of the company's SMS, which is shown to the auditors.

INSPECTION ROUTE

The inspection route is planned at this stage and would include:

- High risk work areas
- Workshops
- Contractor's worksite
- Electrical substations
- Canteens and restrooms
- Process areas

The route should include visiting worksites where lockout is required and where critical tasks, such as confined space entry, are in progress. Any work at heights, or any other critical areas where permits are required, should also be on the inspection list. It should be agreed that the planned route will give the auditors a good idea of the company and workplace processes.

AUDITOR GUIDES

To keep the inspection team as small as practicable, the group then decides who will accompany the auditors as guides during the inspection. These staff members should have keys and access to all areas within the plant. One accompanying member should be appointed to take notes during the inspection. The auditors should obtain permission should they wish to take photos.

SAFETY ORIENTATION

Before embarking on the inspection, the auditors should be subjected to the normal safety orientation required for visitors to the plant. This should include the issue of personal protective equipment or clothing that they may require on the inspection tour.

STAY TOGETHER OR SEPARATE?

There is the idea that if the auditors split up for the inspection, more ground will be covered during the inspection. This may be true, but experience has shown that during the feedback and verification conference, the other auditors cannot relate to feedback from a different inspection team. One auditor sees different thing to the other, and this does not lead to an effective audit. One auditor will want to follow one system that he or she identified during the inspection, which leaves the other auditor in the dark, as they did not see the same thing. It is recommended that the auditors stay together as one inspection team, so that they see the same things and measure the application of the same elements during the inspection.

INSPECTION

The inspection of the work environment, processes, and installations is a key part of the audit. During the inspection, the application of the SMS standards at shop-floor level will be measured.

AREAS INSPECTED

Where possible, all areas of the workplace should be inspected. In a big operation, random samples should be taken to ensure maximum coverage. Offices should also be included in the inspection. Sometimes a route has been preplanned for the inspection. It is always good to deviate from this route and inspect areas off the route to get a good idea of the conditions.

NOTES

The auditors must take notes during the inspection. After a few days of inspecting, it will be impossible to remember the observations made and questions that need to be answered. Experienced auditors have developed a technique of short cryptic notes that they use to note observations. If possible, photographs can also be taken and used as discussion points during the conference.

FOLLOWING THE SYSTEM

It is of vital importance for the auditors to follow and test the safety systems during the inspection. They should enquire where critical tasks are being carried out – for example, tasks that require lockout activities – and ask to inspect where the work is being done. They should then follow the system to the place where the source of energy has been isolated. They should examine the lock, the label, the labeling of the isolator, and other features to judge if the isolation was done in accordance with the energy control standard.

If the standard states that all lifting gear is to be inspected every three months, for example, the auditors must follow the system and inspect lifting gear during the inspection to ascertain if it has been checked. Making a note of a piece of lifting gear during the inspection and then asking to see the checklist during the documentation review is following an item through the system.

EMPLOYEE INTERVIEWS

During an audit, employee interviews must be planned well in advance. The interviews should be open and friendly and will give the auditors an insight into how the SMS is perceived from an employee standpoint. Certain programs can also be confirmed during the interviews. Examples are safety training, employee participation in the SMS, safety communication, and others.

If possible, the inspection should include a visit to the area where confined-space activities are underway. The work and precautions should be examined, and the permits used (if applicable) should be scrutinized. If there are queries, the auditors should request that copies of the permit be made available during the verification session.

CONTRACTOR SITES

Contractor sites should be inspected to ascertain if they conform to the SMS requirements. Observation should be made of the housekeeping of the site; the condition of equipment used, such as lifting gear; the posting of warning signs; and other elements of an SMS. The auditors could request that that particular site's documents be made available during the verification meeting.

Inspections and discussion take time, and the audit inspection should have a timetable to ensure that all areas to be inspected are inspected. Too much time spent in one area will result in a hurried inspection of others.

SAFETY RULES

The safety rules should be followed at all times during the inspection. Appropriate personal protective equipment (PPE) should be worn by the auditors, and if there is any uncertainty, the guides accompanying them should be consulted. During the inspection, the auditors should not put themselves in any danger and should always consult the guide should they wish to enter an area or building. They must set the safety example at all times.

Employee Interview Guidelines

Interviews with certain employees take place during the inspection phase of the audit. A time and place should be arranged for these interviews, and the employees selected could be health and safety representatives, union representatives, element coordinators, or workplace employees. It should be decided who will be interviewed during the opening conference.

The auditors should prepare questions to be put to the employees. They should preferably be open questions which will allow the interviewee to do most of the talking. The interview must be positive, and the questions posed must be information-gathering questions, for example: "How do you think health and safety can be improved here?" or, "What are the biggest hazards in your work area, and how are they controlled?" Another question could be, "How is safety communicated to the workforce here?"

These are positive, open questions that the interviewee will not object to answering. They will also tell the auditors a lot about the employee's perception of the safety processes and programs.

VERIFICATION MEETING AND DOCUMENTATION REVIEW

Once the inspection is completed, the verification review takes place. This should begin on the day after the inspection to allow the auditors to compile and arrange their notes and prepare for the verification meeting.

DOCUMENTS AVAILABLE

To enable a successful audit, all documents, checklists, and other pertinent documents must be made available in the documentation verification venue. This may entail setting up a computer for screening e-documents for the auditors to review.

NO PAPER, NO POINTS!

If a verification document is not produced, maximum points cannot be allocated for that element. All relevant controls, standards, processes, and programs must be supported with verification documents, registers, attendance lists, and so on. Starting from element number one of the SMS, each verification method or document should be identified and made ready for examination. The audit process should start at the first element and proceed in the order of the elements. An absence of, or missing, documents will result in the element not being able to be verified, and thus not being able to obtain full points.

FEEDBACK

During each element verification, the auditors should report on what they found appertaining to the standard during the inspection. Where a program or process was found to be working, they should compliment the organization. Recommendations on improvements, concerns, and opportunities for enhancing the SMS must be given after each element is reviewed. The auditors then enter their score on the protocol. It is important that auditors score the element immediately, while the evidence is still fresh in their minds. Waiting to allocate scores at a later stage is not advised.

AUDITOR'S CAUCUS

Once all the elements have been reviewed and verifications examined, the auditors hold a short meeting to discuss the audit findings and to determine a final percentage for the audit. A list of strengths, weaknesses, threats, and opportunities for the SMS is agreed upon for the close-out meeting.

Each auditor should allocate their own scores during the verification meeting. During the auditors' caucus meeting, the final scores are tallied, the average found, and the final score determined. It is of vital importance that a score to be given at the end of the review of each element.

SCORING TECHNIQUE

Each auditor has different areas of specialty and will see different aspects during the audit inspection; therefore, each auditor's score will differ. The best scoring method is to add each auditor's final scores together and determine an average. This will then be the final audit score.

CLOSE-OUT MEETING

This is the audit feedback session, and it should be a learning process for the organization being audited. Should the auditors wish to prepare a short close-out presentation for the close-out and results, this will add to the professionalism of the audit.

The meeting should start out with the auditors thanking the organization for the hospitality and cooperation that they received. Individuals should also be thanked for their help during the audit. Element coordinators should also be thanked for the presentation and preparation of their elements.

The strengths of the SMS should now be delivered, with emphasis put on the positive findings. These comments could be about the participation of employees in the SMS, the management leadership observed, the neatness of the work areas, the good control over critical tasks, or other elements that stood out as being excellently controlled.

The weaknesses of the SMS are delivered after the strengths have been presented. Concerns noted by the auditors are discussed with possible solutions offered. The auditors must always present the weaknesses in a factual manner and back up the statements with evidence noted during the audit.

Opportunities for SMS improvement are presented next. Positive examples of where the SMS can be improved are given, and specific elements for improvement are listed. Elements that scored below 50% should be included in the presentation of opportunities. A mini action plan should be suggested at this stage, which will be followed up in detail in the audit report.

The audit score is now revealed. The organization should be congratulated on the score achieved. The auditors then thank the management team and all present in the room for the participation in the audit and for the preparation of the verification documentation, and should then hand control of the meeting to the senior representative of the organization, who will thank the auditors and the participating staff.

REPORT

The audit should be followed up by the submission of a comprehensive audit report. This document should list every element and give the findings of the audit for that element. It must be a comprehensive report. The strengths, weaknesses, opportunities, and threats (SWOT) should be stated in the report as well as the final scores and the proposed action plan (Figure 6.1)

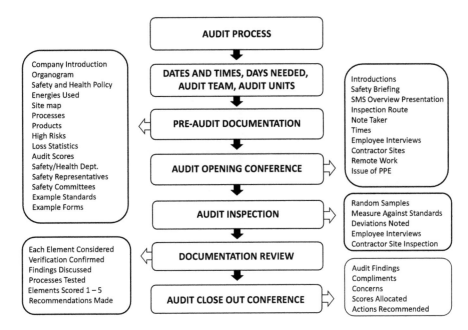

FIGURE 6.1 The Audit Process.

7 Management Principles that Apply to the Implementation of an SMS

A MANAGEMENT FUNCTION

Occupational health and safety is a management function and management's prime responsibility. It entails management leadership and the application of sound management principles and practices. These are essential for the successful implementation of a safety management system (SMS). Some of the most important principles are discussed here, as well as their application in the safety process.

SETTING SAFETY OBJECTIVES

The speed, efficiency, and motivation to implement the SMS is increased if the work is directed towards pre-set safety objectives.

This is often referred to as Management by Objectives (MBO). Management must know what they want to achieve and decide what work is necessary to achieve the safety goal. Safety responsibility must be assigned, and the work relationship must be clearly defined in relation to the safety objectives. The safety policy statement provides a framework for the setting of safety objectives. Objectives for the implementation of the SMS must be time related, practical, and achievable and must allocate responsibility.

Example: The electrical foreman must implement an arc flash protection program within the next 12 months. The risk assessments must be completed within three months, labeling is to be completed during the eighth month, and training of all relevant personnel is to be done within nine months. Suitable protective clothing is to be sourced during the fifth month. The standard to be completed and the complete program must be in place by the twelfth month.

RESISTANCE TO CHANGE

The introduction of safety standards and procedures that differ from the way things were done in the past tends to be met with resistance by the employees involved. The most common comment heard when introducing a new safety concept is, "But we've tried this before ...."

Introducing an SMS is a change that creates an insecure environment. Introduction of safety standards, procedures, and new programs requires adequate preparation and a sound implementation strategy, including timelines and milestones. The best way to introduce a comprehensive SMS is to do so element by element. The smaller the changes, the smaller the resistance to the change.

POLITICS

It has been said that health and safety management is 10% work and 90% politics. The introduction of new standards and procedures will evoke internal politics. Safety is an issue that many resist, as it is a heavy responsibility that is traditionally dumped onto the safety department. Many managers abscond their safety responsibilities and blame employees for any accidental event. Making leadership responsible for safety within their areas of authority creates resistance fuelled by political agendas.

By using the principle of participation and application, resistance to change can be overcome.

COMMUNICATING SAFETY

The more employees and contractors are informed about the safety requirements and achievements, the more they are motivated to participate in safety and accomplish safety results.

Effective communication improves motivation. Reasons should be given as to why certain actions have been taken, why an SMS is being introduced, and how it will be implemented. Highlights, objectives achieved, and safety achievements must be communicated to the entire workforce. Progress of the SMS implementation and goals achieved should be shared on a regular basis. Contractors, interested parties, and the board of directors should also receive this information. A separate SMS element that focuses on safety communication and information sharing is essential.

International SMS guidelines also require organizations to establish, implement, and maintain a process for consultation and participation of workers at all levels and functions. Unions and other worker representation bodies should also be involved in the development, planning, and implementation of the SMS. Employees should also be encouraged to participate in the evaluation and improvement of the system.

PARTICIPATION AND MOTIVATION

Safety motivation increases in proportion to the amount of participation of the people involved. Employees, contractors, and all levels of management must participate in the SMS and its processes.

The SMS calls for the involvement of all management and employees. The various safety programs and processes should involve them all. They should be informed of the facts at all times, and they should be asked to give input and suggestions on aspects of health and safety that directly or indirectly concern them. The more they are involved in the safety process, the more they will participate.

SAFETY DEFINITION

Solutions can only be forthcoming once the real problem is identified. SMSs should treat safety problems and not safety symptoms. Decisions concerning the SMS can only be made if the basic causes of loss-producing events are clearly identified.

Often, directing efforts to the rectification of immediate causes of an accident wastes a lot of manpower. The principle of safety definition states that the root (the real) causes of the event must first be identified before a remedy is prescribed.

SAFETY AUTHORITY

Participation in the SMS and motivation to accomplish results increases if employees are given authority to take decisions concerning safety.

Safety objectives must be set, and employees must know what their safety authority is. Ownership of the SMS, or element of the SMS, gets individuals to participate in the SMS and become active owners of part of the system. Appointing health and safety representatives to conduct monthly workplace safety inspections give those employees ownership of part of the SMS.

Employees and contractors must be encouraged to report hazards and near miss incidents. They should attend safety committee meetings and, where applicable, participate in accident investigations. They should also have the authority to stop unsafe work should it pose a threat to life or limb.

SAFETY REPORTING

Health and safety management is a management science and is a profession that sometimes doesn't get the recognition and support it deserves. The higher health and safety personnel report in the organizational structure, the more effective they will be.

Health and safety departments' true place is advising management and coordinating the activities of an ongoing SMS. They cannot improve safety by accepting the responsibility for safety. They should not directly try to influence the behaviors of employees. Only management can do that.

SAFETY DEPARTMENT

The higher the level to which the health and safety department reports, the more management cooperation they are likely to obtain. Health and safety staff are the catalysts in the SMS and should function as such. Safety coordinators, and advisors, should not be in a line function but rather, in a staff function, that is, in an advisory capacity.

SMSs that originate in and are maintained by the health and safety department will have little effect on the organization. It is estimated that about 15% of a company's problems can be controlled by employees, whereas 85% can be controlled by management. Most safety problems are therefore management problems.

GETMAC

The function of all health and safety departments should be to *guide*, *educate*, *train*, *and motivate* all levels of management, contractors, workers, and unions in the techniques of accident and disease prevention. They should also *advise* on and *coordinate* (GETMAC) the functions within the safety management system (SMS) in a staff capacity.

THE CRITICAL FEW

A small number of causes could give rise to the largest number of safety problems. Eighty percent of accidents are caused by 20% of the tasks carried out at a workplace. A few critical jobs could be responsible for the majority of accidents and injuries occurring within an organisation. A few critical SMS elements could be responsible for the major risks within the workplace. These few critical elements should receive maximum safety control and attention to minimise their potential for causing the majority of problems.

SAFETY ADVOCATES

Normally during the introduction of an SMS, a few employees, the critical few, will stand out as safety advocates and play leading roles in the implementation process. These few advocates will be responsible for much of the SMS's success. On the contrary, a small group will oppose and reject the changes, and will be responsible for the most stumbling blocks encountered during the implementation of the system.

INTEREST IN SAFETY

The workforce will only become interested in safety if management show an interest in the results they achieve, individually or as a group. Management must set the safety trend and help individuals and departments achieve safety objectives. The SMS must be a common interest in the organization.

PAST EXPERIENCE PREDICTS FUTURE EXPERIENCE

An organization's past safety efforts and experience tend to predict the safety effort and experience of the future. The safety culture that is embedded in the organisation tends to prevail in the future. Safety attitudes and behaviors experienced in the past tend to be carried over to the future.

APPLICATION

The principle of safety application is that the more the various elements of the SMS are practised and applied, the more they are understood and accepted as day-to-day activities. The more safety inspections are done, the better the inspection techniques and efficiency will become. The more safety procedures are used, the easier it will become to follow them in the future. The more the safety committee meets, the more effective they will become. The more audits are carried out, the more streamlined and professional future audits will be.

RECOGNITION

Safety motivation increases as people are given recognition for their contribution to the safety effort. Safety has traditionally been a blame and punishment game. This has led to employees not participating in safety activities and management not taking full safety responsibility. Contemporary management styles show that commending and encouraging people for safety goes far in ensuring that those safe actions are repeated. Good safety actions should be praised, and this praise should be made in public where possible.

MANAGEMENT LEADERSHIP AND SAFETY SUCCESS

The chief executive officer of the organization is the leader, and if he or she leads for safety, others will follow. The degree of integration and involvement of safety principles and standards is directly proportional to the amount of management leadership and commitment.

Top management must always set an example for others to follow. Setting an example for safety is of crucial importance in the SMS. Management must set the standards, take the lead, and be prime examples of safety. Involvement in the SMS by the chief executive officer and other members of management is not sufficient; commitment to the SMS is what is required.

HENRI FAYOL

Henri Fayol (1841–1925) was a French coal-mine engineer, director of mines, and modern management theoretician. His scientific management theory forms the basis for business administration and business management.

According to Van Vliet, V., (2009), Henri Fayol proposed 14 principles of management. They include the following:

Division of Work

> In practice, employees are specialized in different areas and they have different skills. Different levels of expertise can be distinguished within the knowledge areas (from generalist to specialist). Personal and professional developments support this. According to Henri Fayol, specialization promotes the efficiency of the workforce and increases productivity. In addition, the specialization of the workforce increases their accuracy and speed. This management principle is applicable to both technical and managerial activities.

Authority and Responsibility

> In order to get things done in an organization, management has the authority to give orders to employees. Of course, with this authority comes responsibility. According to Henri Fayol, the accompanying power or authority gives management the right to give orders to subordinates. The responsibility can be traced back from performance, and it is therefore necessary to make agreements about this. In other words, authority and responsibility go together, and they are two sides of the same coin.

Unity of Command

The management principle *unity of command* means that an individual employee should receive orders from one manager and that the employee is answerable to that manager. If tasks and related responsibilities are given to the employee by more than one manager, this may lead to confusion, which may lead to possible conflicts for employees. By using this principle, the responsibility for mistakes can be established more easily.

Scalar Chain

Hierarchy presents itself in any given organization. This varies from senior management (executive board) to the lowest levels in the organization. Henri Fayol's "hierarchy" management principle states that there should be a clear line in the area of authority (from top to bottom and all managers at all levels). This can be seen as a type of management structure. Each employee can contact a manager or a superior in an emergency situation without challenging the hierarchy, especially when it concerns reports about calamities to the immediate managers/superiors.

Order

According to this principle of the 14 principles of management, employees in an organization must have the right resources at their disposal so that they can function properly in an organization. In addition to social order (responsibility of the managers), the work environment must be safe, clean, and tidy.

Initiative

Henri Fayol argued with this management principle that employees should be allowed to express new ideas. This encourages interest and involvement and creates added value for the company. Fayol argued that employee initiatives are a source of strength for the organization. This encourages the employees to be involved and interested (p.1–7).

SUMMARY

Occupational health and safety is a management function and will always be. Only management can bring about changes in an organization as they have the authority to do so. By applying these principles of management to the implementation and maintenance of a SMS, management will be able to integrate all aspects of health and safety into the ongoing daily management of the organization.

Part 2

Design, Implementation, and
Audit of Occupational Health
and Safety Management
System, Safety Leadership
and Organization Elements

8 Health and Safety Policy Statement

BACKGROUND

Most occupational health and safety management systems (SMSs) must start at a logical point, which is a policy of intent, and must be initiated and followed through by management actions. The health and safety policy statement of intent is the guiding document in health and safety management. Referred to as the *safety policy*, it is a written statement by an employer stating the company's commitment to the protection of the health and safety of employees and to the public.

DESIGN OF AN OCCUPATIONAL HEALTH AND SAFETY POLICY

Policies are defined as *standing decisions, which apply to repetitive health and safety questions and problems.* It is the commitment that the management teams make concerning health and safety, and is also the health and safety commitment that employees, contractors, and other affected parties agree to.

PLANNING

The compiling of a health and safety policy statement is part of the safety management planning function. It is the initiating action and forms the fulcrum of any SMS.

ADVANTAGES

The following are a few advantages of the health and safety policy:

- It gives common points of view concerning occupational health and safety.
- It helps managers at all levels by giving employees the advantage of knowing the executive's point of view on safety.
- It is an indication of the organization's health and safety considerations.
- It provides rational rather than erratic health and safety decisions.
- It allows for delegation of health and safety work.
- It facilitates efficient and effective teamwork.
- It provides guidelines for everybody on how to do the right things concerning health and safety.

ESSENTIAL

The health and safety policy is an essential starting point and driver for the SMS, and is the most important document in the SMS. Dan Petersen said that management often writes the policy and then fails to ensure that it is enforced by managers and supervisors on the job, every day.

SAFETY RULE BOOK

It is advantageous to have a copy of the health and safety policy of the organization reproduced in the safety rule book. This helps during the safety induction process and also serves as an ongoing reminder of the safety culture of the organization.

REQUIREMENTS OF POLICIES

Health and safety policies must be dynamic and realistic, and the objectives set must be tangible. Both management and worker representation should agree upon the policies. This joint policy should be extensively publicized. The policy must suit the needs of the organization and include contractors and others with whom they interact (interested and affected parties).

It must be written in such a way that it is understood by all. It must be practicable and achievable. More tangible than intangible objectives should be set by the policy. The policy should also list practical ongoing steps that will ensure compliance to the policy.

According to the *Encyclopedia of Occupational Health and Safety* (Fourth Edition), International Labor Organization (ILO):

> Having a policy on health and safety seldom achieves anything unless it is followed up with systems that make the policy live. For example, if the policy states that supervisors are responsible for safety, it means nothing unless the following is in place:

- Management has a system where there is a clear definition of role and of what activities must be carried out to satisfy the safety responsibility.
- Supervisors know how to fulfil that role, are supported by management, believe the tasks are achievable and carry out their tasks as a result of proper planning and training.
- Supervisors are regularly measured to ensure they have completed the defined tasks (but not measured by an accident record) and to obtain feedback to determine whether or not tasks should be changed.
- There is a reward contingent upon task completion in the performance appraisal system or in whatever is the driving mechanism of the organization.

> (ILO website) (Copyright © International Labour Organization 2019)

HEALTH AND SAFETY POLICY CONTENTS

Since the policy is the initiating document in the safety management process, it should:

- Include a commitment to injury, ill-health, and disease prevention.
- Refer to continuing improvement of health and safety initiatives.
- Contain a commitment to comply with health and safety legislation.
- Be a commitment to consultation and participation of workers and/or workers' representatives.
- Provide a framework for safety objective setting.
- Be documented, displayed, and maintained.
- Be freely available.
- Be communicated to all relevant parties.
- Be signed and dated.
- Receive periodical review.

COMMITMENT

The health and safety policy should be drawn up with considerable care, and once agreed to, it must be signed. The parties signing the policy would be the senior management and, in some cases, worker representatives as well. In some instances, the entire management team sign the policy as well as the worker representation team.

IMPLEMENTATION OF A HEALTH AND SAFETY POLICY

OBJECTIVE OF THE POLICY

The objective of the health and safety policy statement is to clearly define the organization's intent and commitment to the health, safety, and wellbeing of employees, their families, contractors, site visitors and related organizations.

RESPONSIBILITY

CHIEF EXECUTIVE OFFICER

The Chief Executive Officer should approve the contents of the safety policy and ensure that it is updated in accordance with the needs of the organization.

SENIOR MANAGEMENT

The senior management team of the company shall authorize and sign the health and safety policy statement. They are also ultimately responsible for ensuring that the policy is made available and known to employees, contractors, and other relevant and interested parties.

HEALTH AND SAFETY DEPARTMENT (SAFETY DEPARTMENT)

The safety department, safety engineers, safety coordinators, and other safety staff should be responsible for ensuring that:

- Sufficient copies of the policy are made available.
- The policy is included in all health and safety training presentations and hand-outs, the safety manual, and all other health and safety related publications and materials, where practicable.
- The policy is included in all induction and health and safety training courses and workshops as the first matter of business.
- The policy is in the possession of all contractors on site.
- The update and maintenance of the policy is coordinated.
- The employees' knowledge of the policy is tested during regular audits.
- The policy is made available to other interested parties.
- It is displayed in all training rooms, offices, and other prominent areas.
- The policy is displayed on all company intranet and external websites.

EMPLOYEES

Employees should be familiar with the policy and should:

- Understand the commitments contained in the policy.
- Accept that they play a major role in maintaining a safe work environment and in working safely.
- Understand that they have a responsibility toward themselves, their fellow workers, and their families.
- Report unsafe situations to their immediate superior for rectification.
- Be role models for safety.

LANGUAGE

As per company policy, the policy should be made available in English and other languages if applicable.

POLICY DISPLAYED

The health and safety policy should be posted at prominent positions throughout the organization. To give credibility, the policy should preferably be attractively printed and suitably framed. The display positions must be carefully selected, and employees must constantly be briefed and reminded of the policy during ongoing briefing sessions.

The following guideline offers some examples of how and where the policy should be displayed, promoted, and made visible. A framed version of the policy should be displayed at major offices and departments throughout the organization's facilities:

- In office foyers
- In lunch rooms

- On safety notice boards
- In training rooms
- In meeting rooms
- In workshopsIn addition,
- A copy of the policy should appear in the safety manual.
- The policy should appear in the employee handbook.
- The policy should be included in contractor bid documents.
- A pocket-size version can be laminated and issued to employees.
- All safety training materials and handouts should include a reference to the policy.
- Safety induction or orientation training should begin with the policy contents.
- The company website should display the policy prominently.
- It should be included in other areas and media that are deemed appropriate to promote the policy.

EXAMPLE OF A HEALTH AND SAFETY POLICY STATEMENT

(The Company)

Occupational Health and Safety Policy Statement

Nothing at The Company is more important than the health, safety, and wellbeing of our employees, contractors, and interested parties. The Company leadership believes that identifying and reducing risks will help minimize all forms of accidental loss. As an organization we are determined to achieve our vision of reducing the probability of illnesses and injuries to The Company employees, family, contractors, and visitors, and the communities and environment in which we operate.

We are committed:

- To making risk-based occupational health and safety management a core value that drives performance.
- To holding managers accountable for occupational health and safety in all of our facilities.
- To providing the practices, tools and resources via The Company Health and Safety Management System (SMS).

To achieve our occupational health and safety objectives:

- Each employee, regardless of position or title, must take individual responsibility for health and safety. It is the job of each employee to create a work environment that eliminates occupational health and safety hazards. Further, we encourage all employees to be role models and leaders in health and safety at work, as well as for their families and their neighbors in our communities.
- The Company is committed to complying with, and even exceeding, applicable occupational health and safety laws and international standards. We believe that occupational health and safety laws and regulations can and must be integrated with our effort to produce a world-class environment.

- We will not be satisfied until we have reduced all workplace risks and the probability of occupational injuries and illnesses occurring among our employees and contractors. This is the only acceptable goal, and we are dedicated to achieving it through continuous improvement of our SMS.
- We know we will achieve these results only through each employee's participation in and attention to health and safety and dedication to make working safely an integral part of every job we do.

IMPORTANCE OF A HEALTH AND SAFETY POLICY STATEMENT

The policy is regarded as an occupational health and safety opportunity to enhance health and safety performance. It creates an opportunity to adapt the work environment and processes, to workers and is an opportunity to eliminate hazards and reduce risks. It determines the direction of the SMS and is consequently one of the most important elements in any SMS.

AUDIT OF A HEALTH AND SAFETY POLICY STATEMENT

Since the health and safety policy is a fulcrum point for the entire SMS, specific attention should be paid when auditing its contents and application throughout the workplace.

AUDITING OF THE POLICY STATEMENT AND ITS IMPLEMENTATION

The main question to be answered during an SMS audit is, "Is the health and safety policy known, is it being applied, and is it working?" The audit should examine the policy content and make sure it covers the basic requirements of a health and safety policy.

INSPECTION

During the audit inspection, the auditor should look for policy visibility. Is it prominently displayed? Is it the correct policy, and has it been signed? Is the policy posted on notice boards? Are contractors in possession of the policy?

EMPLOYEE INTERVIEWS

During the employee interview segment of the audit, employees should be tactfully tested for policy knowledge and awareness. Without causing embarrassment, the auditor must ascertain if the employees know of the policy and of at least one of the concepts contained in the policy. Contractors' knowledge of the policy should also be audited.

AN AUDIT PROTOCOL FOR THE SMS ELEMENT, HEALTH AND SAFETY POLICY STATEMENT

This audit protocol contains suggested minimum standards and minimum standard details for a health and safety policy standard. It also recommends questions to be posed during the documentation review session, as well as what to look for during the audit inspection (Figure 8.1).

ELEMENT/PROGRAM/PROCESS	POINTS	QUESTIONS THAT COULD BE ASKED	VERIFICATION	WHAT TO LOOK FOR
HEALTH AND SAFETY POLICY				
Policy signed by Executive and prominently displayed in the workplace?	5	What is the company policy?	See the policy	.Check the following requirements
Are employees aware of and familiar with the policy?	5	What is the company policy?	How are employees taught the safety and health policy?	Is it signed by the management? Ask at least 2 employees to namesome concept contained inthe health and safety policy in their own words.
Is top management committed e.g. attending SMS evaluations and audits, making presentations, etc.?	5	What other involvement does management have in the SMS?	Is the management really involved in the SMS?	Managers partaking in the audit process
Injury/disease prevention	5	Is there a commitment in the policy?	Include a commitment to injury and ill-health and disease prevention	Check policy document
Improvement	5	Is continuous improvement included?	Refer to continuing improvement of safety and health initiatives	Check policy document
Health and safety objectives	5	Are objectives set by the policy?	Provide a framework for safety objective setting	Proactive and reactive measurements
Legal compliance	5	Does the policy state this?	Contain a commitment to comply with safety and health legislation	
Communicated	5	How is the policy disseminated	Be communicated to all affected parties	Induction training/handbook
Displayed	5	Where is the policy displayed?	Be documented, displayed and maintained	Visual confirmation during inspection
Policy updated	5	When was the policy last updated?	Date of update	Check policy issuance
TOTAL	**50**			

FIGURE 8.1 Audit Protocol for the Element – Health and Safety Policy.

9 Health and Safety Policies, Standards, Processes, Systems, and Programs

THE DESIGN OF POLICIES, STANDARDS, PROCESSES, SYSTEMS, AND PROGRAMS

Health and safety policies, standards, processes, systems, and programs are the components and functions that comprise the safety management system (SMS). Together they form the mechanisms and guiding documents of the health and safety management system.

HEALTH AND SAFETY POLICIES

Policies are a set of principles in which the long-term direction is given by management for the support and continued improvement of the SMS. They are written guidelines for each area of risk reduction opportunity, and which stipulate measurable management performance criteria.

HEALTH AND SAFETY STANDARDS

These are written health and safety performance requirements that indicate responsibility and accountability for achieving the listed actions. They are measurable management performance requirements, stipulating certain activities and desired outcomes. Standards should be written for each element of the SMS. These must be applied, be communicated to stakeholders, be consistent with the health and policy statement, and be monitored and updated as required.

HEALTH AND SAFETY PROCESSES

A health and safety process is a series of actions, or steps taken, in order to achieve a particular objective. Processes are ongoing activities within the SMS, and do not cease when the objective is achieved. Examples are the machine guarding process, risk assessment process, and safety orientation process.

HEALTH AND SAFETY SYSTEMS

Health and safety systems are a combination of standards, processes, and programs that operate constantly to form an ongoing risk reduction process. They are a set of interacting elements of an organization which establishes policies, objectives, and processes to achieve the health and safety objectives stated in the health and safety policy statement.

HEALTH AND SAFETY PROGRAMS

Programs are a collection of planned activities and actions that constitute one element of the SMS and which have an objective. Examples are the hearing conservation program, safety training program, and off-the-job safety program.

THE IMPLEMENTATION OF SMS POLICIES, STANDARDS, PROCESSES, SYSTEMS, AND PROGRAMS

When implementing the occupational health and safety policies, standards, processes, systems, and programs, the following questions should be asked:

- What safety policies, standards, processes, systems, and programs are in place, and what need to be written?
- Are the policies, standards, processes, systems, and programs correct and up to date?
- Are the policies, standards, processes, systems, and programs reviewed regularly?
- How are the policies, standards, processes, systems, and programs communicated?

IMPLEMENTATION STRATEGY

The organization now plans for the implementation of the required policies, standards, processes, systems, and programs (initiatives), and this would include:

- The resources, roles, responsibility, accountability and authority
- The competence required, as well as the training and creation of awareness of the initiative
- The communication of the initiative and the participation required from stakeholders.

EXISTING INITIATIVES

Existing initiatives should be examined to see if they comply with the objectives set by the health and safety policy statement and the legal requirements. A gap analysis should be done to see what initiatives still need to be implemented and what standards require drafting.

STANDARD FORMAT

The standards that are missing or inadequate then need to be drafted. Depending on the sophistication of the existing SMS, a team of selected personnel could be used to draft these standards. Certain processes and programs need to be compiled by the experts in that field, and they should be given this task. A standard format should be used. This should conform to the corporate identity documentation format.

Before these initiatives can be implemented, they should be approved by a body that includes worker and management representation. Since health and safety committees represent all stakeholders, they could be nominated as the approval body.

SIGNED

Once approved, the element standard must be signed and dated by top management. Only once this has been done can the standard be cascaded down the line and made known to all. In some instances, briefing sessions or workshops are held to explain the standard to all stakeholders.

TRACKING SYSTEM

Each standard should be grouped under headings or sections, and each element should receive a number relative to that section. This is to give the element an identity as well as for tracking purposes. A master document listing the headings and grouping the elements under those headings should be compiled and used as the SMS master layout plan. In this publication, the following headings (sections) have been used:

    Section 1: Safety Leadership and Organization
    Section 2: Workplace Environment Conditions
    Section 3: Accident and Near Miss Incident Reporting and Investigation
    Section 4: Emergency Preparedness, Fire Prevention, and Protection
    Section 5: Electrical, Mechanical, and Personal Safeguarding

Each element under a section will then be numbered accordingly.

For example:

The element *Health and Policy Statement* will fall under Section 1, and is element number one, so is referred to as Section 1, Element 1.1 Health and Safety Policy Statement (S1, E1.1), this facilitates easier reference to the SMS elements which are now arranged in a logical format.

WRITING OF STANDARDS

Standards must be written in a practical manner and should follow a fixed sequence, listing the objectives of the standard, the responsibilities and accountabilities, and the action that must take place. They should state what the objective of the standards is, and the methods by which this will be achieved. Objectives should be included in the standard and these should be attainable, realistic, and time bound.

THE AUDIT OF POLICIES, STANDARDS, PROCESSES, SYSTEMS, AND PROGRAMS

The purpose of an SMS audit is to measure the adequacy and effectiveness of the actions, and activities to reduce workplace risk, as required by the standards. Standards should be available for all components, processes, systems and programs within the SMS. When auditing the standards, processes, systems and programs of the SMS, the following should be checked:

- Is the standard adequate in relation to the risk reduction opportunity?
- Has it been reviewed and updated?
- Is it signed?
- Does it have a document tracking number?
- Is it cross referenced to other standards?
- Is it on the documentation control system?
- Do stakeholders have knowledge of the standard?

DOCUMENTED VERIFICATION

Documents containing the standards, processes, systems, and programs must be examined closely during the audit documentation verification meeting. These should be scrutinized in relation to what was found happening on the shop floor during the inspection. The audit must be able to confirm if the element is in place, whether it is working, and how effective it is. Is the organization doing what it says it is doing?

CORRECTIVE ACTIONS

Deviations from the requirements of SMS standards, processes, and programs should be pointed out to the organization so that appropriate action plans can be compiled to bring the intervention into conformance. Action plans should also be time related and allocate responsibility and accountability for corrective actions. This may include the modification or updating of the standard, the re-examination of the process, or introducing a different approach to the problem.

10 Occupational Health and Safety Management Systems (SMSs)

INTRODUCTION

The first and best approach to health and safety management is to eliminate hazards and thus create a safe workplace. Although not always possible, the five levels of hazard reduction, and consequent risk reduction, should be applied in order to reduce workplace hazards.

HAZARDS

Hazards in the workplace could be either physical, chemical, biological, or psychosocial. There are five main hazard reduction methods:

ELIMINATION

This is where the hazard is completely eliminated. It is most effective in the design stage, but this does not always occur. This may mean changing the process drastically, or stopping the process altogether. Substances used may need to be changed, or safer substances used. Eliminating the hazard, although the first option, is not always feasible and could prove very costly. This is an ongoing process in the SMS via actions such as risk assessments, change management, management reviews, and safety inspections.

SUBSTITUTION

Here a substitute is used instead of the hazardous process, substance, or chemical. A process could also be replaced with a safer method. A machine could be replaced with another safer one. Robotics are sometimes used in hazardous situations instead of people. This is an example of substitution.

ENGINEERING CONTROLS

By applying engineering controls, the hazard is engineered out. This involves making a physical change to the workplace to remove or contain the hazard. This change often involves placing a barrier between the worker and the hazard. Machine guarding is an example of an engineering control. Ventilation systems that remove hazardous substances from the air are another example.

ADMINISTRATIVE CONTROLS

Administrative controls such as training, scheduling different times of exposure, writing safe work procedures for certain tasks, and so on can be introduced to reduce the hazard exposure. These controls help reduce the duration, frequency, and severity of exposure to hazards and hazardous situations. Good housekeeping practices are an example of administrative controls.

PERSONAL PROTECTIVE EQUIPMENT (PPE)

Where hazard control methods have been applied, or in some instances could not be applied, for example, the final resort is to protect employees against injury by providing PPE. This does not eliminate or lessen the hazard but provides a reduction in an accidental exchange of energy caused by a hazard. The providing of PPE should not be seen as a substitute for the other more effective methods.

ONGOING HAZARD REDUCTION

The elements of the SMS constantly apply and monitor all five hazard reduction methods on a continual basis. All opportunities for risk reduction are identified and explored systematically.

TERMINOLOGY

OCCUPATIONAL HEALTH AND SAFETY MANAGEMENT SYSTEM

An occupational health and safety management system (SMS) (safety system) is a formalized approach to health and safety management through the use of a framework that facilitates the identification, control, and minimization of health and safety risks. It is integrated into other management systems and uses the same methods and strategies.

SAFETY PROGRAM

A safety program is an element, component, or set of components within, and which comprises, a comprehensive SMS. Examples are a bloodborne pathogens program, a respiratory program, and an ergonomics program.

A SECTION OF AN SMS

Elements or programs that have common outcomes are grouped together under a common heading to facilitate easy recognition and administration. Examples are:

Section 1: Management Leadership and Organization
Section 2: Electrical, Mechanical, and Personal Safeguarding
Section 3: Emergency Preparedness, Fire Prevention and Protection

Section 4: Accident and Near Miss Incident Recording and Investigation
Section 5: Workplace Environment Conditions

SMS ELEMENTS

Elements or components of the SMS can be grouped under the above main sections. These could be processes, standards, or programs. At least 70 elements are present in a comprehensive SMS.

SMS Element Standards

Each element is defined by a standard. This document sets standards of performance as well as standards of responsibility. It lists actions and activities to be carried out, as well as time frames for these actions and activities. Together, these create measurable performance criteria. The standards prescribe the minimum standards to be achieved.

SMS Element Minimum Standard

The SMS minimum standard represents the requirements of the standard. In the example given here, the minimum standard is that training in hazard recognition is to be carried out. This is a general requirement of the standard. The detail requirements of the training are stipulated in the minimum standard detail.

SMS Element Minimum Standard Details

The minimum standard is broken down into smaller achievable and measurable components (details) to facilitate easier implementation and adjudication during audits. Each element standard should contain the minimum standard required for compliance to the standard. Legal requirements should always be included in the standard and would be regarded as the absolute minimum standard to be achieved. Minimum standards prescribe what must be achieved, and the minimum standard detail breaks the minimum standards into measurable and quantifiable details.

For example:

Element:

Health and Safety Training

Minimum Standard (1):

Training in hazard identification carried out

Minimum Standard Detail:

Has training been done?
10% of the workforce trained annually
A plant inspection to form part of the training
Tests to be given at the end of the class

Minimum Standard (2):

Employee Refresher Training

Minimum Standard Detail

All employees attended the refresher training
Refresher training annual for employees
Records kept of the training
Health and safety policy included in training
Vendors and site visitor's orientation given

Audit Protocol

An audit protocol is a document which is drawn up to reflect the measurable actions contained in the element standard so that they can be quantified. Each minimum standard is broken down into detail, and each detail is allocated a rating or score. This means each small achievable action can be quantified during the audit process.

The audit protocol must contain all the sections of the SMS, all the elements, and all the minimum standard details so that auditing can be done against the detailed requirements. Maximum scores are shown for each detail so that a score can be allocated. A simple but effective scoring method is to rank each minimum standard detail on a (1–5) scale. This means every aspect of the entire SMS can be scored. A (1) would indicate a 20% compliance, while a (5) will indicate a 100% compliance. The element weighting, dependent on the risk, should be indicated on the protocol for final score allocation. Other scoring methods can also be used.

The protocol should include a guide to the auditors as to what to look for during the inspection, what elements to follow through the system, what questions to ask, and what verification documentation to review.

Systems Approach

A systems approach is an approach whereby a collective group of independent processes constantly interact to form a united whole. A SMS is a systems approach to the prevention of accidental loss. It contains a number of programs and processes that together form the SMS. Rather than being reactive (after the accident), it is a proactive (before the accident), ongoing system that is merged into the daily management of the organization.

OSHA (OCCUPATIONAL SAFETY AND HEALTH ADMINISTRATION) SAFETY SYSTEM SECTIONS

In their publication *Recommended Practices for Safety and Health* (2016), OSHA proposes the core elements (Sections) of a health and safety system (they use the term *program*) as follows:

- Management leadership
- Worker participation

- Hazard identification and assessment
- Hazard prevention and control
- Education and training
- Program evaluation and improvement
- Communication and coordination for host employers, contractors, and staffing agencies.

(OSHA website, p.10)

These seven sections are similar to those of most SMSs and will contain sub-sections or elements similar to most SMSs. There is little difference between health and safety programs and SMSs. The term *health and safety management system* is preferred, as this is in keeping with international standard guidelines such as ISO 45001:2018.

OSHA has developed model safety plans for certain elements of safety systems, which are a good starting point for the creation of a comprehensive safety system, or safety plan.

FLY BY NIGHT PROGRAMS

Numerous safety gimmicks are marketed and promoted as safety programs. These are not fully fledged safety programs but merely novelties to stimulate interest in some aspect of workplace safety; they are not long-lasting, sustainable, or a substitute for a formal integrated safety system.

SUMMARY

Many advisory and legal instances have proposed outlines of health and safety management systems and health and safety programs. The organization's SMS must be a structured approach to safety management and should contain those elements, processes, and programs that it needs dependent on the risks within, and the needs of, the organization.

11 Health and Safety Policies
Management Leadership and Involvement

INTRODUCTION

Despite it being common knowledge that health and safety is a management function, and that management are ultimately responsible for the safety and wellbeing of the employees and other stakeholders, this is not always practiced.

HISTORY

Management have a very demanding job in any organization. Health and safety is an extra burden to them, and is sometimes delegated down the line to becoming the responsibility of the safety department. Contemporary thinking is that management must now own and *commit* to the health and safety process and can no longer simply be involved.

TOP MANAGEMENT

Top management is a person, or group of people, who direct and control the organization. It is the highest decision-making level in the organization, and its members have the authority to initiate and provide resources necessary for the safety management system (SMS). This is where management leadership starts.

POLICIES

Health and safety policies must originate from top management. The SMS should be led by management if it is to be successful. While standards and policies can be drafted and have input from other levels within the organization, top management must sign and approve them.

In some organizations, the health and safety policy is signed by the entire top management team as a visual commitment to its intent. This is management leadership.

MANAGEMENT LEADERSHIP

Safety leading is ensuring that people act and work in a safe manner. It means taking the lead in safety matters, making safety decisions, and always setting the safety example. It also requires the development of standards and support for the implementation of those standards, processes, and programs.

LEADERSHIP

A good definition of leadership is the action of leading people in an organization towards the achievement of goals. Leaders do this by influencing employees. A leader sets a clear vision for the organization, motivates employees, guides employees through the work process, and builds morale. A leader is more like a coach than a manager.

MOTIVATION

Part of leadership is determining the needs of employees, providing them with the resources they need, and then praising them for a job well done. Good leaders communicate with their employees to learn about what they want and their needs. They constantly commend and encourage employees. This is motivation.

COMMUNICATION

Guiding employees involves defining their role in the work process and providing them with tools needed to perform the task. A good leader will explain the tasks, provide the correct resources, direct and participate in the work, and be available to assist employees if they run into problems.

A MANAGER

A manager uses the four functions of management – plan, organize, lead, and control – to get others to do the work. Due to his or her position, a manager has authority, and subordinates must follow his or her directives. They have no choice. Managers must achieve certain goals and must direct the activities of others to achieve these goals.

A LEADER

A leader inspires people to follow them, even though he or she has no authority over them. A leader motivates others to follow him or her. He or she is not in a managerial position, and people follow leaders because of their ability to continue to motivate and inspire them.

To explain the difference between leadership and management, one must acknowledge that leadership is about effectiveness through trust, inspiration, and motivation of people. Leaders often challenge the status quo that managers spend much of their time upholding to bring innovation to organizations. A leader is an agile, visionary, change-savvy, creative, and adaptive person. Managers are more concerned with the bottom line, while leaders spend time looking at the horizon.

SAFETY MANAGEMENT

Managing the complex science of health and safety, managers need to be both managers and leaders. The design, implementation, and auditing of a sound health and safety system requires that authority be given to all levels within the organization. With this authority, the SMS should create responsibilities and hold persons with authority accountable for results achieved.

Authority holders can only be held accountable for the resources over which they have responsibility and cannot be held to account for non-conformances out of their sphere of authority. The cliché "Everyone is responsible for safety" is an example of holding employees accountable for happenings that were beyond their control and scope of authority. A person can only be responsible and accountable for that which they have authority over.

SMS STANDARDS

Each SMS standard must clearly define the authority, responsibility, and accountability for actions that need to be performed to meet the requirements of the standard.

An example from a standard on the element *Accident and Near Miss Incident Recall* follows:

RESPONSIBILITY AND ACCOUNTABILITY

Managers, supervisors, and contractors are responsible and accountable for fully supporting the formulation, administration, implementation, and performance of this standard.

The health and safety department is responsible and accountable for administration and support of this standard, as well as coordinating revisions to this standard as needed.

Health and safety and personnel are responsible and accountable for record keeping of documentation and distribution of safety reports and statistics concerning near miss incident/accident recall.

Employees are responsible and accountable for participating in the daily and monthly accident and near miss incident recall sessions.

TOP MANAGEMENT COMMITMENT AND LEADERSHIP

Top management sets the trend for health and safety initiatives, and other levels must follow this example. Some of the ways in which management show their commitment and leadership to the SMS are by:

- Chairing the monthly executive health and safety committee meeting
- Supporting employees and managers who contribute positively to the SMS
- Constantly monitoring the SMS's effectiveness
- Providing a mechanism to protect whistle blowers

- Providing means for employee consultation and input into the SMS
- Encouraging and supporting continuous SMS improvement
- Constantly and effectively communicating about the importance of the SMS
- Supporting the SMS by providing all the resources needed to maintain an effective SMS
- Combining the organizations production and safety goals
- Committing to providing a healthy and safe workplace

SUMMARY

Implementing and maintaining a sound SMS is a challenge for managers at all levels and requires a subtle mix of management and leadership styles. Managers must be visible participants in the system and its activities. Involvement and participation at all levels can only be successfully achieved if each element of the SMS defines the roles and responsibilities of management, employees, worker representatives, and other stakeholders. These need to be communicated clearly.

12 Safety Objectives, Goals, and Performance Indicators

OBJECTIVES AND GOALS

OBJECTIVES

A health and safety objective is a defined result that a system, or person within that system, aims to achieve by using available resources and within a time frame. Objectives are basic tools that underlie all planning and strategic activities.

Some examples of health and safety objectives include:

- Reduce the number of reported hazards by 80%.
- Appoint 20 safety representatives per year.
- Train 60% of the workforce in safety annually.

In general, objectives are more specific and easier to measure than goals.

GOALS

A goal is an observable and measurable end result having *one or more objectives* to be achieved within a stated timeframe. Goals serve as the basis for creating policy and evaluating performance. Create a healthier and safer workplace would be a goal. Improving a safety culture would also be a goal.

Meeting objectives leads to the accomplishment of the goals of the health and safety policy statement. While goals are the end result or the bigger picture, objectives are the small achievements that help reach the goal. Both are proactive, but objectives are more short term than goals.

LEADING INDICATORS

The best metric for measuring safety performance are leading health and safety indicators. These gauge the degree of achievement of health and safety objectives set in the safety management system (SMS) standards.

Examples of health and safety objectives are:

- The number of completion of planned inspections
- The number of non-compliance detected and rectified
- The number of near miss incidents reported
- The number of near miss incidents closed out

- Risk assessments done
- The number of employees that have attended formal safety training classes
- The number of health and safety representatives appointed and active
- The quality of near miss incident and accident investigations
- The number of safe behaviors observed in relation to high risk behaviors
- The divisional SMS audit scores
- The number and quality of evacuation drills per quarter
- Reduction of number of legal safety citations.

RESULTS MEASUREMENT INDICATORS

Results measurement indicators show to what extent the SMS objectives have been reached by calculating the difference in the results in relation to the objectives set by the action plans within the standards. If housekeeping scored 60% during the last audit and the current audit shows an achievement of 80%, there has been a 20% improvement in this element.

MEASUREMENT OF CONTROL

Leading measurements are measurements of control. They indicate the degree of work being done to reduce risk on an ongoing basis. Management and employees have full control over these measurements, which provide opportunities for hazard reduction.

LAGGING INDICATORS

Injury rates, injury severity rates, days lost, and injury and health costs are lagging safety indicators. They are downstream indicators. They only show what happened in the past and do not measure health and safety efforts and inputs. Inaccuracy and honesty of reporting also means they are not accurate figures for comparison. The safety fear factor – the fear that employees have of reporting an injury – further skews the final numbers, rending them extremely inaccurate.

These figures must, however, be kept and monitored, but they should not be used as the sole safety measurement.

TRENDING INDICATORS

Downstream measurements are trending indicators which help to keep a record of a trend, for example, the change in the number of occupational injuries and diseases over the years. They calculate the rate of progression from one year to another, or over several years.

MEASUREMENTS OF CONSEQUENCE

Lagging indicators are downstream indices and do not tell management where they are going. Rather, they tell them where they have been. They are measures of consequence, and outcomes of undesired events could be fortuitous. Luck factors often determine the outcome and final consequence of an accident and they are therefore not a good gauge of safety efforts.

Many safety professionals concur and agree that, in the early days of safety, safety measures, such as the number of injuries, injury frequency rates, severity rates, and costs, were used to measure safety performance and progress. Even though it became clear long ago that these measures offer little help or guidance, they continue to be used today. Why should we consider other measures? The answer is that these measures of consequence nearly always measure only luck.

HEALTH AND SAFETY KEY PERFORMANCE INDICATORS (KPIS)

Safety improvements have become synonymous with the number of injuries, so much so that it is difficult to move management's thinking from this paradigm. If one understands that the outcome of accidents is largely fortuitous, it will become clear that other, more positive methods of safety performance are required.

In setting up a structured system, managers at all levels should be given achievable, manageable, and time-bound key performance indicators (KPIs). These should start off as simple achievable objectives and should be monitored on a monthly basis. This is giving safety responsibility and creating accountability for positive safety actions.

One organization introduced a number of KPIs for their management. The list included:

- Safety committee established and meetings held
- Health and safety observations reported and rectified
- Workplace safety inspections carried out
- SMS audit results
- Fire drills held
- Number of toolbox talks held
- Health and Safety representatives appointed and active
- Health and safety training completed

Each activity within the KPI was broken down into objectives, and each objective had a scoring system so that performance and achievement of goals could be scored and reported monthly.

An example follows:

Safety Committees (20)

A formal health and safety committee is established in the department/ division = 10 points
The committee meets monthly = 5 points
The committee meets 6 times per year (2-monthly) = 2.5 points
The committee meets 2 times per year (bi-annually) = 1 point
The committee is chaired by management = 5 points
Minutes of the meetings are kept and are available = 5 points

Near Miss Incident Reports (10)

> 8% of workforce submitted near miss incident reports per month = 5 points
> 4% of workforce submitted near miss incident reports per month = 2.5 points
> 1% of workforce submitted near miss incident reports per month = 1 point
> 100% of near miss incident reports have been acted on per month = 5 points
> 50% of near miss incident reports have been acted on per month = 2.5 points
> 20% of near miss incident reports have been acted on per month = 1 point

Safety Observations Reported (written) (10)

> 10% of workforce submitted observations per month = 5 points
> 5% of workforce submitted observations per month = 2.5 points
> 2% of workforce submitted observations per month = 1 point
> 10% of observations reported have been acted on per month = 5 points
> 5% of observations reported have been acted on per month = 2.5 points
> 2% of observations reported have been acted on per month = 1 point

Workplace Inspections Completed (5)

> Weekly safety inspections conducted (50 per annum) = 5 points
> Monthly safety inspections conducted (12 per annum) = 5 points
> Every second month safety inspections conducted (6 per annum) = 2.5 points
> Quarterly safety inspections conducted (4 per annum) = 1 point

SUMMARY

The SMS must have a goal. This is usually the goal laid out in the health and safety policy statement, which is to create a healthy and safe workplace. A number of safety objectives are set by the SMS standards, and these need to be monitored and measured to gauge performance and achievement of objectives. Upstream, leading indicators that can be managed are a far more accurate measure of safety control. Lagging indicators are unreliable but need to be measured. Ideally, a mix of leading and lagging indicators will give management a good idea of the organization's health and safety performance. Key performance indicators should be established for all levels of management and should be monitored monthly.

13 Hazard Identification and Risk Assessment

INTRODUCTION

Hazard identification and elimination is the foundation of any health and safety management system (SMS). It must be an ongoing process as hazards arise, or whenever there are changes in the process or procedures. Contractors' sites may change from day to day and pose different hazards to the employees. The goal of an SMS is to constantly identify hazards, assess , and eliminate them by using a hazard identification and risk assessment (HIRA) process.

DESIGN OF A HIRA PROCESS

According to the Occupational Safety and Health Administration (OSHA) publication *Recommended Practices for Safety and Health Programs,*

> One of the "root causes" of workplace injuries, illnesses, and incidents is the failure to identify or recognize hazards that are present, or that could have been anticipated. A critical element of any effective safety and health program is a proactive, ongoing process to identify and assess such hazards.
>
> **(OSHA website)**

HAZARDS

Hazards can be introduced over time as workstations and processes change, tools and equipment become worn, maintenance is neglected, or good housekeeping practices decline.

DEFINITION

A hazard is a situation or behavior that has potential to cause injury or illness to people, damage to equipment, or harm to the environment.

HAZARD IDENTIFICATION

There are a number of ways to identify hazards in the workplace. Some methods are to:

- Consider hazards that arise from unusual jobs
- Identify accident cause trends
- Analyze near miss incidents for common root causes
- Conduct workplace inspections

- Use checklists that highlight items to look for
- Conduct incident recall sessions

COMPARATIVE AND FUNDAMENTAL METHODS

The two main methods of hazard identification are the *comparative* and *fundamental* methods. The comparative method makes use of checklists, hazard indices, and reviews of historical data and is facilitated by inspections and audits. The fundamental method uses tools such as Hazard and Operability Analysis techniques (HAZOPS), failure mode and effect analysis (FMEA), and failure mode and criticality analysis (FMECA). Failure logic is another method of hazard identification.

QUESTIONS

Some questions that can be asked to identify hazards are as follows:

- What can fail and what will the effect be?
- What components are critical to the process, and what will the effect be if they fail?
- What accidents have occurred in the area?
- What property-damage accidents occurred?
- What near miss incidents were reported?
- What deviations from standards exist, in terms of operating error, instrument failure, process upset, or loss of containment?

When reviewing critical tasks, scenarios should be posed and the question, "So what if it happens?" asked, so that possible hazardous situations and solutions can be brainstormed.

According to *Recommended Practices for Safety and Health Programs* (OSHA),

Many hazards can be identified using common knowledge and available tools. For example, you can easily identify and correct hazards associated with broken stair rails and frayed electrical cords. Workers can be a very useful internal resource, especially if they are trained in how to identify and assess risks.

(OSHA website)

HAZARD ELIMINATION HIERARCHY

When designing an SMS, an ongoing method of hazard identification and elimination must be a component of such a system. The hierarchy of hazard elimination, from the most effective to the least effective method, is as follows:

Hazard elimination – physically remove the hazard.
Hazard substitution – replace the hazard.
Engineering controls – isolate workers from the hazard.

Administrative controls – change the way the work is done.

Personal protective equipment – protect the worker with personal protective equipment.

HAZARD CONTROL PLAN

A hazard control plan describes how the selected hazard controls will be implemented. An effective plan should address major hazards first. Interim controls may be necessary, but the overall goal is to ensure effective long-term control of hazards. It is important to track progress toward completing the control plan and to periodically verify that controls remain effective (at least annually and when conditions, processes, or equipment change).

RISK ASSESSMENT

The accident sequence is often triggered by a failure to assess the risk and set to up the necessary controls in the form of a SMS. A risk is a chance for loss. Safety has often been defined as "acceptable risk."

A risk assessment is the combined effort of identifying and analyzing potential events that may negatively impact individuals, assets, and/or the environment. It analyzes what can go wrong, how likely it is to happen, and what the potential consequences could be.

A risk assessment entails viewing each hazard and asking the following two questions:

- What could happen here? (What is the probability of something adverse happening?)
- If it happens, how bad could it be? (What would the likely consequence be if it did happen?)

The main question to be considered with risks is "How tolerable is the risk?" Risk assessments are tools that attempt to predict the future to enable risk mitigation actions to be implemented.

IMPLEMENTATION OF A HIRA PROCESS

HAZARD IDENTIFICATION

Hazard identification processes need to be built into the SMS system. This should be specified in the elements covering inspections, housekeeping standards, critical task analysis, observation reporting schemes, and incident recall meetings. These should be ongoing processes which strive for continual improvement by constantly reducing hazards.

Risk Assessment

Risk assessments should be kept simple and easy to carry out. The workforce are the experts in their areas of operation, and they should be taught a simple method of risk assessment. The risk assessment process should be incorporated into the following:

- Near miss incident reports
- Accident investigations that caused fatality, injury, or ill health
- Property-damage accidents
- New task procedures
- The beginning of each shift
- Critical tasks before they are done
- Ongoing processes

The risk assessment process will prompt the assessor to consider likely future events and their possible consequence by answering the questions, "What could happen here, and if it does happen, how bad will it be?"

Ideally all risks should be kept as low as is reasonably practical (ALARP). This is accepted business practice. As soon as the risks extend beyond the ALARP level, then the consequences of those risks could be detrimental to the business and the employees working there.

In their publication *The Five Step Guide to Risk Assessment*, The Royal Society for the Prevention of Accidents (ROSPA) presents a simple 5-step sequence for the HIRA process (ROSPA website):

1. Identify the hazards
2. Decide who might be harmed and how
3. Assess the risks and decide on control measures
4. Record your findings and implement them
5. Review the assessment and update if necessary

Risk Register

A risk register is a documented risk tracking process. It is a management tool that records risk, records the possible risk outcomes, prescribes control methods, and allocates responsibility for risk reduction actions.

The risk register should contain the following:

- Risk ID – a unique tracking number
- Risk category – the type of risk
- Risk description – a brief description of the risk
- Possible likelihood and severity – a risk ranking based on a risk matrix
- Risk owners – who is responsible for managing the risk?
- Risk scores – what is the risk ranking?
- Mitigation actions – actions required
- Completion date – date of expected completion of actions
- Completed – date on which risk declared ALARP (Figure 13.1)

#	Risk Description	Category	Probability	Severity	Score	Action Plan	Date	Owner	Date Completed

FIGURE 13.1 Example of a Risk Register.

AUDIT OF A HIRA PROCESS

The audit inspection will indicate the effectiveness of the HIRA process. If a number of hazards are noted, this will indicate that the system is not working satisfactorily. The fewer hazards found, the better the system is functioning. Hazard identification should be incorporated into all inspections, and an ongoing observation reporting system should be in place, so that reported hazards can be identified and eliminated. Incident recall sessions should include information about hazards. Safety training in hazard recognition should take place frequently.

Hazards identified should be risk assessed and these findings should be recorded and tracked. The risk register should be kept up to date.

SUMMARY

A HIRA process forms the foundation of any SMS. Most elements are focused to identify hazards in the workplace and during work procedures. Only by having a continuous system to identify and rectify hazards can workplace risks be reduced. All hazards must be risk assessed to determine their potential for loss and the possible severity of that loss. Simple systems of hazard identification and risk assessment must be employed so that shop-floor employees can be involved in the process. A risk register will ensure that risks are tracked until they have been driven down to a tolerable level (Figure 13.2).

ELEMENT/PROGRAM/PROCESS	POINTS	QUESTIONS THAT COULD BE ASKED	VERIFICATION	WHAT TO LOOK FOR
HAZARD IDENTIFICATION AND RISK ASSESSMENT (HIRA)				
HAZARD IDENTIFICATION	5	What hazard identification methods are used?	See examples	Cross check with hazards noted during inspection
Inspections	5	How often are inspections done?	Copy of a completed checklist	Is the entire area covered?
Walkabouts	5	How often are walkabouts done?	Copy of a completed checklist	Proof of hazard identification
Checklists	5	Are checklists used?	Copy of a completed checklist	Is it applicable?
Incident Recall sessions	5	How often are inspections done?	Copy of minutes/records	Are hazards being recalled at these sessions?
RISK ASSESSMENT				
Risks Assessed	5	How are risks assessed?	Example	Check for probability/severity and ranking
Matrix Used	5	Is a risk matrix used?	Example of completed matrix	Is it being used?
Risk reduction efforts	5	What risks have been reduced during the last 12 months?	Examples of risk abatements	Is the system working?
Risk Register	5	Is a risk register kept?	Inspect register. Up to date?	Is the register kept evergreen?
TOTAL	45			

FIGURE 13.2   Audit Protocol for the Element – Hazard Identification and Risk Assessment.

14 Employee Communication, Consultation, and Participation Processes

DESIGN OF AN EMPLOYEE COMMUNICATION, CONSULTATION, AND PARTICIPATION PROCESS

Systems must be built into the health and safety management system (SMS) that allow employees to communicate and participate in the day-to-day activities of the systems, programs, and processes. Existing systems should be modified and new avenues created for employee participation. The number and structure of these activities such as safety committees, safety observation processes and safety training programs, will depend on the nature and size of the organization.

IMPLEMENTATION OF AN EMPLOYEE COMMUNICATION, CONSULTATION, AND PARTICIPATION PROCESS

Employees are the safety experts in their particular work areas and in their field of expertise. They can, therefore, contribute greatly to the safety process. Systems and avenues that allow for two-way communication must be integrated into the SMS so that constant communication and participation is maintained.

SMS ELEMENTS, PROCESSES, AND PROGRAMS

Below are a number of SMS elements, processes, and programs that facilitate communication, consultation, and participation on the part of employees, and in some cases, management as well.

SAFETY COMMITTEES

Employees should be represented on all health and safety committees. This is an ideal platform for two-way communication on health and safety. They should give and receive information at these meetings. This will ensure all are informed on safety matters, and safety concerns can be expressed and discussed and action plans drawn up. Contractors and contractor employees should also be members of this committee. Monthly meetings should be held, and an agenda of items to be discussed should be compiled to ensure input from all members. A member of management should chair the meeting.

HEALTH AND SAFETY REPRESENTATIVES

The most successful method of getting employees to participate in the SMS is to nominate health and safety representatives. These employees could be nominated by their fellow workers or by the workers' representative organizations. Often they are volunteers. At least 10% of the workforce should be appointed as health and safety representatives. These appointments should ensure that all work areas have coverage. Off-site work areas should also have health and safety representatives, as well as office and administration buildings. The role of health and safety representative offers an ideal opportunity for employees to play an important role in safety at the organization.

SAFETY TRAINING

A key ingredient in the SMS is health and safety training. This training should include an 8-hour annual refresher training session for all employees. Health and safety representatives should undergo a special one-day training class in hazard recognition and risk assessment, and they should be shown how to complete the health and safety representative inspection checklist. Management should receive basic safety training.

The training programs will depend on the nature of the company but should be ongoing processes, presented by well experienced trainers who know how to make safety training effective.

FIRST AID TRAINING

Selected employees can be trained as first aiders. In some industries, this is a legal requirement. Training employees in first aid also helps increase safety awareness and prepares the organization for when first aid assistance is required. Some workplaces have trained EMS (Emergency Medical Services) or full-time paramedics on site. First aid training is beneficial as it can be used in the home, or during recreation activities.

SAFETY SUGGESTION SCHEMES

The safety management principle of participation states that the more employees participate in the safety process, the more they are motivated to continue to contribute. Safety suggestion schemes are a part of the SMS and allow all employees to contribute to the overall safety and productivity of the plant by volunteering their own input in the form of suggestions. Without participation from the workforce, the SMS can never be completely successful.

INSPECTIONS

Employees must be involved in safety inspections. This could be either the regular health and safety representative inspections or ad hoc inspections by the safety department. Their knowledge should be called on during the inspection, as they know the work area and understand the processes.

ACCIDENT INVESTIGATIONS

When investigating accidents, it is a good idea to include in the process employees from the area where the accident took place. They can offer insight during the investigation and become involved in solving the problem. In some instances, accident investigation committees, comprising employees and managers, are appointed to investigate accidents.

INCIDENT RECALL

Regular accident and near miss incident-recall sessions are an important element of the SMS. These sessions should be used to encourage employees to recall events that happened in the past, or events that were not reported via the normal channels. The recall and discussion of off-the-job near miss incidents and road accidents all offer a lesson learned and should be encouraged.

PURCHASING OF PERSONAL PROTECTIVE EQUIPMENT (PPE)

Employees should participate in the selection of personal protective equipment (PPE). Ideally, a PPE committee is formed, and this committee is comprised of the purchasing department, production departments, and employees from other areas. This way, employees have a say in the selection of PPE. Participating in decisions concerning safety leads to employees feeling a part of the safety system.

JOB SAFE PRACTICES

Job safe practices (JSPs) are required for all high-risk tasks. Employees who perform these tasks should be encouraged to participate in the writing and updating of these procedures. They are well versed in the performing of these tasks and should be the ones who know how the task can be carried out safely and effectively.

NEAR MISS INCIDENT REPORTING

Involving employees (and line management) in the reporting of near miss incidents is beneficial as near miss incidents are often accident precursors. Employees should be recognized for reporting such incidents, and no blame must be laid on employees involved in the near miss incident. Action should be taken after a near miss report so that employees see something happen as a result of their report.

FIRE DRILLS

Employees can take up the role of area fire wardens who ensure that all employees have vacated the area in emergencies. They can participate in the planning and execution of practice runs. Certain employees could be trained to inspect fire extinguishers and other equipment.

CHANGE MANAGEMENT

Changes in processes, tools, materials, or methods usually gives rise to new hazards. Employees need to be involved in the change management program. Their knowledge of the workplace and processes is invaluable, especially during changes.

SMS AUDITS

Internal and external audits will involve workers throughout the workplace. Employees should be encouraged to participate in the audit inspection, give the auditors information, and be a part of the documentation review process. Participation in housekeeping competitions and toolbox talks also allow for employee participation.

SAFETY NEWSLETTERS

Safety newsletters are a convenient and ideal method of communicating safety information. They are easy and cheap to produce and are effective in disseminating information about health and safety.

SAFETY COMPETITIONS

Safety competitions get employees involved in the challenge of maintaining a healthy and safe workplace. Competitions should be based on upstream activities and actions that employees can achieve. Any competition or reward scheme based on injuries will mean that injuries will be driven underground in departments' efforts to be the best. These types of competitions should be discouraged.

SAFETY VIDEOS

The viewing of safety videos is an effective method of informing employees about certain aspects of safety. The video should be introduced before being viewed and a discussion on the contents should follow. A good objective is to have all employees exposed to at least one video per year. These sessions should be taken seriously, and attendance registers should be kept.

TOOLBOX TALKS

Toolbox talks, or tailgate meetings, are discussions on safety topics at the worksite. They take place before the task commences and cover a specific topic. Sign-in sheets should be completed after the talk. These could also take the form of task risk assessments, where a mini risk assessment is conducted before a task is tackled.

SAFETY PUBLICITY BOARDS

Safety publicity boards and notice boards carry safety information and are a vital part of the safety promotional network. Meetings, group discussions, and one-on-one personal contacts also serve to inform and enlighten people.

POSTERS AND SIGNS

Posters and signs also inform employees. The signage in a workplace must be standardized. Signs should be kept clean and in good order. Where possible, pictograms should be used, especially if the workforce is multilingual. Employees must be able to recognize the signs and understand their meaning. Signs that are no longer applicable should be removed. An annual sign survey will indicate the strengths and weaknesses of the signage.

WEBSITE

Most organizations maintain a website and intranet system. These media are ideal for communicating the organization's information concerning health and safety. Lots of safety information is shared via emails, and many newsletters are sent out in electronic format. Some organizations send safety reminders to employees' mobile phones.

AUDIT OF AN EMPLOYEE COMMUNICATION, CONSULTATION, AND PARTICIPATION PROCESS

Employee communication, consultation, and participation systems and programs are intertwined in many elements of the SMS. The auditor must examine each element and determine how employees are informed, how they are consulted about the health and safety process, and how fully they participate.

Employee interviews during the audit inspection are ideal opportunities to test the degree of communication, consultation, and participation of employees. Documented verification must be scrutinized to ensure this interaction is happening (Figure 14.1).

ELEMENT/PROGRAM/PROCESS	POINTS	QUESTIONS THAT COULD BE ASKED	VERIFICATION	WHAT TO LOOK FOR
EMPLOYEE COMMUNICATION, CONSULTATION AND PARTICIPATION				
Communication	5	What methods are used to communicate with employees?	Verification of methods	Notice boards, signs, banners
Committees	5	Do employees have representation of safety committees?	Copy of committee minutes	
Accident Investigation	5	Do employees participate in accident investigations?	Example of a recent investigation	Employees involvement in the investigation
Incident Recall Sessions	5	Do employees participate in these sessions?	Copy of notes of recall session	Do employees recall accidents/near miss incidents?
PPE Selection Process	5	How do employees participate in the PPE selection process?	Committee/ work group on PPE	Is there employee participation in this process?
Health and Safety Representatives	5	What percentage of employees are health and safety representatives?	Letters of appointment	At least 10%. Updated appointments
Inspections	5	Are employees involved in inspections?	Example inspection checklist	Health and safety rep. checklist and other inspections
Audits	5	Are employees involved in internal and external audits?	Written verification	Are employees involved in audits?
Newsletters/Website/Signs	5	Is there a newsletter? Website?	Copy of newsletter. View website	Correct signs used? Pictograms?
Change Management	5	How do employees participate in change management projects?	Examples of employee involvement	Check for involvement
Job Safe Practices (JSPs)	5	Do employees contribute to JSPs?	JSPs signed by employee(s)	JSPs up-to-date and employee consultation
TOTAL	55			

FIGURE 14.1   Audit Protocol for the Element – Communication, Consultation, and Participation.

15 Health and Safety Representatives

WHO ARE HEALTH AND SAFETY REPRESENTATIVES?

Management is not always in a position to identify hazards created by specific processes and items of machinery, and therefore they need the assistance of employees to act as safety observers. In his book *Industrial Accident Prevention*, W. H. Heinrich wrote about "safety observers." Safety observers are the eyes and ears of management. They are employees nominated to assist management by carrying out safety inspections. During these inspections, they complete a report on their findings, which is submitted to management for action.

DESIGN OF A HEALTH AND SAFETY REPRESENTATION SYSTEM

Health and safety representatives are employees appointed, volunteered, or nominated to assist and participate in the ongoing health and safety management system (SMS) in an organization. They represent employees in specific workplaces and contribute greatly to the health and safety of the workplace, and they assist in the identification and elimination of hazards. Health and safety representatives are also important for liaison between employees and different levels of management.

In some instances, worker unions nominate and appoint full-time health and safety representatives as their formal nominated persons to co-ordinate the activities of the SMS, and also to negotiate safety and health issues on their behalf.

Duties and Functions of Health and Safety Representatives:

- To inspect the workplace, including any article, substance, plant, machinery, or health and safety equipment at that workplace, on a monthly basis with a view to the health and safety of the employees
- To present a completed inspection report to management after each inspection
- To follow up on the rectification of deviations reported
- To attend meetings of the health and safety committee and also accept nomination to this committee
- To identify hazards which have potential to cause injuries
- To assist the employer to investigate and examine the causes of accidents
- To investigate any complaints by employees concerning that person's health or safety
- To make representations to the employer, or the health and safety committee, concerning hazards and threats to employees' safety and health
- To participate in ongoing safety audits
- To attend formal accident inquiries

IMPLEMENTING A HEALTH AND SAFETY REPRESENTATION SYSTEM

NOMINATIONS

Health and safety representatives should be nominated or selected according to the processes within the company. At least 10% of the workforce should be nominated as health and safety representatives. All work areas should be covered by a health and safety representative, including storage areas and offices. Signs should be erected in those areas indicating who the health and safety representatives are. Appointments should be for a 12-month period.

A formal training class should be attended by health and safety representatives to ensure that they get an understanding of hazard recognition and risk assessment and that they fully understand their roles and functions. In some countries, this is a legal appointment required by safety and health regulations. This training should be presented each year as a refresher class.

INSPECTION CHECKLIST

Inspections are always more efficient when a checklist is used. Checklists should cover basic safety elements and, in some cases, they need to be customized according to the work area or processes being inspected.

AUDIT OF A HEALTH AND SAFETY REPRESENTATION SYSTEM

The objective of an SMS is to create a healthy and safe workplace, free from hazards. The health and safety representative system is an important part of this endeavor. The auditor must establish if sufficient representatives have been appointed, that their training is effective, and that hazards are identified, reported, and actioned. A completed inspection report should be reviewed to ensure that action has been taken to reduce the hazard identified by the health and safety representative (Figure 15.1).

ELEMENT/PROGRAM/PROCESS	POINTS	QUESTIONS THAT COULD BE ASKED	VERIFICATION	WHAT TO LOOK FOR
HEALTH AND SAFETY REPRESENTATIVES				
Sufficient safety representatives appointed (10%)	5	How many are appointed?	At least 10% of workforce. Appointmentletters	
Do all representatives/appointees complete a monthly checklist based on the SMS elements?	5	Do health and safety representatives conduct regular, monthly safety inspections of their work areas?	Copy of completed checklist	Have hazards been reported
Do the inspections cover the entire area for which they are responsible?	5	Is a checklist used?	Check at least 8 items on checklist for SMS elements	Notices indication health and safety representative areas
Are high risk conditions reported?	5	Is the checklist based on the SMS?	Check some of the health and safety representatives checklists.	
Are high risk behaviors reported?	5	Are the checklists up to date and done correctly?	Check dates, signatures	
Are positive recommendations made?	5	What is a recent example of hazards found and rectified?	Is management taking action to rectify nonconformance's?	Follow the system to see if the hazards have been addressed.
Has the health and safety representative been made aware of all the hazards in the area by responsible the departmental supervisors ?	5	How was this done?	Verification of discussion/training	
Health and safety representative training	5	Have all health and safety representatives been trained?	Copy of the training records and syllabus	Do they have a good idea of their duties?
REPORTS CONSIDERED AND ACTIONED				
Are all reports forwarded to management (assigned person or deputy?)	5	Does management review these checklists and authorize necessary action?	Check some reports and see where management has authorized action where necessary.	Is the system working?
TOTAL	45			

FIGURE 15.1 Audit Protocol for the Element – Health and Safety Representatives.

16 Critical Task Identification and Job Safe Practice (JSP) Processes

DESIGN OF A CRITICAL TASK IDENTIFICATION PROCESS

OBJECTIVE

Job safe practices (JSPs) are required in order to reduce the possibility of risk to employees and damage to equipment while performing work tasks, specifically critical tasks (CTs). A critical task is a task which has the potential to cause major loss to people, property, process, or the environment if not carried out properly.

Written work procedures, properly used, serve as a base from which tasks can be continually modified to improve work methods, employee and contractor safety, and productivity.

The objective of a JSP process is to reduce accidental losses and to:

- Develop written job safe practices (JSPs) for critical tasks to be followed that will identify and control hazards that might not otherwise have been identified or highlighted.
- Improve the safety, productivity, and quality of tasks and improve work methods by analyzing the tasks, identifying the risks for each step of the task, and then establishing written, correct task methods, with inbuilt controls to mitigate or avoid the risks identified.

IMPLEMENTATION OF A CRITICAL TASK IDENTIFICATION PROCESS

JOB SAFE PRACTICES (JSPs)

According to the management principle of the critical few, of all the tasks undertaken in an organization, some 20% (minority) of these have the potential to cause 80% (majority) of the accidental losses, such as injuries, damage, or pollution. These are known as critical tasks.

Some of the hazards in the work environment are inherent in the location, the equipment or the materials used. In many cases, those hazards are impossible to eliminate, which means the method for safe work execution must ensure that losses are not caused by incorrect work methods or incorrect work-step sequences.

The first consideration for protection against these hazards should be *engineering controls* such as barriers, shields, special containers, and so on.

The other means is to *identify* the *high-risk tasks*, analyze them, and write structured step-by-step procedures (JSPs) to carry out the task correctly and safely. Employees are then trained in the correct job method as laid down by the JSP.

The JSP process is designed to give employees the information and training they require to carry out the task safely, despite the inherent hazards of the task.

DEVELOPING AND IMPLEMENTING JSPs

The following method could be used to establish a systematic method of identifying and controlling the hazards associated with critical and other tasks. A team consisting of employees who are required to do the job or task should be used to write the JSP. Attendance at an 8-hour JSP writing course will assist them in writing the JSP.

The manager, supervisor, or contractor (responsible persons), should develop the JSP in the following sequence:

- The professions/trades of employees in the area/department are identified and a list of all the jobs/tasks carried out by them is entered on the critical task identification form.
- A critical task identification exercise is then carried out by using the form to determine the critical jobs/tasks by means of a risk ranking.
- A critical task inventory sheet is then compiled listing the critical tasks, from the most critical down to the least critical, according to the risk ranking produced by the critical task identification exercise.

CRITICAL TASK ANALYSIS

Starting with the most critical tasks (high risk), the tasks are now analyzed, which involves listing the steps, the hazards, and the controls, in draft, using the JSP form. The draft should be reviewed with the employees to solicit their comments on actual and potential hazards as well as the required controls to eliminate the hazards. This process is often referred to as a *job safety analysis.*

WRITE THE JSPs

Using the draft analysis, which includes the steps, the hazards, and the controls, as a basis, the JSP is now written. (Ideally, an observation of the task being done should form the basis of the analysis.)

Each JSP developed should be reviewed by the prospective section supervisor and approved by the manager prior to its inclusion in the JSP manual. JSP manuals should be maintained in the department, as required, to allow for ready access for each supervisor and all employees.

PLANNED JOB OBSERVATIONS

Regular planned job observations (PJOs) are carried out to monitor the performance of the employee carrying out the task and the quality of the training he or she received, and also to verify the correctness and accuracy of the JSP. Observations should be a learning exercise and not a fault-finding exercise. After the observation, a discussion with the employee should be held to discuss their performance in relation to the JSP.

AUDIT OF A CRITICAL TASK IDENTIFICATION PROCESS

This is a critical element in the safety management system (SMS) and could give rise to a number of losses if not applied and maintained correctly. During the inspection segment of the audit, an effort must be made to visit the site of a critical task being carried out. Notes should be taken and the task observed closely. During the verification meeting, the auditors should call for that particular task's JSP and compare its contents with what they observed in the field. Dates of updating of the JSP as well as employee training should be confirmed (Figure 16.1).

ELEMENT/PROGRAM/PROCESS	POINTS	QUESTIONS THAT COULD BE ASKED	VERIFICATION	WHAT TO LOOK FOR
CRITICAL TASK IDENTIFICATION				
TASKS LISTED				
Tasks listed	5	Have all tasks been listed?	List of tasks	Visit sites where critical tasks are executed
Critical task identification done	5	Has a critical task identification been done?	Analysis and risk assessment chart	
Tasks risk ranked	5	Have critical tasks been identified and ranked?	Tasks ranked from high to low	
Critical task list	5	Is a list of critical tasks available?	Critical task inventory	
JOB SAFE PROCEDURES				
JSPs written and available	5	Have JSPs been written for all critical tasks?	Example of JSPs	Scrutinize at least five
Training conducted	5	Has training in the JSPs been done?	Training syllabus and attendance sheets	
JOB OBSERVATION				
Observations done	5	How often are observations done?	Proof of this	Observe critical tasks being done during the inspection
Discussions held	5	Are discussions held with the employee being observed?	Written acknowledgement	
Action taken	5	Is action taken if nonconformance's are noted?	Examples of changes to JSP ? Retraining of employee, etc.	
TOTAL	45			

FIGURE 16.1   Audit Protocol for the Element – Critical Task Identification.

17 Safety Induction Training Program

DESIGN OF A SAFETY INDUCTION TRAINING PROGRAM

Safety induction training is safety orientation training session for new employees, contractors, or employees who have not been in the working environment for a substantial period of time.

It is intended to orientate the trainee so that the trainee is aware of the walkways and working areas and also the safety required for that particular work environment. Orientation makes the new employee aware of the dangers, hazards, processes and dos and don'ts of the workplace to ensure their own safety.

NEW EMPLOYEES

The orientation also serves to familiarize new employees with the work environment and to help him or her to get settled in by emphasizing the safety factors of that work environment. Safety induction training immediately orientates the employee towards the safety culture of the company or, "the way we do it here." It teaches employees the safety approach practiced by the employer.

SAFETY RULES

Safety induction training spells out the safety rules, the occupational hygiene controls in place, the various tests that the employee will go through during his or her employment, and the type and nature of hazards that could be expected in the workplace. It also explains particular risks attached to the process.

The induction process could also bring about an awareness of the accident causation factors and help the trainee become familiar with the machines, the process, and the particular hazards they create. Personal responsibility for their own safety is also spelt out during the induction training. The trainees become aware of their own contribution to safety that is expected by the employer. The training indicates to the employee that the employer cares, and this generates a feeling of security within the new employee.

UNFAMILIAR ENVIRONMENT

The employee may be in an industrial or mining environment for the first time in their career. This could be their first introduction to machinery, electricity, materials, material handling, chemicals, and other items that form the backbone of that industry. Perhaps the new-hire has never ever worked with electricity, motorized transport, or other industrial processes, and the safety induction training is vital in getting the person familiar with the process, the nature of the business, and the noises present during the process, as well as the general plant layout. The location of emergency exits, clocking stations, first aid stations, and so on forms part of the training.

IMPLEMENTATION OF A SAFETY INDUCTION TRAINING PROGRAM

An example of a safety management system (SMS) standard for a safety induction program is as follows:

OBJECTIVE

The objective of this SMS standard is to ensure that all employees, management, contractors, and other affected persons receive the necessary health and safety induction and ongoing training to perform their work in a safe and productive manner.

RESPONSIBILITIES

Managers, supervisors, and contractors (Responsible persons) are responsible for ensuring that their employees are nominated for and attend the new employee induction training and other training as deemed necessary by this standard.

STANDARD

All new employees must receive basic safety and health training. This is part of the new employee induction training arranged by the human resources department.

All employees, as well as all contractors, who will be on the site for a period exceeding 8 hours continuous must receive basic safety and health induction training before being allowed to obtain a security pass badge to access the work site.

For contractors, this induction is valid for 12 months only. Thereafter, re-induction is given every year, or after periods of absence from the site exceeding 3 months.

Employee safety rules in the form of the company safety rule book are handed out to all new employees and contractors after training. This book contains the company health and safety policy and general safety rules. Issued books are signed for and records are kept.

All personnel will receive task specific training with regards to the health and safety risks of their specific work area. This is done during the area site-specific safety induction session. This also applied to transfers and promotions.

All employees are to be trained in job safe procedures (JSPs) applicable to their specific work. Planned job observations (PJOs) are to be done to ensure that training in the JSP process is effective.

Supervisors are to train their employees in all applicable standards, procedures, and work instructions related to their responsibilities before work commences, and they are to hold daily 5-minute safety talks with their employees and keep attendance registers.

Health and safety and training, as required, will be presented periodically to keep management and employees abreast of the latest trends and developments in the health and safety field.

SAFETY RULE BOOK

The safety rule book should form the basis of the safety induction orientation training session. This should ideally be a small pocket book, which the new employee can carry with him or her. To make the safety message attractive, the book should be colorful and where possible, pictures, sketches, and diagrams should be used.

The rule book should carry a safety message from the chief executive officer. The trainee should also sign a receipt acknowledging that they have received a safety rule book, have been trained in the rules contained therein, and agree to abide by the rules. Some organizations have their safety policy statement signed by the chief executive officer on the inside front cover.

INDUCTION TRAINING PRINCIPLES

As with any form of safety training, there are certain principles which the supervisor or the person doing the training should be aware of. If applied correctly, they can make the induction training a meaningful experience for the new-hire and also ensure that the training is effective.

RELATE FROM THE KNOWN TO THE UNKNOWN

The induction should move from the easy and simply understood principles to the more difficult principles. During the training session, the trainer should compare situations that the trainee has experienced or can identify with. The trainer should move from the tangible to the intangible, slowly, and at all times should recheck to ensure that the trainee is following. One of the basic principles of learning is to repeat the main points over and over, thus emphasizing their importance.

FOLLOW-UP TRAINING

As with any training there should be follow-up refresher training, and ongoing training, to ensure that the training received is not just a once-off session, which will have little or no effect on the attitude of the trainee.

When the trainee proceeds to his or her work situation and adheres to the safety rules, their immediate supervisor should commend them and congratulate them on their positive actions. Positive behavior which is recognized acts as a motivator for repeating positive and safe behavior.

VISUAL AIDS

We only retain a small percentage of the information we hear. The percentage increases with the more senses that are used. Visual aids in the form of digital projectors, models, and perhaps even unsafe hand tools and damaged equipment (used as models) will always increase the retention of the learning session. The flow process of raw materials into the plant and the finished products leaving the plant could be depicted by means of visual aids.

Samples of different types of fire extinguishers, pictures and sketches of different types of ladders, and a book containing certain accident and near miss incident case studies are ideal visual and teaching aids to complement the learning process in induction training.

SAFETY MUSEUM

A safety museum where actual unsafe objects which have been confiscated or removed from service are displayed is ideal for safety induction training. A display of the standard personal protective equipment used can also be part of the museum, and any item of personal protective equipment that has been damaged whilst protecting the wearer from injury are also interesting items to add to this museum.

ON-THE-JOB SAFETY INDUCTION

Once the classroom induction training period is completed, the trainee should then be taken into his or her particular work area. The induction training concerning the immediate work environment, the risks involved in the environment, and the various processes and the general dos and don'ts of safety in that area should commence.

AUDIT OF A SAFETY INDUCTION TRAINING PROGRAM

The auditor must establish that safety induction training takes place. This induction must be given to new employees and employees who have been away from work on extended vacations, as well as contractors and part-time or temporary workers. A written syllabus should be available, and ideally some form of testing should be part of the training. A safety rule book should also be part of the training. Ideally the company health and safety policy should be included in the book. Some form of on-the-job training program should follow the classroom training (Figure 17.1).

ELEMENT/PROGRAM/PROCESS	POINTS	QUESTIONS THAT COULD BE ASKED	VERIFICATION	WHAT TO LOOK FOR
SAFETY INDUCTION TRAINING PROGRAM				
INDUCTION IN PLACE				
New employees	5	Is there a safety induction program for new employees?	Copy of the program	
Other employees	5	Who else must attend?		
Contractors	5	Do contractors attend?	Proof of this	
SYLLABUS USED				
Syllabus followed	5	Is a fixed syllabus followed?	Copy of syllabus	Health and Safety policy included?
SAFETY RULE BOOK				
Safety rule book issued	5	Is a safety rule book issued?	Safety rule book copy	Is the rule book up to date?
Test method used	5	What test method is used after training?	Example of testing method	
ON-THE-JOB TRAINING				
On site training	5	Is there an on-site orientation process?	Example of this	
Follow up	5	What follow up is there after induction?	Example of this	
TOTAL	40			

FIGURE 17.1   Audit Protocol for the Element – Safety Induction Training.

18 Health and Safety Committees

DESIGN OF A HEALTH AND SAFETY COMMITTEE SYSTEM

OBJECTIVE

The objective of this element is to establish and sustain a system of occupational health and safety committees (safety committees) throughout the organization. These will facilitate the management of health and safety issues and provide a forum for health and safety communication, safety management system (SMS) implementation, and decision making in line with single point accountabilities at all levels within the organization.

COMMITTEE STRUCTURE

The committee structure will need to match the company hierarchy and allow for an executive committee at the highest level, led by the chief operating officer, down to committees at shop floor and contractor level. Some special committees may also be needed for ongoing or ad hoc projects. Examples are the protective equipment selection committee and the suggestion scheme committee.

IMPLEMENTATION OF A HEALTH AND SAFETY COMMITTEE SYSTEM

The following is a guideline for the implementation of a safety committee system:

Safety committees should be established at different levels and in different departments throughout the organization, for the purpose of providing forums for communication, decision making, and SMS implementation.

Each safety committee should meet on a regular monthly basis, and these meetings need to be scheduled in advance to ensure attendance is given priority. Meetings should generally be limited to one hour in duration.

The secretary should submit a prepared agenda of items for discussion to the committee members one week before the actual meeting. Members are to submit discussion points to the committee chairperson at least one day before the meeting.

MINUTES

Brief minutes of the meeting, noting the decisions, actions, and assigned responsibilities, should be taken and circulated within three days of the meeting by the secretary of the committee to all committee members. A copy is sent to the next higher-level committee chairperson.

Minutes will be in the form of an action plan listing:

- WHAT must be done
- WHO will do it
- WHEN it should be done

Where possible, minutes of the committee meeting should not be longer than one page and should be issued within three days of the meeting.

AUDIT OF A HEALTH AND SAFETY COMMITTEE SYSTEM

The auditors need to satisfy themselves that there is an effective safety committee structure in place. Managers from different levels need to chair these meetings, not safety personnel. Safety personnel should coordinate the meetings and play a secretarial role for the committee. It is important to check that management and employees are represented on committees. Are the minutes kept? Has some action been taken on agenda items? Is the committee system providing a platform for joint health and safety consultation and SMS implementation. (Figure 18.1)

ELEMENT/PROGRAM/PROCESS	POINTS	QUESTIONS THAT COULD BE ASKED	VERIFICATION	WHAT TO LOOK FOR
HEALTH AND SAFETY COMMITTEES				
COMMITTEE(S) ESTABLISHED				
Committees established according to standard and needs of company or legal requirement	5	How many committees have been formed?	List or chart of the committees or the list of members.	Committees established to meet the requirements of the standard and/or the needs determined by management, or legal requirements
Health and safety representatives	5	Do health and safety representatives participate in meetings?	Copy of minutes	Minutes
Do all health and safety representatives serve on a committee?	5	Who is the chairperson?	Copy of minutes	
Managers chair the meetings?	5	Are all departments represented? Do managers chair the committee meetings?	Copy of minutes	
MEETINGS ONCE PER MONTH				
Regular meetings	5	Do committees meet monthly?	Check minutes of meetings to ensure monthly meetings	
MINUTES KEPT				
Record of meeting	5	Are minutes kept of safety committee meetings?	Copy of Minutes	Follow up action taken?
Is the ratio of health and safety representatives/management appointments correct?	5	Who is represented on the committees?	Is there worker representation?	Meetings once a month.
TOTAL	35			

FIGURE 18.1 Audit Protocol for the Element – Health and Safety Committees.

19 Safety Management System Continuous Improvement Program

DESIGN OF AN SMS CONTINUOUS IMPROVEMENT PROGRAM

A safety management system (SMS) needs to be continually improved or else it stands the chance of stagnating. New developments and initiatives should be introduced to improve the system and keep employees engaged in its processes. The suitability of the SMS and its effectiveness should be frequently reviewed to improve safety controls.

Planned improvements should be set as objectives with completion dates. Records of improvements should be kept for reference. Ongoing inspections, reviews, and audits will provide scope for further system enhancements. Keeping the system and its elements evergreen will be a task for the leadership team, supported by a strong, proactive safety department.

The continuous improvement program must focus on improving the health and safety controls, maintaining a strong safety culture, and constantly promoting and encouraging the participation of employees in the SMS improvement processes. The improvements made should be communicated to all within the organization via existing health and safety communication systems.

IMPLEMENTATION OF AN SMS CONTINUOUS IMPROVEMENT PROGRAM

Plan, Do, Check, Act

The Plan, Do, Check, Act methodology can be used to implement and maintain a continuous improvement program.

Plan – Identify an opportunity for change and set objectives for improvements to the SMS and its elements.

Do – Implement the improvements on a small scale.

Check – Use data to analyze the results of the change and determine whether it made a difference.

Act – If the change was successful, implement it on a wider scale and continuously assess your results. If the change did not work, begin the cycle again.

SMALL CHANGES

Continual improvements to the elements of the SMS should be made in small changes. Incremental changes are easy to implement and do not cost a lot of money to carry out. If employees are involved in suggesting and helping with these small changes, they will be inclined to take ownership of the improvements. The changes must be measurable and more than likely can be repeated. Constant feedback should be provided to keep participants informed and involved in the changes.

Suggested changes could be brainstormed by forming small groups and requesting them to come up with improvements to certain elements, or to help solve certain health and safety issues. Safety committees could also propose improvement ideas, and the safety suggestion scheme is also a means to obtain ideas for improving the SMS.

AUDIT OF A SMS CONTINUOUS IMPROVEMENT PROGRAM

A record of continuing improvement to the SMS should be retained in the files. This record should reflect the improvements made since the last audit. Improvements to certain programs and processes should be measurable and the auditors should identify this (Figure 19.1).

ELEMENT/PROGRAM/PROCESS	POINTS	QUESTIONS THAT COULD BE ASKED	VERIFICATION	WHAT TO LOOK FOR
SMS CONTINUOUS IMPROVEMENT PROGRAM				
PROGRAM IN OPERATION				
Continuous improvement standard	5	Is a program in operation and is a standard available?	Copy of the standard	Is the system working?
REVIEW METHODS				
Suggestions	5	How are improvement suggestions handled?	Example of suggestions	Suggestions implemented
Past accidents	5	Are past events used to make improvements	Example of lessons learned	Are the examples positive
Inspections	5	What improvements and changes have been made as a result of inspections?	Example of improvements	Improvements and changes made to SMS
Reviews	5	How often are SMS reviews held?	Copy of review	
Committees	5	Do committees suggest improvements?	Example	Are committees making suggestions for improvements?
CHANGES MADE				
Changes tracked	5	What changes were made during the last 12 months?	Example of changes	Positive improvements
Objectives for further improvements	5	Is there an improvement objective set?	Copy of improvement objective	
TOTAL	40			

FIGURE 19.1 Audit Protocol for the Element – Continuous Improvement Program.

20 Safe Management of Change Process

SAFE MANAGEMENT OF CHANGE

Change is inevitable, but change to processes, procedures, and layout at the workplace often brings progress. However, ineffective management of change has been the cause of many major accidents in the past and creates potential for future accidental events. Unmanaged changes increase risks that, if not properly managed, may create conditions that could lead to injuries, property damage, or other losses. The main types of change within an organization are as follows:

- Changes to infrastructure
- Changes to processes equipment or product
- Changes in personnel
- Use of different materials
- Changes brought about by the health and safety management system (SMS)

Ideally, no modification should be made to any plant, equipment, control systems, process conditions, operating methods, or health and safety procedures without authorization from a responsible manager. In some cases, third party approvals may be necessary.

The hazards encountered and risks posed by these changes should be assessed and the necessary controls put into place before the change to reduce the probability of the change resulting in accidental loss.

IMPLEMENTING A SAFE MANAGEMENT OF CHANGE PROCESS

There are a number of ways to implement the safe management of change. All achieve the same objective of ensuring that the change does not create additional risks; is of benefit to the organization, its employees, and its processes; and is communicated to all. A change management checklist and flowchart is vital in change management. An example of change management is as follows:

- Identify the Change
  The change must be identified and clearly defined. Departments, machinery, or processes that will be affected must be listed and consulted.
- Risks and Rewards of the Change
  The risks created by the change must be identified and assessed. The benefits of the change should be clear and measurable. Affected departments should use this data to approve or reject the change.

- Change Approval
  Most change initiatives need approval from the applicable authority level. Budgets need to be established as well as a plan of action which is approved by all affected parties. Once approved, a change management document should be opened.
- Change Team
  In some instances, a change management team or committee may be needed to manage the change and give feedback on the progress of the change.
- Communicating the Change
  Before any change takes place, the change should be communicated to all interested and affected parties. The benefits of the change should be stated as well as the commencement and completion date of the change.
- Risk Mitigation
  Any risks identified as a result of the change should be identified before the change takes place, and risk control measures should be instituted to mitigate these risks. In all change interventions, the benefits must outweigh the risk.
- Implement the Change
  The change should be implemented by following a plan of action which allocates authorities, responsibilities, and accountabilities to bring about the change. The change management form will guide the change owners through the correct procedure. A timeline should be established as well as budget requirements.
- Training
  Depending on the change, additional training of employees or contractors may be needed to enlighten them on the changes. All affected parties should undergo this update training.
- Confirm Effectiveness of Change
  Once the change is completed, data should be collected that quantifies the efficiency of the change.
- Follow up
  A follow up on the change is the final step of the change management process. This follow up would check that the change was implemented according to plan, and that the change has created the benefit envisioned in the planning stage. This step would include final sign off of the change document.

AUDITING A SAFE MANAGEMENT OF CHANGE PROCESS

The auditors must establish that the organization has a safe management of change process in place. This should be documented, and a standard should be available as well as a change tracking and control document. Examples of communicating the change to employees and other affected parties should be reviewed. A risk assessment of the change to be made should be available as well as the risk mitigation plan. The auditors should review a change or modification that took place during the past 12 months (the audit period) and follow it through the system from beginning to end, reviewing the notifications, risk assessments, training, inspections, and benefit analysis of the change (Figure 20.1).

ELEMENT/PROGRAM/PROCESS	POINTS	QUESTIONS THAT COULD BE ASKED	VERIFICATION	WHAT TO LOOK FOR
SAFE MANAGEMENT OF CHANGE				
PROGRAM				
Program in place	5	Is there a safe change program in place?	Copy of program	Visit a site where recent changes have been made
Standard written	5	Is a SMS standard available?	Copy of standard	
RISK ASSESSMENT				
Risk of change considered	5	Has a risk assessment been done?	Risk assessment copy	
CHANGE DOCUMENT				
Flow sheet	5	Is there a change document/flow sheet?	Example of the document used	Follow the flow sheet and compare with what was seen
CHANGE AUTHORIZATION				
Person in charge	5	Is a person appointed responsible for the change project?	Appointment letter	
BENEFIT ANALYSIS				
Benefit of change identified	5	Have the benefits of the change been identified?	Document	
Follow up	5	What follow up is done after the change?	Document	
EMPLOYEE COMMUNICATION				
Communication	5	How is the change communicated?	Examples of how this was done	Employee interview question
Informing others	5	How are others informed?	Examples	
CHANGE TRAINING				
Training needed	5	Has a need for training in change been identified?	Training needs analysis	
Training done	5	Has training been done?	Copy of training material	
TOTAL	55			

FIGURE 20.1   Audit Protocol for the Element – Safe Management of Change.

21 Health and Safety Training Program

DESIGN OF A HEALTH AND SAFETY TRAINING PROGRAM

INTRODUCTION

Lack of knowledge and skill is one of the root causes of accidents. Safety training creates an awareness of what causes accidents and what constitutes injuries and diseases, and it teaches the difference between near miss incidents and accidents. It also imparts knowledge about other safety topics.

Safety training carries the message that the majority of accidents are preventable. It helps teach employees how to do their job correctly, and indicates what dangers may be present in the work environment. Safety training can be presented to individuals, safety committees, small groups, and work task teams.

Safety training is of vital importance as it forms an important base on which to form a comprehensive health and safety management system (SMS). Both management and the workforce should attend appropriate training programs. All employees should attend the annual safety refresher training.

TRAINING NEEDS ANALYSIS

The organization should conduct a health and safety needs analysis to ascertain which safety and health training needs to be presented. This needs analysis should indicate who should attend the training and how often. Line management should be included in this analysis.

IMPLEMENTATION OF A HEALTH AND SAFETY TRAINING PROGRAM

TRAINING VENUE

A suitable training room should be used for the health and safety training classes. This venue should be equipped with all the visual aid equipment necessary and provide a place for the permanent display of personal protective equipment, safety equipment, and other exhibits that relate to health and safety.

TYPES OF HEALTH AND SAFETY TRAINING

Safety training can take many forms, and can either be general or specific.

General Health and Safety Training

- Induction training is normally given to new employees to ensure that they are familiar with the work environment and the risks relating to the workplace and the particular work they will be performing.
- Refresher training is normally a follow up and can be given on an annual basis, or when a person returns to the workplace after a leave of absence.
- Training in the philosophy of safety is important as it helps people understand the cause of accidents, the effects, and the results. Training employees to understand acceptable safety standards is another vital aspect of safety training. This training program could include teaching employees the safety rules of the organization as well as the safety dos and don'ts.
- Training in basic safety management can be presented to all supervisory staff as well as managerial staff. First aid training and training in CPR (cardiovascular pulmonary resuscitation) and mouth-to-mouth resuscitation makes trainees aware of their safety responsibility within a workplace, and also prepares them for emergencies. Rescue and evacuation training as well as firefighting courses are beneficial to both the individual and the SMS.

Specific Health and Safety Training

Depending on the industry, specific health and safety training could cover topics such as:

- Accident/near miss incident investigation
- Modern safety management
- Safety for supervisors
- Hazard communication (HazCom)
- Training the trainer to teach classes
- Regulatory safety requirements
- Firefighting

HAZARD COMMUNICATION TRAINING

Hazard communication, also known as HazCom, is a set of processes and procedures that employers and importers must implement in the workplace to effectively communicate hazards associated with chemicals during handling, shipping, and any form of exposure.

CRITICAL TASK TRAINING

An important aspect in carrying out critical or hazardous tasks is the training that is given to enable the operator to understand the critical task procedure. Retraining after a job observation is the best method to ensure that operators follow the critical task procedures.

TECHNICAL SAFETY TRAINING

A lot of safety training is technically orientated and this could include training on:

- Vehicle safety
- Occupational hygiene
- Pressure vessel safety
- Ladder safety
- Permit issuance and receiving
- Confined space team member
- Lifting gear safety, and so on
- Energy control (lock-out)
- Trenching and shoring
- Material safety data sheets (MSDS)
- Confined space entry
- Asbestos awareness

HEALTH AND SAFETY COORDINATORS

Ongoing safety training for health and safety coordinators is important and would help keep them updated concerning modern safety techniques such as:

- Risk management
- Risk evaluation
- Risk financing
- Ergonomics
- Sick building syndrome
- Carpal tunnel syndrome

AUDIT OF A HEALTH AND SAFETY TRAINING PROGRAM

The auditors must satisfy themselves that all legal training requirements have been met; that line management are being trained in basic safety concepts; that all employees attend an annual refresher training class; and that an employee rulebook is issued and used as a basis for general health and safety training. The on-the-job health and safety training should be aligned with the risks that the employee will encounter at the workplace. Since hazardous communication (HazCom) is a general weak area in many organizations, the auditors should determine if it is being done effectively (Figure 21.1).

ELEMENT/PROGRAM/PROCESS	POINTS	QUESTIONS THAT COULD BE ASKED	VERIFICATION	WHAT TO LOOK FOR
HEALTH AND SAFETY TRAINING PROGRAM				
TRAINING PROGRAMS				
Employee Training	5	What training do employees undertake?	Copy of training schedule	Training sufficient?
Contractors	5	What training do contractors undertake?	Copy of training schedule	Training sufficient?
Legal training	5	What legal training requirements are there?	Copy of training schedule	Training sufficient?
CRITICAL TASK TRAINING				
Specific critical task training	5	Is training on JSPs done?	Copy of an example	
HAZARD COMMUNICATION				
Hazard communication training	5	How often is HAZCOM training done?	Attendance registers	Does this meet the legal requirements?
MANAGEMENT TRAINING				
General health and safety for managers	5	What training does management attend?	Copy of training schedule	Training sufficient?
HEALTH AND SAFETY DEPARTMENT				
Department training and development	5	What training and development is there for safety staff?	Examples	Is this sufficient for the department?
OTHER TRAINING COURSES				
General health and safety courses	5	What other training is presented?	Examples	Does the company do more than basic training required by law?
TOTAL	**45**			

FIGURE 21.1 Audit Protocol for the Element – Health and Safety Training.

22 Health and Safety Management System Auditing

DESIGN OF A HEALTH AND SAFETY MANAGEMENT SYSTEM AUDITING PROGRAM

INTRODUCTION

A health and safety management system (SMS) audit is the systematic and documented verification process to obtain and evaluate evidence objectively to determine whether an organization's SMS conforms to the SMS audit criteria set by the organization, and the communication of the results of this process to management.

The purpose of auditing a SMS is to offer checks and balances and verify that a system is in place, is appropriate for the risks, and is effective when compared to the company's SMS standards.

REQUIREMENTS

The organization must have an active, functioning SMS in place before a comprehensive audit can be done. If this is not the case, a baseline audit should be conducted using a generic audit protocol. Smaller divisions and office blocks should have customized audit protocols containing the SMS elements applicable to them.

Trained auditors must be available to conduct the audit. If it is an external audit, then reputable, qualified SMS auditors should be used. Suitable audit protocols must be made available. These should reflect the requirements of the SMS standards for each element of the system.

IMPLEMENTATION OF A HEALTH AND SAFETY MANAGEMENT SYSTEM AUDITING PROGRAM

Internal audits should be scheduled for twice a year, and external audits should take place annually. The audits should be a learning exercise, and a professional approach is required by the auditors. For external audits, all arrangements must be made well in advance to ensure the venue is booked, permits are issued, and other company requirements are fulfilled.

In some instances, certain manufacturing processes are trade secrets and auditors will not be able to inspect those specific work areas. This is acceptable, as the auditors can get a good idea of the working of the SMS by visiting other areas.

SMS AUDITING STANDARD

An example of an SMS standard covering the internal and external audit programs is given below.

Objective

The objective of this standard is to ensure that both internal and external audits of the company SMS are carried out at prescribed intervals, in all divisions, to measure the degree of conformance to standards and to evaluate the health and safety effort. It is also to specify what SMS internal and external audits are conducted and to determine who conducts them, how they are conducted, and at what intervals.

Procedure

Internal audits do not result in outside recognition or accreditation by any authorizing body. They encompass audits of each division and result in internal recognition and grading (scoring) of the division.

Auditable Units

Auditable units are self-contained units within the company that are geographically, operationally, and organizationally (GOO) together as a unit, are under one manager/supervisor, and which can maintain a SMS which can be audited. This would mean that at least 50 SMS elements are applicable to that division. Examples of auditable units are production houses, power plants, warehouses, training centers, maintenance facilities, vehicle maintenance facilities, and contractors' worksites and yards.

Office buildings and small worksites can seldom manage a comprehensive SMS even though some elements are applicable. Specific audit protocols will be compiled and used to audit such work areas.

External Audits

External audits are carried out by an external agency or body selected by the company, and they result in external accreditation or recognition. They encompass the entire company, including all sites, divisions, and subsidiaries, and result in a grading (scoring or ranking) of the company as a whole. The auditors will spend three days (for example) examining the physical conditions and one day (for example) reviewing the verification documentation. The final company grading score is derived by means of random samples of each division selected by the external auditors. The company SMS audit protocol should be used as the audit protocol for external audits. The company external audit score will be obtained by averaging the scores allocated.

Internal Audits

During the year, formal internal audits will be conducted to measure the effectiveness and implementation of the SMS and to correct deviations from standards.

- Each division will be audited internally six-monthly.
- All internal audits are to be conducted by company Accredited Internal Auditors (AIAs).
- All elements of the SMS are considered during audits.

FORMAL AUDIT AND REPORTING

Internal self-audits will be initiated and coordinated by the health and safety department in conjunction with the divisional managers. The audit team will consist of company AIAs assisted by the divisional safety coordinators. A member of the audit team will be made responsible for producing a report on the audit within a month of the completion of the audit.

METHODOLOGY

Internal audits will have management, supervisor, and health and safety representative and contractor participation. At least four working days shall be spent at each division for internal auditing purposes. One of those days shall be used for the verification documentation review.

For internal audits, the simplified version of the company SMS audit protocol will be used with a reference to the audit protocol. Audit reports will be comprehensive and will include recommendations for corrective measures.

PROCESS

The audit team will meet at the beginning of each day and plan the workday. At the end of each day, the audit team will review the day's findings. A detailed SMS element percentage scoring will be given to each division at the end of the audit. Based on the audit scores, an internal ranking will be issued which the division will display on their safety notice boards.

PERFORMANCE METRICS

Achieving the percentage as listed below will determine the ranking issued.

AUDIT SCORE	RANKING
40%+	Below average
50%+	Good
60%+	Very good
74%+	Excellent
91%+	Safety Achiever

A ranking shall only be valid for 12 months. Audits will measure what activities took place in the 12-month period preceding the audit.

RESPONSIBILITY AND ACCOUNTABILITY

The health and safety department is responsible for the initiation and coordination of the audits. Managers, supervisory staff, and contractors are to be active audit participants during the physical inspections of their areas of responsibility.

The health and safety personnel in each division are responsible for compiling the inspection program and for ensuring all necessary control documentation is available in the SMS element sequence in a central location. Health and safety personnel are responsible for site-specific safety induction of internal and external auditors if and where applicable, as well as for the issue of applicable personal protective equipment (PPE) to the auditors.

AUDITING OF A HEALTH AND SAFETY MANAGEMENT SYSTEM AUDITING PROGRAM

External auditors will examine the effectiveness of internal audits. They will determine what training the internal auditors have had, the frequency and depth of the audits, and the resultant action plans for improvements recommended after the audit. All forms of internal audits will be adjudicated by the auditors to verify their applicability and effectiveness. The audit process will also compare audit scores to verify if the continuous improvement process is working (Figure 22.1 and Figure 22.2).

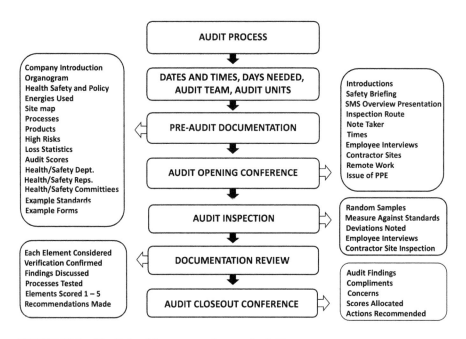

FIGURE 22.1   The Safety Management System Audit Process.

ELEMENT/PROGRAM/PROCESS	POINTS	QUESTIONS THAT COULD BE ASKED	VERIFICATION	WHAT TO LOOK FOR
HEALTH AND SAFETY AUDIT PROGRAM				
INTERNAL AUDITS				
Internal audit program	5	Is an audit program in operation?	Copy of standard	Does the audit program meet the standard?
Every 6 months	5	Are audits done internally every 6 months?	Copy of audit	
Ranking given	5	Is some form of score or ranking given	Example	Are scores or ranking displayed?
EXTERNAL AUDITS				
Audits done	5	How often are audits done?	Documented audits	Are audits done annually?
Every year	5	Is an audit done every year?	Documented audits	Documented audits
INTERNAL AUDITORS				
Qualified internal auditors	5	Are there internal qualified auditors?	List of auditors	
Training program	5	What training is there for them?	Example of training	
AUDIT PROTOCOL				
Audit protocol	5	Is an audit protocol used?	Copy of audit protocol	Does the protocol match the SMS?
All elements considered	5	Are all elements considered?	Score sheet and protocol	
Report issued	5	Is a report issued?	Examples of audit reports	Are the audits effective? Has action been taken on reported findings?
NON AUDITABLE UNITS				
Audit protocol (non auditableunits)	5	Are non auditable units also audited?	Examples	
Offices and other areas audited	5	What about office areas and similar?	Examples	
TOTAL	60			

FIGURE 22.2 Audit Protocol for the Element – Health and Safety Management System Audits.

23 Safety Management System Review

DESIGN OF A SAFETY MANAGEMENT SYSTEM REVIEW PROCESS

It is important for top management to review the health and safety management system (SMS) to determine if there are changes necessary to improve or correct the system, and for them to plan future improvement initiatives. Nonconformities are also reviewed at these meetings.

The objective of the review would be to suggest changes to the SMS, determine the effectiveness of the elements of the system, decide if additional resources are needed, and ensure that the policies and procedures are up to date and that the performance required is being achieved.

IMPLEMENTATION OF A SAFETY MANAGEMENT SYSTEM REVIEW

A scheduled review of the health and safety performance should take place at lease bi-annually. A suitable venue should be arranged and line managers invited to attend. An agenda containing the items to be reviewed should be compiled and circulated before the meeting by the health and safety department.

The review could take place at a scheduled executive health and safety committee meeting, as a formal review is preferable to an informal review. The review should have an agenda and the following points should be covered:

- Review of injury, damage, and other loss events since last review
- Status of accident and high potential near miss incidents investigations
- Changes made within the SMS
- Review of achievement of health and safety objectives
- Feedback from external parties
- Improvement opportunities
- Participation of employees in the SMS
- Internal and external audit results
- Recommended improvements and suggestions
- Legal requirements being met
- Follow up on previous review

An action plan should be drawn up after the review, and this plan must allocate responsibilities for actions to make any changes or improvements arising from the review. The findings of the management review should be made known to employees and employee representation organizations.

AUDIT OF A SAFETY MANAGEMENT SYSTEM REVIEW

When auditing this element of the SMS, the auditors should review the management review process and check documentation that refers to the review meetings. Who sits in on the reviews? Are notes kept? Are action plans drawn up? These are some of the questions that need to be asked (Figure 23.1).

ELEMENT/PROGRAM/PROCESS	POINTS	QUESTIONS THAT COULD BE ASKED	VERIFICATION	WHAT TO LOOK FOR
SAFETY MANAGEMENT SYSTEM REVIEW				
Management Reviews	5	How often are management reviews held?	Schedule	At least annually
Attendance	5	Who attends the reviews?	Attendance lists	Management attendance/worker representation
Agenda	5	Is an agenda prepared for reviews?	Copy of the agenda	
Items reviewed	5	What items are reviewed?	Agenda	Injury/damage/changes/objectives/feedback/participation/legal compliance/improvements/audits/Investigations
Review Frequency	5	How often are reviews held?	Check dates	
ACTION PLANS				
Notes Kept	5	Are notes kept of the review?	Copy of minutes	Do notes correspond with actions?
Action Plans	5	Are action plans compiled?	Action plan	Are there dates and responsibilities assigned?
Follow up	5	What follow-up is there after the review?	Follow-up notes	Deadline dates
TOTAL	**40**			

FIGURE 23.1   Audit Protocol for the Element – Safety Management System Review.

24 Employee Job Specifications

DESIGN OF AN EMPLOYEE JOB SPECIFICATION PROGRAM

To enable an organisation to function safely, an all-out endeavour should be made to get the correct employee to do the work for which they are best suited. This would ensure placing the correct person in the correct job, so that there is no mismatch. The possibilities of accidents can be reduced by selecting employees with the correct attributes for the work that they are to perform.

EMPLOYEE JOB SPECIFICATION

An employee job specification is *a detailed description of both the physical and cognitive attributes required of a person to fill a specific work function.*

The specification specifies the physical and cognitive aptitudes and attitudes required for the person who is to do the work. The job specification can be referred to as a checklist to ensure that the correct person is selected for the correct job.

SPECIFICATION LIST

All of the variables, employee specifications, and requirements should be compiled into a checklist and used when selecting employees. The person requisitioning the employee should complete the checklist. This checklist will then form an outline of the type of person required for that specific job.

The employee specification should be used for the correct selection and training of employees, and should be taken into consideration when employees are transferred or promoted. Obtaining the correct person for the correct job will reduce the chances of frustration, mismatching, and stress, which could lead to accidents.

IMPLEMENTATION OF AN EMPLOYEE JOB SPECIFICATION PROGRAM

PRE-EMPLOYMENT MEDICAL EXAMINATION

Before a person is employed, they should attend a pre-employment medical examination and be interviewed by a selection panel. The objective of the medical examination will be to ensure that they have the physical attributes and requirements specified for the type of work that they have applied for.

The medical examination will examine the applicant to ensure that they possess the necessary physical requirements for the post, and that he or she is in good health and is capable of fitting into the work environment.

PHYSICAL, HEALTH, AND COGNITIVE REQUIREMENTS

The employee specification would list the various physical, health, and cognitive requirements demanded by the particular job. The person requesting that the position be filled would indicate to the medical department what specific attributes are required.

These could include eyesight, and the doctor may be required to check depth perception, the vertical and lateral phoria, color vision, and also acuity. The latter is an important attribute especially for vehicle and equipment operators.

To ensure that the candidate can heed warning signs and signals, their hearing acuity should be tested and a general overview of their health obtained. Many organizations require drug testing for all new employees.

If the position calls for physical manual handling, the specification may require a person to be of a suitable build, a certain height, and a certain weight.

PERSONAL PROTECTIVE EQUIPMENT

The employee specification will list the items of personal protective equipment that the employee might have to wear. The medical examination will determine whether or not the person is able to wear safety shoes, hard hat, safety glasses, or whatever else maybe required during the work. If breathing apparatus is to be worn, the employee would require a medical certificate stating that they can wear a respirator. Respirator test fitting would then follow.

EDUCATIONAL QUALIFICATION AND EXPERIENCE

Depending on the position being filled, the person requesting the manpower will specify what general education is required, what degrees or diplomas are required, and how many years of work experience is required. The general intelligence of the person may be tested as well as the applicant's comprehension and memory. If needed, the specification will list other specific requirements for the position.

SPECIAL APTITUDES

When completing the employee specification, special aptitudes required for the job may be listed. These aptitudes could include mechanical ability and manual dexterity, including hand and eye co-ordination or hand, eye, and foot co-ordination. Reaction ability may be required, and the ability to speak local languages may also be specified.

PERSONALITY

If a person is to be placed in charge of other workers, they must fulfil certain personality requirements. The job specification may list certain leadership requirements such as communication skills, flexibility, initiative, tenacity, and ability to train others. A supervisor or leader lacking in some of these attributes may create a situation where friction and stress occurs in the workplace, which in turn could give rise to accidents.

PHYSICAL WORK CONDITIONS

The employee specification will also specify special circumstances under which the person may work, such as the working hours and the physical work conditions, such as heat, cold, noise, and special activities (climbing, standing, and bending.) The incumbent may be required to work shift work or over-time, or to be on standby over weekends.

Physical work conditions could include working in a noise zone; in dirty, dusty areas; or in a hot or cold environment, or they may involve working with heavy equipment or other hazardous substances such as explosives. The task may even be repetitive and monotonous, which would require a certain disposition.

AUDIT OF AN EMPLOYEE JOB SPECIFICATION PROGRAM

The main question that auditors need answered when auditing the employee job specification element is, "Is there a structured system of selecting the correct employees for the specific work they are to perform?" There should be an example of the employment process, the medical examination requirement, and special attributes for different work positions. This should include critical positions such as crane operators. Requirements for different levels of management should form part of the job specification process.

DOCUMENT VERIFICATION

This element is best audited during the documentation verification process. Here the specifications can be examined and the organization questioned concerning their selection and placement program.

FOLLOWING THE SYSTEM

To follow the system, the auditors should identify an employee during the inspection (a worker who works at heights, or a worker who works with hazardous material) and ask for the employee specification for that job category. This should then lead to the kinds of tests that were administered during the hiring process, as well as the training given to the employee. The system is functioning when all efforts have been made to match the employee with the position (Figure 24.1).

ELEMENT/PROGRAM/PROCESS	POINTS	QUESTIONS THAT COULD BE ASKED	VERIFICATION	WHAT TO LOOK FOR
EMPLOYEE JOB SPECIFICATIONS				
Medical examinations	5	Are pre-employment medicals held for all employees and is medical history, including previous injuries, obtained?	Have all employees attended a pre-employment medical examination?	
JOB SPECIFICATIONS AVAILABLE				
Employee job specifications available	5	To ensure the right person is placed in the position, is a job specification completed and sent to the doctor?	Copy of what aspects are examined by the doctor?	
Job specifications used to recommend placement or suitability for job	5	Does it cover physical requirements as well as cognitive requirements, such as reaction time, phobias, temperament, etc.?		
Job specifications updated when tasks or environment in which job is carried out change	5	When was this last done?	Examine a few completed job specifications forms for a few different types of employees.	
Biological monitoring and medical surveillance for workers performing listed work conducted where necessary?	5	What listed (hazardous as identified by law) is carried out on this site?	Record of monitoring and surveillance results.	
REGULAR MEDICALS CARRIED OUT				
Hazardous substance handlers checked regularly	5	Are regular medicals carried out for employees who work with hazardous substances. Senior management , equipment operators, crane drivers, etc.		
Job categories with requirements for regular medicals or biological testing identified	5	Have these jobs been identified?	List of job categories applicable.	
Medicals conducted at predetermined intervals	5	What are the intervals?	Copy of standard of intervals	
Remedial action taken	5	If any deterioration is discovered – what action is taken?	List/matrix of who should be checked for what and how often	
JOB SPECIFICATIONS AVAILABLE AND USED				
Employee specifications for all job categories	5	Are the employee-job specifications available?	Examples/copies of employee job specifications,qualifications, skills, etc.	
Job specifications used in the selection process	5	Are they used?		
Effort to match people to the job (physically, mentally, ergonomically)	5	What other effort is made to ensure the right person is placed in the right position?		
TOTAL	60			

FIGURE 24.1   Audit Protocol for the Element – Employee Job Specifications.

25 Return to Work Program

DESIGN OF A RETURN TO WORK PROGRAM

A return to work (RTW) program is a proactive, formal plan that helps injured workers remain at work or safely return to suitable work. It also outlines the steps that workers, supervisors, and others within the organization need to take if an injury occurs. An RTW standard should be written and a coordinator appointed to manage all aspects of the RTW program.

IMPLEMENTATION OF AN RTW PROGRAM

EXAMPLE OF AN RTW POLICY

Our company has implemented an RTW program that is intended to bring employees back to work as soon as they are physically able, to perform work that is meaningful, without aggravating their injury or illness.

An RTW program has many benefits for the employee, as well as the employer. It helps reduce the financial burden of being out of work, it often helps in the healing process by keeping the employee physically and mentally active, and it keeps the employee connected to their friends and co-workers. Therefore, our company will do its best to arrange temporary, alternate, or modified work or transitional duty assignments whenever possible for employees who are ill or injured.

ELEMENTS OF AN RTW PROGRAM

- Immediate reporting of work related injuries and illnesses
- A job bank of potential transitional duty tasks or functions
- A coordinated team approach among the company, the injured employee, the medical provider, and workers' compensation insurance
- Training of employees in the elements of the RTW program

RTW PROGRAM COORDINATOR

Ideally, a return to work coordinator (RTWC) should be appointed and trained in all aspects of the RTW program. Once medical treatment has been provided, the RTWC should obtain the following from the treating physician:

- Jobs or work assignments that the employee is capable of performing
- Tasks that the employee is restricted from performing, and time of restriction
- A treatment schedule that includes dates for any follow-up treatment(s)
- Written acknowledgment that the physician has explained restrictions to the employee
- Estimated date the employee should be able to return to normal duty

SUITABLE WORK

Suitable work must:

- Be within the worker's functional abilities
- Not put the worker or co-workers at risk or hinder recovery
- Restore pre-injury earnings, where possible
- Be meaningful and promote the worker's recovery

Suitable work means that the work should serve a purpose or valuable function to the organization. Is it something that the employer would pay someone to perform?
Suitable work may involve changes to:

- Job tasks or duties – includes alternate duties that are not normally performed by the worker, differing methods to complete job duties, organizing the job tasks, and so on.
- Workload – work schedule or hours of work
- Equipment – modified equipment or new equipment purchased to assist in the completion of job duties
- Environment – includes the work area and may include set-up, lighting, climate, and so on.

AUDIT OF AN RTW PROGRAM

During the audit, the RTWC should be present to answer questions concerning the RTW program. A copy of the company standard should be scrutinized as well as examples of employees who have returned to alternate work after an occupational injury or disease. The auditor should try to follow a case study through the system. The auditors must be satisfied that a policy or standard is in place, it has employee buy in, and that the program is working (Figure 25.1).

ELEMENT/PROGRAM/PROCESS	POINTS	QUESTIONS THAT COULD BE ASKED	VERIFICATION	WHAT TO LOOK FOR
RETURN TO WORK PROGRAM (RTW)				
RTW Program in place	5	Is there a RTW program in operation	See a program overview	A written program
Standard or policy written	5	Is there a standard or RTW policy?	Copy of policy	
Employees and employee representative organizations consulted	5	How were employees and employee representative organizations consulted?	Verification of their participation	
COORDINATOR APPOINTED (RTWC)				
Coordinator appointed	5	Has a coordinator been appointed?	Letter of appointment and duties	
Alternate work identified	5	Has alternate work been identified and listed?	Examine the list of alternate work	
Medical and workers compensation	5	Do medical and workers' compensation feature in the RTW program?	Documented proof of this	
Training in RTW program	5	Who receives training about the RTW program?	Copy of training program and attendance registers	
Participants	5	How many employees went through the program in the last 12 months?	Follow one case through the system	Did the employee do alternate work? Is the program fair and beneficial?
TOTAL	40			

FIGURE 25.1 Audit Protocol for the Element – Return to Work Program.

26 The Health and Safety Coordinator

THE DESIGN OF THE HEALTH AND SAFETY COORDINATION FUNCTION

The function of the health and safety professional is to guide the organization in structuring and maintaining a health and safety management system (SMS) that meets the requirements of one of the national or international SMS guidelines. Many organizations operate internationally, and achievement of the ISO 45001-2018 standard may be a future requirement.

HEALTH AND SAFETY DEPARTMENT

When planning the health and safety department, many factors will influence the structure of the department. Factors such as the number of employees, the risks within the workplace, and the type of industry will determine the staff required. More than one safety coordinator may be required, as well as a full-time industrial hygienist, a fire coordinator, and other positions.

QUALIFICATIONS

The person appointed in the role of coordinator should have the necessary formal qualifications and should be a member of a professional body. It is important to select the right person for this position, as they will coordinate the activities of the SMS.

FUNCTIONS OF THE HEALTH AND SAFETY DEPARTMENT

The function of all health and safety departments should be to *guide*, *educate*, *train*, and *motivate* all levels of management, workers, and unions in the techniques of accident and disease prevention, and to *advise* on and *coordinate* the functions within the SMS (GETMAC). This should be a staff function, and not a line function.

THE IMPLEMENTATION OF THE HEALTH AND SAFETY COORDINATION FUNCTION

EXAMPLE OF A HEALTH AND SAFETY PRACTITIONER'S JOB DESCRIPTION

- To guide, educate, train, and motivate all levels of management, unions, contractors, and the workforce in the techniques of accident prevention, occupational, and environmental control, in an ongoing effort to reduce risk to an acceptable level in order to prevent injury and illness to employees, damage to property, and harm to the environment.

- To implement and coordinate the company's SMS in his or her areas of responsibility. To offer support to management, unions, and workers concerning the safety management system in an effort to achieve national or international occupational SMS accreditation.

INTERPERSONAL RELATIONSHIPS

One of the main requirements for a good safety practitioner is excellent interpersonal relationships with others. Unless a person with the right communication skills, approach, and motivation is appointed, constant clashes could occur.

OTHER DUTIES

The safety practitioner should meet with the manager(s) of his or her areas of responsibility on safety and occupational hygiene matters, once a week, for feedback and discussion on the state of the SMS in the respective areas.

He or she must coordinate and ensure the implementation of the SMS in his or her respective areas and must be knowledgeable on safety, health, and environmental regulations, policies, and standards.

The practitioner should conduct six-monthly internal SMS audits using all elements of the SMS and is responsible and accountable for maintaining the safety element files. He or she must advise all levels on safety, health, and environmental regulatory compliance requirements and should be knowledgeable and proficient on all aspects of the SMS.

He or she must work with safety representatives, managers, superintendents, supervisors, and employees to ensure that proactive goals are met; he or she must also coordinate and participate as a resource in safety committee meetings, and should be an active resource and participant in disabling (lost-time) injury and high potential near miss incident investigations.

One of the practitioner's most important tasks is to ensure the completion of monthly risk assessments in his or her areas of responsibility, and to follow up on corrective actions. He or she should also coordinate recognition, suggestion, and observation schemes.

One function vital to safety success is the coordination of incident recall sessions. Another is to test and document deviations of critical systems such as lock out, tag-out procedures, permits (confined space, hot work, and others), lifting gear, fall protection, and contractor safety.

PROACTIVE ACTIVITIES

The practitioner has many more functions. Most of them are proactive activities which help maintain management and employee interest in the SMS and which also ensure ongoing checks and balances focused on workplace and behavior risk. Safety practitioners should focus mainly on proactive activities, rather than post-contact injury management actions.

THE AUDIT OF THE HEALTH AND SAFETY COORDINATION FUNCTION

The audit should ascertain if the staffing of the health and safety department (sometimes including environmental control, fire protection, and quality) is sufficient for the organization, and that the correct persons have been selected as health and safety coordinators. Their qualifications and experience should be reviewed as well as their job description. Is there an ongoing program of professional skills development laid out for this person? Is the incumbent a member of a professional body? (Figure 26.1)

ELEMENT/PROGRAM/PROCESS	POINTS	QUESTIONS THAT COULD BE ASKED	VERIFICATION	WHAT TO LOOK FOR
THE HEALTH AND SAFETY COORDINATOR				
PERSON(S) MADE RESPONSIBLE FOR OCCUPATIONAL HEALTH AND SAFETY COORDINATION				
Health and safety department in place	5	Who do they report to?	Copy of the organogram or similar	Sufficient coverage
Health and safety coordinator(s) appointed	5	Who has been appointed?	Copy of letter of appointment.	Legal requirement?
Membership of professional bodies	5	Members of a professional body? (ASSP/AIHA) or similar	Copies of membership certificates	
Occupational hygiene coordinator been appointed either full-time or part-time	5	Is the appointment in writing?	Copy of duties defined. Note: the duties must not read "Responsible for health and safety"	
Health and safety coordinator job description	5	Is there a job description?	Check job description	Clear job description
Duties and responsibilities	5	Are their duties clearly defined?	Review the job description	
Have the health and safety coordinator(s) attended formal health and safety training?	5	What training/workshops have been attended?	Copy of certificates	
Health and safety coordinator(s) attended other training	5	What other formal training has been attended?	Copy of attendance list or certificates.	
TOTAL	**40**			

FIGURE 26.1 Audit Protocol for the Element – The Health and Safety Coordinator.

27 Industrial Hygiene Program

DESIGN OF AN INDUSTRIAL HYGIENE PROGRAM

Occupational or industrial hygiene can be described as the science dealing with the influence of the work environment on the health and safety of employees. It is defined as *the science and art devoted to the anticipation, recognition, identification, evaluation and control of environmental stresses arising out of a workplace, which may cause illness, impaired well-being, discomfort, and inefficiency on the part of employees or members of the surrounding community.*

INDUSTRIAL HYGIENE HAZARDS

The main industrial hygiene hazards faced are as follows:

Chemical Hazards – chemical hazards include gasses, fumes, dusts, vapors, mists, and smoke. Some chemical hazards become respiratory hazards as they are inhaled, while others can be absorbed into the skin, causing burns or other irritations.

Physical Hazards – physical hazards include extreme temperature, ionizing radiation, non-ionizing radiation, noise, and vibration, which can cause effects such as sunburn, frostbite, radiation exposure, or hearing loss.

Biological Hazards – biological hazards include viruses, bacteria, mold, yeast, fungi, and organisms that can cause sickness or disease.

Ergonomic Hazards – ergonomic hazards include hazards caused from twisting, awkward posturing, working overhead, kneeling, lifting, gripping, static posturing, overreaching, forceful exertion, contact stress, repetitive motion, vibration, and bending. Most ergonomic hazards result in bodily pain or injury.

The industrial hygienist normally coordinates the industrial hygiene elements or sub-elements of the safety management system (SMS).

IMPLEMENTATION OF AN INDUSTRIAL HYGIENE PROGRAM

IMPLEMENTATION STEPS OF AN INDUSTRIAL HYGIENE PROGRAM

The three steps of an industrial hygiene programme are the *recognition* step, the *evaluation* process, and finally the *control* methods.

RECOGNITION

The recognition phase of an occupational hygiene program begins with obtaining knowledge of the processes and materials used and conducting personal observations during a thorough survey to determine what industrial hygiene stressors may be present in the workplace.

EVALUATION

The evaluation step is when the exposure to the identified occupational hygiene stressors is measured and quantified. This may necessitate monitoring, dust counts, noise level and lighting measurements, and it could also involve personal monitoring to determine exactly the extent of exposure to the hazard.

The evaluation would also include a risk assessment of the situation by asking the following questions: What is the potential *severity* of the exposure? How *frequent* are employees exposed to the hazard? What is the *probability* that the exposure will result in adverse effects on the worker.

CONTROL

Control of the occupational health hazards is a difficult aspect, as it normally involves actions that cost money and may hamper the production output of the facility. The items that are normally considered during the control phase are:

- The costs involved
- The degree of rectification obtained
- Adverse effects on production
- The practicality of the control method

THE INDUSTRIAL HYGIENIST

Industrial hygiene is an important aspect of any occupational SMS and should be managed by a professional industrial hygienist (IH). The incumbent should have a comprehensive job description that directs them in the functions of implementing and maintaining an industrial hygiene program within the SMS.

AUDIT OF AN INDUSTRIAL HYGIENE PROGRAM

It must be shown to the auditors that a comprehensive survey of hygiene stressors has been carried out, that they have been evaluated, and that efficient and adequate controls have been implemented. Should a full-time IH be employed, the incumbent should be well qualified, experienced, and a member of a professional organization. A job description should be available.

During the inspection, the auditors should look for seating comfort, access points, manual handling and environmental stressors, and how they are being controlled (Figure 27.1).

ELEMENT/PROGRAM/PROCESS	POINTS	QUESTIONS THAT COULD BE ASKED	VERIFICATION	WHAT TO LOOK FOR
INDUSTRIAL HYGENE PROGRAM				
INDUSTRIAL HYGENIST				
IH appointed	5	Has an IH been appointed?	Letter of appointment	
Qualifications/professional body member	5	Qualifications and membership?	Review membership	
Job description	5	Is there a job description?	Review duties and functions	
IH PROGRAM				
Recognition of stressors	5	Recognition survey been done?	How was this done?	Chemical/Physical/Biological/Ergonomic
Assessment of stressors	5	How was this done?	List of stressors available	During the inspection identify where stressors are and check controls
Control measures	5	What controls are in place?	Were the controls effective?	Are they still in place?
Ongoing monitoring	5	Is there ongoing monitoring of stressors?	Ongoing program documents	
Ergonomic program	5	Is there an ongoing ergonomic program?	Documented proof	Were any ergonomic nonconformities noted?
Hearing conservation program	5	Is there an ongoing hearing conservation program?	Documented proof	
Blood borne pathogen program	5	Is there an ongoing blood borne pathogen program?	Documented proof	This may be a separate SMS element
Other IH program in place	5	Is there any other program operating?	Documented (heat/stress/vibration)	
TOTAL	55			

FIGURE 27.1   Audit Protocol for the Element – Industrial Hygiene Program.

28 Annual Report – Health and Safety

DESIGN OF AN ANNUAL REPORT ON HEALTH AND SAFETY

Most organizations publish an annual report of the company's activities during the preceding year. This is to inform shareholders and the public how the company performed and what new initiatives it has undertaken or changes it has made to its organizational structure or work processes.

A segment of this report should be dedicated to the health and safety activities of the company. This report should highlight achievements during the year and also list the health and safety improvements made during the period, as well as the status of the health and safety management system (SMS). Statistics can form part of this report, but they should include leading indicators as well as lagging indicators.

IMPLEMENTATION OF AN ANNUAL REPORT ON HEALTH AND SAFETY

Space should be provided in the annual report for the section on health and safety activities. The report could contain information on:

- Number of employees who received health and safety training
- Number of active health and safety representatives
- Health and safety committees
- Audit results
- Injury/property damage/fire statistics
- Inspections carried out
- Employee participation in the SMS
- Improvements made to the SMS
- Future plans

This report will give interested and affected parties a good idea of the health and safety activities of the organization.

AUDIT OF AN ANNUAL REPORT ON HEALTH AND SAFETY

The annual report of the organization should include a report on health and safety activities during the period under review. The report should contain at least one paragraph of health and safety information which should give a snapshot of the company's annual health and safety activities (Figure 28.1).

ELEMENT/PROGRAM/PROCESS	POINTS	QUESTIONS THAT COULD BE ASKED	VERIFICATION	WHAT TO LOOK FOR
ANNUAL REPORT–HEALTH AND SAFETY				
ANNUAL REPORT PRODUCED				
Health and safety included	5	Is safety included in the annual report?	Annual report	Is health and safety featured in the annual report?
Statistics included	5	Are statistics reproduced?	Proactive and reactive statistics	
Safety achievements	5	Health and safety achievements mentioned?	Health and safety achievements reported	
Audit scores	5	Audit scores given in report?	Audits mentioned	
Committee work	5	Mention made of safety committee work?	Copy of the report	
Posted on website	5	Is the report on the company website?	View the website	
TOTAL	30			

FIGURE 28.1   Audit Protocol for the Element – Annual Report: Health and Safety.

Part 3

Design, Implementation, and Audit of Occupational Health and Safety Management System, Workplace Environment Conditions

29 Business Order (Good Housekeeping Program)

DESIGN OF A GOOD HOUSEKEEPING PROGRAM

First impressions are lasting impressions. The immediate impression one receives of the housekeeping at a company reflects the standard of health and safety of that organization. Business order, which is defined as *a place for everything and everything in its place, always*, is the foundation on which to build an effective health and safety management system (SMS).

Once there is an SMS in place, the work environment needs to be brought up to standard. Most organizations lack business order. The workplace housekeeping needs to be improved and maintained at world's best practice level. This means that the workplace must be immaculate.

If an organization cleans up the workplace, it also cleans up the thought processes of the employees in that workplace. Maintaining a spotless workplace does more to improve health and safety at an organization than many other efforts, systems, or controls.

IMPLEMENTATION OF A GOOD HOUSEKEEPING PROGRAM

IMPLEMENTATION STEPS

A standard on business order should be written and implemented. Regular inspections should be implemented to identify deviations from accepted practices. Areas should be allocated to health and safety representatives for monthly inspections, and local management must understand that they are responsible for the housekeeping in their areas of control. Toolbox talks should emphasize the importance of good housekeeping.

The SMS has a number of ongoing processes, checklists, and balances to ensure that once the physical work areas are in order, they remain so. Many of the SMS elements are aligned to create a safe and healthy workplace. These help ensure that business order is maintained.

SMS controls that help maintain good business order include housekeeping competitions, plant inspections, stacking and storage, demarcation, signage, and observation reporting.

AN EXAMPLE STANDARD FOR BUSINESS ORDER

This is an extract from a standard on business order which gives an idea of the items that are to be controlled to bring about good business order.

Physical Requirements for Business Order

- All surplus (redundant, not in immediate use) materials must be removed and be neatly and correctly stored in designated demarcated areas, in a manner prescribed by the environmental standards.
- All unusable materials must be disposed of in specifically allocated areas.
- All storage areas are to be demarcated. Labels should identify materials in shelves, racks, and bins.
- Storage sheds and storage areas must be laid out in an orderly manner and kept neat and tidy.
- Sufficient demarcated walkways must be provided to allow easy access to all items and areas.
- Walkways and roadways should be suitably demarcated, where practicable.
- All excess spillage or waste is to be removed on a regular basis, and areas are to be cleaned and returned to their normal condition.
- All items that are no longer required should be removed from the workplace and stored in the correct area.
- Storage facilities, racks, bins, shelves, and pallets should be made available as needed to ensure proper housekeeping and tidiness.
- Racks, bins, and shelves that are no longer usable shall be discarded and replaced as needed.

Procedure to Implement Business Order

- Once per month, all offices, work areas, and warehouse facilities are to be inspected and deviations noted.
- All work areas and yard areas, both interior and exterior, including offices, are to be included in the inspection.
- Managers and supervisors are to ensure proper compliance to the written standard on business order, and promote the awareness of a clean, orderly, and tidy workplace.
- All managers, supervisors, health and safety representatives, and employees are accountable for their areas of responsibility. This includes completing the monthly housekeeping checklist and retaining it for audit purposes.
- The monthly checklist will list all items to be corrected. The supervisor will do the follow-up. He or she will list the items and give dates by which corrections will be made, and who will do them.
- Departmental managers and supervisors will ensure compliance with housekeeping standards.
- Supervisors and health and safety representatives shall conduct regular (minimum monthly) formal and informal inspections of their areas of responsibility.
- Contractors are to abide by this standard.
- Departmental health and safety personnel will offer support and be a resource as needed.

AUDIT OF A GOOD HOUSEKEEPING PROGRAM

The auditors should inspect all aspects of business order during the inspection stage of the audit. All things should be in their correct place, and there should be no superfluous material, tools, or equipment lying around, both in and outside the plant. Demarcated walkways and storage areas should be visible to allow for good housekeeping practices. Windows should be clean as should machines and workstations. Are areas delegated to individuals for ownership of housekeeping duties? The appearance of the workplace should reflect the requirements of the written standard which is *a place for everything and everything in its place, always.*

FOLLOW THE SYSTEM

Auditors should select a work area and see if the name of the responsible person for housekeeping is posted. They should inspect a specific area and make notes of positives and nonconformances. During the documentation review, they should call for the checklist of the last inspection of that selected area and compare it with their findings. The main criteria is, "Is the housekeeping system working"? (Figure 29.1)

ELEMENT/PROGRAM/PROCESS	POINTS	QUESTIONS THAT COULD BE ASKED	VERIFICATION	WHAT TO LOOK FOR
BUSINESS ORDER (GOOD HOUSEKEEPING)				
Standard	5	Is there a written standard for business order?	Review the standard	
Supervisors responsible	5	Are supervisors made responsible for housekeeping in their areas?	Check if in standard	
Health and safety representatives appointed	5	Are all areas covered by health and safety representatives?	Ask for a plan showing the areas covered	Inspection
Housekeeping inspections	5	How often and who conducts housekeeping inspections?	Copy of some completed checklists	
Checklist used	5	Is a housekeeping checklist used?	Copy of the checklist – is it applicable?	
Housekeeping competitions	5	Is there a housekeeping competition?	Competition rules / judging sheet	
Part of induction training	5	Is business order part of the induction training?	See the induction syllabus	
Workstations tidy	5	Auditor feedback		Physical inspection
Contractors work areas in order	5	Auditor feedback		Physical inspection
Workplace in order	5	Auditor feedback		Follow specific area through the system	Physical inspection
TOTAL	**50**			

FIGURE 29.1   Audit Protocol for the Element – Business Order.

30 Plant Hygiene Amenities

DESIGN OF A PLANT AMENITIES PROVISION AND MAINTENANCE PROGRAM

Plant hygiene amenities are important areas as they include, inter alia, toilets, change rooms, kitchens, and other facilities which should be kept neat, tidy, and hygienic at all times.

Hazards may exist and accidents may occur in plant amenity areas, and there could also be a risk of illness or occupational disease occurring. The housekeeping and business order within these areas should conform to the highest standards. The cleanliness of the amenities is also a direct reflection on the importance that the organization places on plant hygiene and neatness.

The table gives an idea of the items to check in a plant amenity; from this list, individual checklists can be compiled for site specific inspections (Figure 30.1).

Regular cleaning of all plant amenities should take place, as they must be kept hygienic at all times. Ongoing maintenance is essential to ensure that any unsafe conditions are rectified as soon as is practically possible.

Unsafe conditions in amenities could also prove to be unhygienic and could include cracked and dirty floors, cracked wash-hand basins, malfunctioning toilets, defective lighting, or inadequate ventilation.

IMPLEMENTATION OF A PLANT AMENITIES PROVISION AND MAINTENANCE PROGRAM

A simplified 8-step process is recommended as follows.

STEP 1 – LIST AMENITIES

This would entail making a list of all the toilets, ablution facilities, lunch rooms, change rooms, kitchens and canteens, and other amenities throughout the entire plant. This could include emergency eye-wash stations and showers.

STEP 2 – INSPECTION

A thorough inspection of each of these amenities should now take place. Where necessary, experts and consultants could be used to carry out this top-to-bottom thorough inspection. Notes should be made of every single nonconformance identified, and recommendations proposed on the inspection report.

Ovens	Walls	Effective vermin control	Microwaves	Floors
Colour coding of hot and cold water taps	Food lockers	Refrigerators	Flow of hot and cold water	Hygiene of shower curtain/door
Soap and soap holder	Extractor fans (where applicable)	Toilet and other seats	Tables	Trash cans
Fire equipment (if applicable)	Floor and Wall Tiles	All eating utensils	Adequate supply of towels	Ashtrays (if applicable)

FIGURE 30.1　List of Hygiene Amenities to be Inspected.

Step 3 – Action Plan

An action plan to rectify the deviations from standard should now be compiled, stating:

- What action is to be taken
- Who should take the action
- By when the action should be completed

This might involve having to budget for capital items such as replacement of wash-basins, replacement of ceilings, replacement of tiles, or, in some instances, redoing plumbing or electrical circuits.

Step 4 – Deviations Rectified

The deviations are now tackled on a priority basis according to a schedule. Contractors could be used, or the internal maintenance divisions could be given the task of recti-fying the deviations. Once the deviations have been rectified and long-term projects, which involve major expense, have been initiated, checklists are now drawn up.

Step 5 – Site-Specific Checklists

Site-specific checklists should now be compiled. The purpose of a checklist is to act as a guide to the person carrying out the inspection. They are also working docu-ments, and follow-up action and completion dates can be entered on the checklist. Different checklists should be provided for different amenities.

Sub-committees may be used to compile separate checklists for ablution facilities, restrooms, and other amenities. A selected group can be given this task. The check-lists are then incorporated into the SMS standards and distributed to all concerned.

STEP 6 – APPOINT RESPONSIBLE PERSONS

Responsible persons are now appointed to control the condition of the particular amenity. Cleaning teams are appointed or cleaning contracts negotiated to ensure that regular cleaning and replenishing of essential supplies takes place.

STEP 7 – ONGOING INSPECTIONS

Persons should be appointed responsible for inspecting the amenities. The amenities are placed on the inspection schedule and receive ongoing inspections by these inspectors who use the site-specific checklists for the inspections. Responsibility must also be allocated for rectifying deviations found during inspections.

STEP 8 – MONITOR PROGRESS

The progress to ensure conformance to standard is now monitored on a regular basis. This could be by means of formal or informal inspections and audits.

AUDIT OF A PLANT AMENITIES PROVISION AND MAINTENANCE PROGRAM

A physical inspection of plant amenities during the audit inspection is the best way to see if the standard is adequate and effective and is being applied. All hygiene amenities, including toilets and eating areas, should be inspected. Fridges, stoves, and microwave ovens should be checked for clean and healthy conditions. All areas and items associated with plant amenities should be inspected. Public areas should also be inspected.

FOLLOW THE SYSTEM

The auditor should select an amenity and inspect it thoroughly. During the documentation review session, the checklists for that amenity should be called for so the auditor can correlate what they saw in relation to the checklist. Again, the prime question is, "Are the amenities adequate, and is the system of inspecting and maintaining them working"? (Figure 30.2)

ELEMENT/PROGRAM/PROCESS	POINTS	QUESTIONS THAT COULD BE ASKED	VERIFICATION	WHAT TO LOOK FOR
PLANT HYGIENE AMENITIES				
ADEQUATE FACILITIES PROVIDED				
Toilets and sinks facilities adequate, according to legislation	5		Visual	
Facilities adequate	5	Are kitchen, break rooms and storage facilities adequate?	Visual	
Cleaning arrangements	5	Are there sufficient cleaning tools (brooms, chemicals, squeegees,?)	Visual	
Waste bins and removal system	5	Are sufficient waste bins provided?	Visual	
AMENITIES CLEAN AND HYGIENIC				
Amenities clean (tiles, floors, walls, fixtures, and fittings)	5	Who does the cleaning? Maintenance? How often?	Visual	Toilets, urinals, basins, floors, sinks, tiles, kitchens, fridges, walk-in refrigerators, water coolers etc.
Soap and towels	5	Is there soap, towels and toilet paper?	Visual	
Lockers and change-rooms sufficient and tidy	5	Cleaning schedule	Visual	
Kitchen and canteens clean and pest free	5	Pest control program in place?	Visual	Pest control stations. Visual.
NO FOOD IN UNAUTHORIZED AREAS				
Food in labs, chemical areas, areas with bio hazards, areas with critical electronics	5	Where can food be eaten in the workplace? What are authorized areas?	Policy document on food storage and eating.	Food in workplace: Evidence of eating. Empty, dirty, cold drink bottles. Lockers, toolboxes or food near chemicals or other unauthorized areas.
Food storage	5	Has provision been made for food storage (break rooms, refrigerators, kitchens, etc.?)		
REGULAR MONTHLY INSPECTIONS				
Regular inspections of facilities	5	Are the facilities inspected monthly?	Copy of checklists.	Are the facilities clean and in a hygienic state as a result of ongoing inspections?
Steps taken to correct deviations	5	Who does the inspections - is this a regular, structured inspection? What action is taken?	Action list	Follow the system
CHECKLIST USED				
Checklists for different amenities	5	Is a checklist used for inspections?	Copy of a completed checklist for area	
TOTAL	**65**			

FIGURE 30.2 Audit Protocol for the Element – Plant Hygiene Amenities.

31 Permit to Work Systems

DESIGN OF A PERMIT TO WORK SYSTEM

This element of a health and safety management system (SMS) is one of the critical elements, and although the requirements differ greatly from workplace to workplace, the basic principles apply. A risk assessment of work done at an organization should be undertaken to ascertain what specific high risk tasks require a *permit to work*.

A permit to work system is a formal written system used to control certain types of work that are potentially hazardous. A permit to work is a document which specifies the work to be done and the precautions to be taken. Permits to work form an essential part of safe systems of work for many maintenance activities.

OBJECTIVES OF PERMITS TO WORK

The objectives of permits to work are to reduce the risk of injuries, occupational diseases, fires, and other undesired events occurring during critical work, maintenance, repairs, or other work. They allow work to start only after safe procedures have been defined, and they provide a clear record that all foreseeable hazards have been considered.

IMPLEMENTATION OF A PERMIT TO WORK SYSTEM

Health and safety legislation dictates that certain tasks must be carried out only on issue of a permit to work. These legal requirements should be regarded as the minimum requirements. Once a risk assessment has been done, the type of permits needed can be listed and permits to work drafted. The permits must be ideally re-issued daily, and the lapse time and date must be clearly indicated on the permit.

This is an example of the types of permits to work that could be required (Figure 31.1).

A *hot work permit* can be issued for carrying out hot work (flame producing) in an explosive area or an area where the fire risks are high. This would include hack-sawing, hammering, drilling, or filing. Open flame work in an explosive area would include tasks such as lead burning, grinding, arc welding, soldering, and

Confined space entry	Work at height permit	Diving permit	Blasting permit	Excavation permit
Hot work permit	Cold work permit	Electrical switching permit	Contractors permit	Work on live electrical installations permit

FIGURE 31.1 Examples of Permits to Work.

oxyacetylene cutting or welding. Hot work in general would include grinding, arc welding, soldering, and oxyacetylene welding or cutting.

Cold work permits would include permits to work on electrical installations or mechanical installations. Cold work permits could be either electrical isolation permits, or physical isolation permits which are not electrical. This type of permit would include closing and locking valves, inserting slip plates, and physically disconnecting pipelines or blanking off live ends.

Confined space entry permits are used for vessel entry, or whenever work is to be carried out in underground passages, pipes, ducts, openings under columns, sewers and gutters, pits, or canals. These permits would also be required when entering fermentation tanks, metal storage tanks, autoclaves, and other vessels.

A *work at height permit* would be issued for employees about to work at the top of tall stacks, on high roofs, and in any elevated position where the chances of falling are high.

An *underwater diving permit* would be issued for specialized applications when work has to be carried out underwater. The two types of diving permits are a sea diving permit and a fresh water diving permit.

An *excavation permit* would be issued for any excavation deeper than 6 inches (150 mm). The reason for this is the risk of buried utilities that may have not been marked on the site plan. Working in deeper excavations is high risk work and should be covered by a permit to work.

A *contractor's work permit* should be issued to all contractors before the commencement of work. Normally this permit is issued for any work to be undertaken by contractors on the site.

THE THREE PHASES OF A PERMIT TO WORK SYSTEM

PHASE ONE – COMMENCING WORK

The following actions take place before work commences:

- Identification of hazards
- Providing proper personal protective equipment (PPE)
- Using correct tools
- Isolating and locking out
- Testing for sources of energy
- Notifying other departments
- Arranging necessary standby
- Receiving the permit from the issuer

PHASE TWO – DURING THE WORK

The following precautions are taken during the work:

- The permit should be displayed by posting it at the worksite entrance.
- The permit will specify what PPE is to be worn by the workers.

- Specific safety requirements are to be followed.
- Standby workers are in place if needed.
- The necessary fire-fighting equipment is available, and other precautions such as having a water hose available or providing continuous toxic gas monitoring is executed.

Phase Three – After the Work

Once the work is completed, the following is done:

- The permit will call for the work site to be checked by the issuer to ensure that the work has been carried out satisfactorily.
- The general housekeeping of the area will be noted and all equipment and tools used must be removed.
- Before removing the lock out or isolation, the necessary persons will be warned and if necessary the site be cleared.
- The receiver, when handing back the job, will get the permit dated and signed off by the issuer.

PERMIT ISSUERS AND RECEIVERS

Only authorized, trained, and licensed *permit issuers* should issue permits to work. The work permit must be signed off at completion of the task by the *receiver* of the permit. The issuer's and receiver's names must be on the work permit. During the carrying out of the work, supervisors should check the physical state of the work area against the requirements specified by the permit.

Permit Issuer

The permit issuer is an experienced and authorized employee of the organization requiring the work to be done. The issuer has been trained in all aspects of the hazards of the work, and he or she issues the permit prior to the commencement of the work, subject to the precautions and limits listed on the permit to work.

Permit Receivers

Employees or contractor teams carrying out the work must have a trained and authorized permit receiver. This person is responsible for ensuring that the requirements of the permit are adhered to. Once the work is finished, the receiver must complete the completion of work portion on the permit and hand it back to the issuer for final inspection of the worksite, after which the issuer will close the permit.

AUDIT OF A PERMIT TO WORK SYSTEM

The best way to audit the permit system is to visit a site where a permit to work is required, and follow the permitting process through the system. On the work site, the permit can be examined and work conditions compared to the permit requirements. The validity of the permit and the issuer and receiver information can also be ascertained from the permit, which should be posted at the entrance to the worksite. The auditors should check the issue dates and the duration of the permit (Figure 31.2).

ELEMENT / PROGRAM / PROCESS	POINTS	QUESTIONS THAT COULD BE ASKED	VERIFICATION	WHAT TO LOOK FOR
PERMIT TO WORK SYSTEM				
AREAS / TASKS IDENTIFIED WHERE PERMITS REQUIRED				
Risk assessment undertaken to identify the areas where permits to work are required	5	What types of work permits are needed here?	Copies of filled-in permit	Mechanical, electrical, hot work, work at height, excavation, etc.
Written standard been established	5	Is there a SMS standard?	Copy of Standard and forms	
Supervisors aware of where and when permits are required	5	Are supervisors trained in permitting?	Training for supervisors	
Permits always issued, displayed and closed off at end of job	5	Are permits issued, received and closed off when the job is finished?	Copy of list	Check a site where a permit is required Signing authority validity Condition of permit met?
TRAINED ISSUERS		Are appointed Issuers trained?	Training records / license	
Permit issuers trained	5	Are issuers trained and licensed?	Copy of appointments	When checking the permit ensure issuer and receiver have valid authorizations
TRAINED RECEIVERS				
Receivers trained	5	Are appointed receivers trained?	Copy of training / license	
TOTAL	30			

FIGURE 31.2 Audit Protocol for the Element – Permit to Work System.

32 Safety Inspection System

DEFINITION

A *safety inspection is a monitoring function to endeavor to locate, identify, and eradicate unsafe conditions (hazards) and high risk acts, which have the capacity to lead to accidental loss in the work area.*

BACKGROUND INFORMATION ON SAFETY INSPECTIONS

A thorough safety inspection, guided by a hazard control checklist, is one of the basic, best, and widely used methods of identifying physical hazards as well as high risk practices. The hazards, once identified, should be ranked as to their classification by using a simple rating system, such as: High Risk – A, Medium Risk – B, and Moderate Risk – C.

All work areas should be inspected to identify hazards. Once hazards are identified, a risk assessment of the hazard should be done. This hazard identification and risk assessment (HIRA) process is applied to all aspects of risk within the workplace. All processes, machinery, tools, and equipment used should be included in the inspection, and environmental conditions should be sampled and tested. These would include the level of illumination, ventilation, noise levels, and so on.

PURPOSE OF INSPECTIONS

The prime purpose of inspections is to identify hazards that have the potential to cause loss. During an inspection, many high risk work conditions and practices can be identified and noted for corrective action.

The inspection of the physical workplace not only includes the work area itself, but also the process being carried out and the movement of material, raw product, and finished goods, as well as the actions, working conditions, and general safety of the employees. Short cuts, high risk behavior and high risk processes can also be detected during an inspection. Once these facts are identified, positive remedial measures can be taken to rectify them as part of the proactive safety process.

MEASUREMENT

Inspections help detect hazards and are one of the most important pre-contact control mechanisms of a health and safety management system (SMS). What gets measured, gets done. The most effective way of measuring compliance to SMS standards is by conducting a safety inspection. Often referred to as *management by walkabout*, plant inspections are part of visible felt management leadership.

Inspections can be conducted over and over again with no impact or benefit if the nonconformances found during the inspection are not rectified. Regular inspections act as follow-up tours for actions that were detected during the previous inspection, and which should have been rectified.

WHERE TO INSPECT

Often, only the prime work areas are included in safety inspections. Although these areas may pose more of a threat to the workers, all work areas must be inspected regularly. The frequency of the inspections will be determined by the hazardous nature of the work environment and the number of employees in that environment. Also to be considered is the process and the potential for major loss in the form of injury, fire, explosion, or other risks.

DESIGN OF A SAFETY INSPECTION SYSTEM

The safety inspection processes, checklists, and frequency will be determined by the nature of the workplace. Guidelines will be offered by the risk assessment process as to how often certain inspections need to be done. Each inspection should follow a checklist and should result in the necessary follow-up actions.

TYPES OF INSPECTIONS

Safety inspections can vary greatly from workplace to workplace and could include inspections such as those indicated in Figure 32.1.

OTHER TYPES OF INSPECTIONS

SAFETY SURVEYS

A safety survey is a thorough safety inspection of the work environment, which is followed by a report on the findings. It also includes an inspection of control systems in place. Normally, a safety survey is the first step in introducing a long-range SMS, and would highlight the most prominent deficiencies in the physical conditions and

Ergonomic inspections	Post-accident / near miss incident investigation inspections	Legal inspections by the local legal authority	Housekeeping inspections	Annual audit inspections
Safety competition inspections	Occupational hygiene inspections	Contractor's site inspections	Self-audit inspections	Permit to Work inspections
Safety signage inspections	Critical PPE inspections	Fire and explosion risk inspections	Risk management inspections by insurers, etc.	Other specific inspections

FIGURE 32.1 Types of Inspections.

control systems. The safety report produced after the safety survey acts as an action list for management to initiate an ongoing SMS.

RISK ASSESSMENT INSPECTION

A risk assessment cannot be carried out successfully without firstly conducting an on-site inspection of the physical conditions, the raw products, the materials used, the processes, and the machinery as well as the transportation routes. Only once the entire process and exposures have been examined by a safety inspection can a thorough risk assessment of the most hazardous situations be compiled. A risk assessment without some form of physical hazard identification inspection is virtually impossible. Based on the risk assessment, the organization should determine what inspections are required, their frequency, and who should carry them out.

REGULATORY (LEGAL) COMPLIANCE

A legal compliance audit involves an inspection to confirm compliance to regulations and laws governing the work conditions. This inspection will inspect the work areas and installations and may include an examination of documents, safety records, report forms, and training records, as well as various appointments under different regulations.

THIRD PARTY INSPECTIONS

Another type of safety inspection is an inspection carried out by an external risk or safety consultant. The inspection may be as a result of certain problems or an annual prerequisite prior to being assessed for safety performance achievements or insurance purposes. The third party inspection may be a legal inspection by safety authorities.

INFORMAL SAFETY WALKABOUT

An informal inspection should take place on a regular basis, preferably daily. These are sometimes referred to as management tours but correctly termed, they are safety inspections.

PLANNED INSPECTIONS

Planned inspections are those inspections that are planned (weekly, monthly, or three-monthly) on a regular basis. They normally follow a predetermined route and are carried out by a team comprising the safety coordinator, the supervisor of the area, and possibly the health and safety representative of that area.

HEALTH AND SAFETY REPRESENTATIVE INSPECTIONS

Health and safety representatives are appointed because of their knowledge and familiarity with the work environment and work process. No one is better equipped to carry out a safety inspection of a particular area than the person who works in the area, knows the process, and has many years' experience in their work environment. Health and safety representatives' reports must receive prompt attention by management.

HEALTH AND SAFETY MANAGEMENT SYSTEM AUDIT INSPECTIONS

A safety audit inspection is a thorough examination of the physical conditions, the equipment, the machinery, and the systems in place, measured against an established and quantifiable standard of measurement. The safety audit inspection would indicate *what has been done*, *who did it*, and *the frequency with which it was done* to determine if the requirements of the SMS standards have been met.

SAFETY REVIEW INSPECTIONS

Depending on the SMS in operation, a review or evaluation of the entire system will include an inspection of the physical areas, the control systems, critical items of machinery, and apparatus, and will include control documents appertaining to control processes.

CRITICAL EQUIPMENT INSPECTIONS

Specific equipment inspections are routine inspections of items of equipment which are used regularly and which are essential to the health, safety, and wellbeing of employees. These could include critical parts and components. They could include firefighting equipment, electrical equipment, fixed electrical installations, new equipment, ladders, pressure vessels, boilers, lifting gear, personal protective equipment (PPE), and so on.

IMPLEMENTATION OF A SAFETY INSPECTION SYSTEM

The objective of the safety inspection system is to ensure that a regular and structured inspection system is in place and working to identify unsafe conditions, unsafe acts, and deviations from safety standards so that corrective measures can be taken to reduce risks and prevent accidental loss. A SMS standard should be established and written for this element of the SMS.

EXAMPLE OF A STANDARD FOR THE IMPLEMENTATION OF A SAFETY INSPECTION PROCESS

The following inspection standards and procedures will apply to all company (and affiliate companies) workplaces and sites and include all areas, equipment, and machinery within the company. This standard also applies to contractors and their employees.

Responsibility

Manager/supervisor or contractor (Responsible person)

The manager/supervisor or contractor (Responsible person) will ensure that all the work areas, buildings, and installations under their control are subject to a formal safety inspection on a monthly basis as a minimum, where practicable. Inspection priority shall be determined by the number of employees exposed to risk and the criticality of the area, equipment, or process (Figure 32.2)

If a risk assessment ranking of the *criticality of the area* (ranked on a 1–5 scale) and the *number of employees* exposed to the risk (ranked on a 1–5 scale) are in the black zone on the matrix (extreme–extreme) (25), then more frequent inspections will be required.

Risks that fall in the darker shaded zones (high–high) (16–20) need less frequent inspections than those in the black zone.

Risk that fall in the lighter shaded (medium high–medium high) (9–15) zones still need inspections but less frequent than those that fall in the black or darker shaded zones.

Risk that fall in the lighter shaded zones (medium–medium) (4–10) need fewer inspections than risks in the white zones (low–low) (1–5), which still need to be inspected but less frequently than those that fall in the black or darker shaded zones.

All areas, sections, departments, and workplaces are to be inspected on a periodic basis (minimum monthly) based on the risk of the area and exposure of employees, where practicable.

The manager/supervisor or contractor (Responsible person) is responsible for ensuring that these inspections are carried out. The inspections will be undertaken accompanied by the departmental safety coordinator, where practicable. The inspection should be carried out using the appropriate inspection checklist, which may be modified to suit the area or workplace being inspected. This checklist should be completed after the inspection and submitted to the manager or his or her nominee.

FIGURE 32.2   Inspection Frequency Risk Assessment.

After the inspection, unsafe acts and high risk conditions noted should be assessed and appropriate actions carried out within an agreed timescale.

Health and Safety Personnel, Safety Coordinators, and Safety Inspectors

Health and safety personnel should accompany the inspection team on the inspection, whenever possible, and give advice on any unsafe act or condition that has been identified. They should monitor the follow-up corrective action.

Inspection Schedule

The manager/supervisor or contractor (Responsible person) should ensure that a schedule of dates and times is produced for carrying out these inspections at the beginning of the year, and ensure that inspections are carried out according to the schedule.

Employees

Employees should inspect their immediate work area on a daily basis and ensure all hazards are corrected or reported to the responsible person or his or her nominee. Employees may accompany any inspection team on their inspection.

Health and Safety Representatives

Health and safety representatives should conduct an inspection of their work areas as allocated to them for inspection purposes. These inspections will be conducted monthly using the safety representative checklist.

The completed inspection checklist is to be discussed with the responsible person of the area, who will note the deviations and set action plans in motion to rectify the hazards noted. They should acknowledge the results of the inspection by signing the inspection checklist. Copies of completed checklists should be retained in the SMS file for audit purposes.

Health and Safety Personnel Formal Inspections

Inspections by members of the health and safety department should be carried out once every month, or as determined by the risk matrix.

All departments and/or work areas should be inspected, where practicable, as per a predetermined schedule produced by the health and safety department, based on the risk assessments, at the beginning of each year.

A safety coordinator or inspector from the health and safety department will undertake the inspections accompanied by the responsible person and the safety representative.

They should inspect all areas, buildings, installations, and workplaces under their area of control and also conduct random inspections and participate in other inspection activities.

The completed inspection checklist will be discussed with the manager of the area, who will note the deviations and set action plans in motion to rectify the hazards noted. He or she will acknowledge the results of the inspection by signing the inspection checklist. Copies of completed checklists should be retained in the SMS file for audit purposes.

AUDIT OF A SAFETY INSPECTION SYSTEM

The audit inspection will indicate if regular and efficient safety inspections have been carried out during the period prior to the audit. If a number of deviations from standards (hazards) are found during the inspection, it will indicate a system failure. Critical items should be examined and verification of inspections should be requested for review during the verification conference. High risk acts should also be looked for during the inspection. These deviations will also indicate a failure of some other SMS element or process. An absence of hazards and deviations will indicate to the auditors a system and process that is working.

The auditors should call for a recent inspection checklist for an area they have inspected and correlate their findings with the contents of the checklist (Figure 32.3).

ELEMENT/PROGRAM/PROCESS	POINTS	QUESTIONS THAT COULD BE ASKED	VERIFICATION	WHAT TO LOOK FOR
SAFETY INSPECTION SYSTEM				
Risk matrix used	5	Is a risk assessment method used to determine inspection frequency?	Copy of risk assessment	High risk areas/processes
MONTHLY INSPECTIONS BY HEALTH AND SAFETY REPRESENTATIVES				
Health and safety representativescomplete a monthly checklist based on the SMS elements	5	Do health and safe representatives or supervisors conduct regular, monthly safety inspections of their work areas? Are the checklists up to date and done correctly?	Copy of checklist.	Monthly inspections by health and safety representatives/supervisors of their own areas and reports being submitted.
Inspections to cover the entire area for which they are responsible	5	Aae all areas covered? Is a checklist used?	Check at least 8 items from the SMS	Is it obvious that a health and safety representative or supervisor has inspected the area and taken action to rectify hazards?
High risk conditions reported	5	Does the checklist includeconditions?	Check some of the health and safety representative's checklists.	Checklist based on SMS being used?
High risk behaviors reported	5	Does the checklist include unsafe practices?	Are they on the form?	
Positive recommendations made	5	Are positive actions taken?	Example of actions taken	
Hazard training	5	Has the health and safety representatives been made aware of all the hazards in the area by the departmental supervisors ?	Training/on-site training done	
REPORTS CONSIDERED AND ACTIONED BY MANAGEMENT				
All reports forwarded to management (assigned person or deputy?)	5	Does management review these checklists and authorize necessary action?	Check some reports and see where management has authorized action if necessary.	Reports considered and actioned by management
Remedial action	5	Does management take action on the report findings and recommendations?How is this done?	Call for the checklist of that area and crosscheck	Note one area that has basic deviationsand follow through the system
Feedback given to the health and safety representatives who submit the reports?	5	How and when is this done?	Refer to copies of report	
BI-ANNUAL INSPECTION BY SAFETY DEPARTMENT				
Health and safety department conduct bi-annual inspections of the entire worksite	5	Do the health and safety coordinators conduct inspections of the entire premises?	Look at checklist/inspection form used	
Other inspections	5	What other safety inspections take place??	Examples	
Findings of the inspection reported to management.Inspector follow-up on all inspection reports.	5	Are the findings reported to management? Is there a follow-up?	Example of a follow-up after an inspection	
TOTAL	**65**			

FIGURE 32.3   Audit Protocol for the Element – Safety Inspection System.

33 Stacking and Storage Practices

DESIGN OF A STACKING AND STORAGE SYSTEM

INTRODUCTION

In any process, items need to be stacked and stored. These items could be raw material, finished products, products in process, or material for repairs and maintenance as well as a variety of other types of substances, equipment, and stock. These goods need to be stacked and stored safely. Injuries and fires are caused every year by poor stacking practices. Stacking and storage procedures take place both inside and outside the plant.

Depending on the nature of the workplace, stacking and storage methods and equipment should be implemented as an element of the SMS and monitored continuously. Where necessary, racks and shelving should be provided, and demarcated stacking and storage areas should be clearly signposted and defined. The definition of business order is *a place for everything and everything in its place, always*, which necessitates good stacking and storage practices.

IMPLEMENTATION OF A STACKING AND STORAGE SYSTEM

The introduction of safe stacking and storage practices should be guided by a health and safety management system (SMS) standard. Basic stacking and storage rules should be incorporated, and frequent inspections undertaken to ensure these standards are being applied in practice.

GENERAL RULES OF STACKING

Stacking should be carried out under the supervision of a person qualified and knowledgeable in stacking and storage procedures. The base upon which the stack is built must be level, firm, and capable of carrying the load, and the heavy items must always be stacked at the bottom of a stack, shelf, or rack, and the lighter items on the top.

Only goods of the same size, shape, and weight should be stacked one on top of the other, and if pallets are to be used, they must be in a good condition. Any stacks that are unsafe or incorrectly built must be unpacked and rebuilt under supervision.

It is advisable to mark, by means of a line painted against the wall, the maximum height of a stack. The maximum weight capacity of racking, mezzanine floors, and shelves should be clearly marked on the rack or shelving. Sheets of heavy wrapping paper laid on the top of pallets of tins, for example, prevents the stack from shifting and helps bind the goods being stacked.

Stacks must never be broken down from the bottom. Stacks should be broken down from the top, and no-one should be allowed to climb on a stack. Ladders or other safe means should be used to access stacks. Ensure that employees walking on a stack cannot reach into unguarded machinery, and ensure that the corners of stacks are protected and not bumped by moving vehicles.

AUDIT OF A STACKING AND STORAGE SYSTEM

This element is audited during the audit physical inspection, during which stacking and storage procedures are scrutinized. Actual stacking and storage practices noted during the inspection should be compared with the SMS standard (Figure 33.1).

ELEMENT / PROGRAM / PROCESS	POINTS	QUESTIONS THAT COULD BE ASKED	VERIFICATION	WHAT TO LOOK FOR
STACKING AND STORAGE PRACTICES				
ASSIGNMENT OF RESPONSIBLE PEOPLE				
Competent, experienced employees assigned with responsibility for safe stacking	5	Are competent, experienced employees assigned with responsibility for safe stacking?	Copy of assignment / letter	
STACKING NEAT, STABLE AND CONTROLLED				
Are stacks properly constructed? (NB: Remember max H = 3 x shortest base distance)	5	Are stacked arranged according to standard?	Visual	Check all stacking, scrap yards, storage yards
Stacks bonded	5			
Stacks in authorized places	5	Is there a standard for this element?	Visual	Inspect stacking areas
Unstable or hazardous stacks	5	What action taken if an unsafe stack is noted?		
STORAGE IN CUPBOARDS / ON SHELVES NEAT AND TIDY				
Cupboards neat and tidy	5		Visual	Inspect in cupboards. All shelves, outside areas also
Shelves neat and tidy	5		Visual	
UNAUTHORIZED STACKING			Visual	
Top of cabinets clear	5		Visual	Visual check of windowsills and cupboard tops
Unsafe storage noted	5		Visual	Check stack and storage areas
TOTAL	45			

FIGURE 33.1 Audit Protocol for the Element – Stacking and Storage.

34 Structures, Buildings, Floors, and Openings

DESIGN OF A SYSTEM TO MANAGE STRUCTURES, BUILDINGS, FLOORS, AND OPENINGS

INTRODUCTION

Everyone who works in a building, moves around a structure, or walks on floors in work areas can be exposed to hazards due to the structure, building, or walkway being unsafe.

STRUCTURES

Structures should be clean at all times and should be maintained in a good state of repair. Often, structures and buildings are damaged as a result of accidents which are never reported. Repetitive damage could lead to a situation where the building could suffer irreparable damage, in which case it would then pose a hazard to employees.

DAMAGED STRUCTURES

Structures should be inspected regularly for damage. Vehicles, forklift trucks, overhead (or other) cranes or other items could cause damage. Walls of buildings and structures should not be broken or damaged or pose a threat to the safety of employees.

Are the doors of the structures sound and secure? How safe are the balustrades? Regular inspections should cover all these aspects, and accidental damage to garage and hanger doors should be immediately identified and reported.

STRUCTURE MAINTENANCE

Structures should be cleaned regularly and dirt removed. Where necessary, the structure should be painted, and ongoing maintenance will ensure that the structure is cleaned and kept in a safe and hygienic condition. Only authorized structures should be allowed, and these should be constructed according to the local building regulations.

BUILDINGS

Buildings are those structures built to accommodate the process to manufacture the product. Parts of the buildings such as the roof, gutters, walls, doors, and windows are also included in the definition of a building. Buildings should be sound, secure, and without defect. They should not constitute a hazard to the people working in them.

Buildings are also subject to accidental damage by vehicles, forklift trucks, cranes, and other sources. These damage-causing accidents all have potential to injure people, and therefore it is important that they be reported and investigated.

FLOORS

Floors include walkways, working areas, stacking areas, yard areas, parking areas, and outlying storage areas. Any area where employees walk can be classified as floors where there is a hazard of unguarded openings or slippery, unstable surfaces.

Floors should be kept free from spills and must provide a safe walk and work area for employees. All openings which constitute a hazard should be barricaded or closed, and the floor area should be safe at all times.

HOUSEKEEPING

Good housekeeping will ensure that the floors are free of superfluous material, which will eliminate trip and fire hazards. Walkways must be kept in a safe state of repairs at all times.

OPENINGS

As with structures and buildings, these openings should be kept in a good state of repair and free from any accidental damage or natural deterioration. Windows should be cleaned regularly, and if skylights are fitted on the roof, they should be demarcated or somehow highlighted to indicate their danger to people who may happen to work on the roof. Manhole covers must be in place, and there should be no openings through which a worker can fall.

Falls from or on stairs cause numerous injuries. Stairways should not be used for storage and should at all times be kept free from oil, grime, grease, and other substances which could make them slippery and unsafe. No stacking should be allowed under stairways, as should this material catch alight, it will render the stairway impossible to use as an evacuation route.

IMPLEMENTATION OF A SYSTEM TO MANAGE STRUCTURES, BUILDINGS, FLOORS, AND OPENINGS

An example of an SMS standard for the element Structures, Buildings, Floors, and Openings is as follows:

The objective of this standard is to ensure that:

- Buildings and floor areas, inside and outside, utilized for the business processes are appropriate for the needs and pose no hazards to the work performed.

- Areas of responsibility are designated to appropriate persons to ensure the detection and rectification of deviations.
- Fixed structures are included in the planned maintenance program to ensure their ongoing integrity.

RESPONSIBILITY AND ACCOUNTABILITY

Each manager, supervisor, and/or employee is responsible for the application of this standard in their work area(s). Each area supervisor will be accountable for the compliance to this standard in his or her work area. Managers responsible for new facilities should ensure that new facilities comply with this standard.

DELEGATION OF RESPONSIBILITY

- All office areas, warehouses, and workplaces shall be allocated to nominated persons for inspection purposes. This responsibility can be designated in writing or on a plan.
- The person responsible for inspections may also be the designated health and safety representative.
- The name of the person responsible for inspecting the area should be displayed in a prominent place in that area.
- The responsible person should inspect their area of responsibility at least once per month and report any deviations through the checklist inspection sheet.

STRUCTURES AND BUILDINGS

- Buildings shall be appropriate for the work performed in them, and shall allow for adequate and safe movement of people, equipment, materials, and appropriate vehicles.
- Buildings shall meet the company construction specifications and any other legal requirements, and shall be designed to withstand the likely weather conditions of the region.
- Structures such as roofing, walls, and support columns shall be free from damage and cracks that could affect their structural integrity.
- Gutters and down-pipes shall be adequate for weather needs and maintained free of blockages.
- Doors and doorframes shall not be damaged and shall maintain adequate support of the structure as well as providing sealing from the environment.
- Any wall door or structure that forms part of any passive fire protection shall not be breached or compromised. All services passing through the barrier shall be suitably fire stopped and sealed.
- Windows and frames shall be of appropriate strength and broken or cracked panes replaced. Any glazing used in doorways or near traffic ways shall be safety glass.
- Fences and gates shall be sound and shall be maintained and kept free of hazards such as loose wire, and so on.

FLOORS

- All floors shall be of sufficient structural strength to maintain the maximum working load that they may be subjected to.
- Floor surfaces and carpeting shall be free of holes and uneven or unsafe surfaces that pose a risk of people falling and the upset of mobile equipment.
- Roadways and walkways shall be even, unobstructed and free of debris such as nails, sharp objects, cords, pipes, and so on.
- Where a temporary situation requires a cable or pipe to be run over a walkway or roadway, a suitable sound cable/pipe bridge or ramp should be provided and maintained for the duration of work.
- Drains shall be maintained free from debris to ensure adequate runoff during rain and water discharges.
- Bathroom and change room floors shall be of non-slip material.

AUDIT OF A SYSTEM TO MANAGE STRUCTURES, BUILDINGS, FLOORS, AND OPENINGS

The physical inspection will indicate any damaged or hazard structures, walkways, and buildings. Walkways should be inspected for hazardous openings. A system of delegating sections of the workplace to employees is a good method of ensuring that damage events are reported and the damage duly rectified, so no risk is posed to employees. This allocation of areas also facilitates regular inspections of the areas. These areas should have signs indicating who the responsible person is.

Walkways should be demarcated and good housekeeping should be evident throughout the workplace. A system of planned maintenance should be in operation and cleaning schedules in place. An inspection of a specific area should be followed up during the documentation review and cross referenced to a completed checklist for that specific area (Figure 34.1).

ELEMENT / PROGRAM / PROCESS	POINTS	QUESTIONS THAT COULD BE ASKED	VERIFICATION	WHAT TO LOOK FOR
STRUCTURES, BUILDINGS, FLOORS AND OPENINGS				
STRUCTURES				
Safe	5	Is there a standard for this element?	Visual	Deteriorating structures. Unauthorized. Unsafe structures
Maintained	5		Visual	Evidence of maintenance and repairs
On inspection checklist	5	How often are structures inspected?		
BUILDINGS				
Safe condition	5		Visual	No unsafe, unhygienic buildings
Maintenance program	5	Are buildings on a maintenance program?	Copy of maintenance schedule.	Evidence of maintenance
Inspection checklist	5	Are inspections done using a checklist?	Copy of checklist completed	
FLOORS				
Free from obstruction	5		Visual	No slip, trip or fall hazards
Demarcated	5			Walkways clear, travel ways clear
Inspection routine	5	How often are floors and walkways inspected?	Copy of standard	
OPENINGS				
No unguarded openings	5		Visual	No unguarded openings
Skylights guarded	5		Visual	Guards or fall protection in place
TOTAL	55			

FIGURE 34.1 Audit Protocol for the Element – Structures, Buildings, Floors, and Openings.

35 Demarcation of Walkways, Work Areas, and Storage Areas

DESIGN OF A SYSTEM FOR THE DEMARCATION OF WALKWAYS, WORK AREAS, AND STORAGE AREAS

To bring about business order in a workplace, it is necessary to mark off walkways, work areas, and storage areas so that there is a place for everything, and everything is in its place, always. This introduces order into the workplace.

No successful production or manufacturing area can have good housekeeping, business order, and improved safety without the demarcation of various areas, walkways, and features. Demarcation reduces fire hazards and makes a good impression on the people working in the area, and it is essential for the safe passage of workers and materials, as well as for the correct storing of tools and products. Demarcation provides a safe workplace for all.

One of the main advantages of demarcation is that housekeeping (business order) is improved. Order means *a place for everything and everything in its place, always.* Demarcation defines stacking areas, working areas, walkways, and other areas. Fire hazards are reduced because there is a correct place to store material, and superfluous material is not allowed to accumulate. Firefighting equipment is readily available and unobstructed as a result of the "no parking" areas demarcated below the equipment.

IMPLEMENTATION OF A SYSTEM FOR THE DEMARCATION OF WALKWAYS, WORK AREAS, AND STORAGE AREAS

STANDARDIZATION

The color of demarcation lines is important, and should tie in with the organization's color code. Where possible, the demarcation should be restricted to one or two colors, as more can lead to confusion amongst the workforce. The width of the demarcation line is important, and it should be standard throughout the entire organization. If there are various work sites at different locations, the need for the standardization of demarcation is important.

AREAS IDENTIFIED

Before demarcation commences, the various areas and features that need to be demarcated should be identified and described. They could include the following: work areas, stacking areas, storage areas, exits, assembly areas, scrap bin locations, "no parking" areas, motorized transport roadways, repair bays, canteen and coffee stations, "no stacking" areas, and "no pedestrian crossing" areas.

STANDARDS SET

A standard must first of all be set for demarcating, and this standard would include the following: size of demarcation, method to be used, width of demarcation lines, where to demarcate, how to demarcate, who must demarcate, and by when the demarcation must be done. This standard should be communicated to all concerned, and employees should receive a briefing session as to the purpose and advantages of demarcation.

IMPLEMENTATION STEPS

The following steps are suggested:

- Set a demarcation standard.
- Do temporary demarcation.
- Make changes to temporary demarcation.
- Demarcate, paint, and mark out.
- Re-check and make minor changes.
- Set up a demarcation maintenance system.
- Monitor by inspection.

AUDIT OF A SYSTEM FOR THE DEMARCATION OF WALKWAYS, WORK AREAS, AND STORAGE AREAS

The first impression one gains when entering a work area that has been correctly demarcated is one of order. The auditors must inspect to see that demarcation has been carried out throughout the facility. Is the line width and color according to the standard? Are walkways clearly demarcated? Are work areas and storage areas demarcated? The standard on demarcation should be examined by the auditors and cross referenced to what was noted during the inspection (Figure 35.1).

ELEMENT/PROGRAM/PROCESS	POINTS	QUESTIONS THAT COULD BE ASKED	VERIFICATION	WHAT TO LOOK FOR
DEMARCATION OF WALKWAYS, WORK AND STORAGE AREAS				
FLOORS DEMARCATED				
Demarcation been done	5	What standard for demarcation is followed?	Visual compare with standard	Areas, parking bays, work areas, storage, off-loading/walkways/hazards
All areas been covered	5		Visual	Are all possible features demarcated?
Aisles and storage areas demarcation uniform	5	How often is the demarcation redone?	Maintenance schedule	Sufficient, enough space, uniform.
UNIFORM DEMARCATION CODE USED				
Lines uniform in color	5	What is the standard?	Visual and standard for demarcation/color code board	Same color? Same size?
Lines uniform in width?	5	What is the standard?		Is the demarcation the same in all areas?
DEMARCATION ADHERED TO				
Obstructions in aisles	5		Visual	Check during inspection
Stacking protruding beyond demarcation	5		Visual	Check during inspection
DEMARCATION UNDER SWITCHGEAR				
Switchgear demarcated with "Keep clear" zones	5		Standard for demarcation	Check under all switchgear that needs to be accessible
Fire equipment demarcated	5	What is the standard for fire equipment?	Visual	Check demarcation of fire equipment
TOTAL	45			

FIGURE 35.1 Audit Protocol for the Element – Demarcation of Walkways, Work Areas, and Storage Areas.

36 Labeling of Switches, Controllers, and Isolators

DESIGN OF A PROGRAM FOR THE LABELING OF SWITCHES, CONTROLLERS, AND ISOLATORS

INTRODUCTION

The objective of this SMS element is to ensure that the correct equipment, circuit, or process is operated, especially in an emergency, by labeling all valves, switches, isolators, and contact breakers. Labels also warn of electrical arc flash danger.

A number of fatal accidents have occurred as a result of confusion with switches, isolators, or valves because they were not clearly marked. Identifying and labeling ensures that the proper equipment or machinery is stopped, started, or isolated when required. Furthermore, it assists employees unfamiliar with machinery or the plant to readily identify and locate equipment or circuits, switches, isolators, and valves.

ARC FLASH LABELING

Labels on electrical equipment should also warn of the possibility of an arc flash occurring, and should indicate what level of protective clothing is required when operating such equipment.

IMPLEMENTATION OF A PROGRAM FOR THE LABELING OF SWITCHES, CONTROLLERS, AND ISOLATORS

To implement the labeling program, there should be a written standard which stipulates the methods to be used for the labeling of switches, controllers, and isolators. The standard should also indicate responsibilities for the labeling program.

RESPONSIBILITY AND ACCOUNTABILITY

Managers, supervisors, and contractors (Responsible persons) should ensure that conformity is maintained regarding standards applicable to labels, their method of display, and their position within their areas of responsibility. They should ensure that equipment is correctly identified and correctly marked or labeled, and that labeling is inspected on a random basis in their areas of responsibility.

They should also assist their department in developing practical standards for the identification of all equipment and circuits, and inspect new plant and equipment designs for correct identification of equipment and circuits.

GENERAL LABELING REQUIREMENTS

Labeling must be permanent and standardized throughout and be in the main languages of the organization. All fixed equipment should be clearly labeled with the name by which it is commonly known, for example, *Fire Pump Number 2.* Individual units of a number of similar machines could be identified with numbers, or letters, with one sign for the complete group, for example, *Air Conditioners: AC No. 28 and AC No. 29,* and so on.

The source of supply should be indicated on the label so that the circuit can be traced to the isolator or circuit breaker controlling the unit or circuit. No detailed specification can be given for all applications, but every effort must be made to standardize labeling wherever possible, in size and in proportion to the equipment.

AFFIXING LABELS

Attached labels should be clearly visible, ensure maximum legibility from the working area, and be affixed where they are unlikely to be damaged or obliterated. They should not be affixed to a machine, or part of a machine, which is interchangeable, but should be attached to base plates, steelwork, or walls adjacent to the equipment. All valves, switches, and isolators should be marked to indicate ON and OFF and OPEN and CLOSED positions.

ELECTRICAL LABELING

The voltage of distribution panels should be identified on the front and rear of panels and doors. The electrical switchgear and remote stop and start stations should be labeled using the same name as that on the equipment.

All circuit breakers inside a distribution panel should be labeled with the number and circuit description of the outlet system being fed. All distribution panels should be labeled on the outside of the panel door, with the number and circuit description of the outlet system being fed.

All electrical equipment should be subject to an arc flash risk assessment. If equipment poses an arc flash risk, it should be adequately labeled indicating the arc flash warning, hazards, and boundaries, as well as the level of arc flash personal protective equipment required.

VALVES AND PIPELINES

All pipelines should be identified in accordance with the company color coding requirements.

Critical valves (including emergency shut-off valves) should be clearly labeled as to their purpose or use by means of a metal disc attached to the valve or other similar means.

Arrows should be painted or affixed to the pipe to indicate direction of the flow of contents of the pipe, adjacent to the valve, adjacent to the wall where the pipe goes through the wall on both sides, and adjacent to the corner where the pipe bends on both sides.

AUDIT OF A PROGRAM FOR THE LABELING OF SWITCHES, CONTROLLERS, AND ISOLATORS

A standard should be available for this element. The standard should indicate methods of isolator, switch, and controller identification and assign responsibility for the implementation and maintenance of the labeling program. The audit inspection should include examining labeling practices to ensure there are no nonconformances that could cause confusion (Figure 36.1).

ELEMENT/PROGRAM/PROCESS	POINTS	QUESTIONS THAT COULD BE ASKED	VERIFICATION	WHAT TO LOOK FOR
LABELING OF SWITCHES, CONTROLLERS AND ISOLATORS				
ALL ISOLATORS AND CONTACT BREAKERS LABELED				
All switchgear marked with a permanent label system (i.e. not peeling or faded)	5	What labelling systems are used?	Visual	During the inspection, were all circuit breakers labeled? Were all isolators, switches, starter buttons, clearly labeled as to what equipment they control?
Emergency stop buttons red	5		Visual	
Switch panels marked front and rear	5	What languages are used?	Visual	
Standardized system used	5	Is marking system standardized?	Visual	Was there a standardized system used?
Electrical arc flash labelling	5	Has an arc flash risk assessment been done?	Visual	Check for electrical rooms and panels
CRITICAL VALVES AND CONTROLS IDENTIFIED				
All critical valves identified (natural gas, main water supply, process emergency shut off, etc.)	5	What critical valves are there on site?	Are valves physically identified. Are critical valves identified on a map for use during emergency situations?	Are critical valves such as main steam valve, main compressed air supply, main gas supply, emergency shut-off valves, clearly identified?
Labeling clear and descriptive	5		Visual	
Staff familiar with the critical switches, CB's, valves and control locations and the appropriate actions to take in an emergency	5	How are they informed?	Visual	Location of critical valves marked
All critical valves identified (natural gas, main water supply, process emergency shut off)	5	Are valves physically identified. Are critical valves identified on a map for use during emergency situations?	View the site plan	
TOTAL	**45**			

FIGURE 36.1   Audit Protocol for the Element – Labeling of Switches, Controllers, and Isolators.

37 Color Coding of Plant and Machinery

DESIGN OF A COLOR CODING SYSTEM FOR PLANT AND MACHINERY

INTRODUCTION

Color coding is the organized, standardized, and systematic process of painting certain items in workplaces in specific colors. Color coding is used for the speedy recognition of hazards. It also informs the user of danger and helps eliminate errors as it ensures a standardization and quick recognition of items. Color coding is a common safety language, and helps improve the appearance of the workplace as it contributes greatly to good housekeeping.

IMPLEMENTATION OF A COLOR CODING SYSTEM FOR PLANT AND MACHINERY

A health and safety management system (SMS) standard for color coding should be written and implemented. An important aspect of color coding is that the color coding should be standardized and be the same as that recommended by the national or international standards authority within the country. The color coding must be universally applied throughout the plant, divisions, or group of companies.

A training program should be embarked on to ensure that all in the workplace are aware of the purpose of color coding and what the various colors mean. Color coding key charts should be erected in work areas indicating which color is used to indicate which hazard.

This training should be built into the induction training, and training sessions should be held with all employees to notify them of the color coding and its purpose. The employee safety rulebook should also contain the color code and its application.

The color coding of plant and machinery entails painting certain pieces of equipment specific basic colors. The basic color coding colors (which could differ from country to country) could be as follows:

- Red and red and white stripes
- Yellow and yellow and black stripes
- Green
- Orange
- Blue

Color coding can be used to identify a machine, positioning of fire equipment, floor demarcation, positions of electrical switchgear, and bump-against hazards, such as low level pipelines. Color coding entails the selection and application of colors for the demarcation of parking areas, work areas, and safety signs. Color coding is also used on drums and on pipelines to indicate the contents.

Depending on local standards, the basic plant and machinery color coding colors and their general usage could be as follows:

RED AND WHITE

Red is the background color normally used with white letters or stripes to indicate danger, positioning of firefighting equipment, and warning lights on barricades. Red barricades and lights also warns of explosives being used in the area. Electrical emergency stop buttons are usually red.

YELLOW AND BLACK STRIPES

Yellow is the basic color, used on its own or with black stripes, to indicate areas where caution should be taken. Yellow and black indicates where employees can trip, fall, or collide with something. These are commonly referred to as *bump-against* hazards.

Examples of yellow and black striping are the hooks of cranes, overhead obstructions in passages, the edges and sides of roll-up doors, different floor levels, all protruding levers, and protruding platforms.

GREEN

Green can be used in conjunction with white for symbolic safety signs indicating information and location. Emergency equipment can be color coded green, as can other emergency facilities such as emergency exits, positions of breathing devices, and emergency showers.

BLUE

Blue, used in conjunction with white, normally indicates mandatory actions such as the wearing of personal protective equipment.

ORANGE

Orange can be used to indicate electrical current, distribution boards, and switchgear. Orange can also be used to paint the inside of machine guards. This would ensure that a guard is immediately visible if it is removed and not replaced.

PIPELINE COLOR CODING

The objective of color coding of pipelines and conduits is to indicate the contents and flow direction of the contents of pipes, cables, and other conduits.

The color coding of pipelines differs from basic color coding of plant and machinery as numerous substances, chemicals, fluids, liquids, and gases are transported in pipes.

Basic Color

A basic color is the basic pipeline color code, and the entire pipeline can be painted in this color if so desired. Due to cost considerations, this is not always possible, and therefore a basic color band of at least 6 inches (150 mm) can be painted on the pipeline at regular intervals, indicating its content.

Indicator Band

The color code indicator is a band superimposed on the basic color indicating the contents of the pipeline. This indicator band can be painted in bands over a basic color where the pipeline has been painted with a basic color. In certain instances, there maybe two or three color indicator bands. These bands must be painted next to each other, and the basic color code color must extend for at least 6 inches (150 mm) on each end. The basic color and the superimposed color code indicator band(s) then indicates the content of the pipeline. Valves in the pipeline should also be color coded the same color as the pipeline.

Descriptive Code Indicator

The ideal is to have a descriptive code indicator on the pipeline or conduit. This is a sign or label indicating the contents of the pipeline. The contents description can be printed on adhesive labels, stenciled onto the pipeline, or printed onto a small metal plate hanging from or affixed to the pipe. Ideally, the flow direction of the contents should be indicated by means of arrows, either on the pipe or on metal plates.

AUDIT OF A COLOR CODING SYSTEM FOR PLANT AND MACHINERY

The auditors must confirm that a standard for color coding is available and that color coding has been applied according to the standard. The inspection of the work area will indicate the use of standard colors to highlight items and warn of other hazards. Pipelines should be labeled or color coded, and the demarcation of aisles, walkways, and other areas should be done according to the requirements of the standard (Figure 37.1).

ELEMENT/PROGRAM/PROCESS	POINTS	QUESTIONS THAT COULD BE ASKED	VERIFICATION	WHAT TO LOOK FOR
COLOR CODE PLANT AND MACHINERY				
UNIFORM COLOR CODE APPLIED THROUGHOUT				
Pipelines color coded or labeled	5	Is a color code applied?	Visual	Pipeline code in place (labeled or marked)
Equipment (pumps, motors, valves, etc.) color coded or labeled	5	How is equipment identified?	Copy of the color code.	Is there a basic color applied?
Electrical switchgear color coded or labeled?	5	How is this done?	Is it consistent with the physical application?	Is it consistent? Faded?
Emergency stop buttons/trip wire switches labeled	5	What color is used?		Isolated areas? Are the pipelines color coded, or labeled and flow direction indicated?
Low doorways/structures color coded or labeled.	5	Are bump-against hazards color coded?		
COLOR CODE KEYBOARD DISPLAYED				
Color code legend or display readily available for employees.	5	What standard of color code is used?	Display of colorcode boards at the department where applicable.	A color-code board must be displayed for each section at least.
Colors conform to legend at the plant or facility?	5			Does it indicate all the colors used?
KNOWLEDGE OF COLORS				
Employees/Contractors	5	How do they learn about the color code?	Training syllabus, other?	Employee interview question.
TOTAL	40			

FIGURE 37.1 Audit Protocol for the Element – Color Coding of Plant and Machinery.

38 Scrap, Waste, and Refuse Removal System

DESIGN OF A SCRAP, WASTE, AND REFUSE REMOVAL SYSTEM

INTRODUCTION

Scrap, waste, and refuse lying around a work area constitutes superfluous and unwanted material. Housekeeping cannot be maintained and fire hazards are increased. Containers, receptacles, and holders are needed for the storage and removal of recyclable material and the removal of other material from the workplace.

- Scrap is any piece of waste material.
- Waste is any reject or excess material.
- Refuse is rejected, discarded, or worthless matter.
- Recyclable material is material that can be recycled.

OBJECTIVE

The objective of providing recyclable material, waste, and refuse bins is to keep the work area clean, safe, and free from fire and other hazards, and to create business order. Good housekeeping is easily maintained if a regular system of removing superfluous material generated in the work process is implemented. Bins and containers should be provided at strategically located positions so that scrap, waste, and refuse can be placed in them. The accumulation of waste and scrap takes up valuable workspace and also constitutes trip hazards and obstacles to the employees working in that area.

IMPLEMENTATION OF A SCRAP, WASTE, AND REFUSE REMOVAL SYSTEM

The *Plan, Do, Check, Act* methodology can be used to implement this element. The steps to implement a scrap, waste, and refuse removal system are the following:

- Do a scrap, waste, and refuse bin requirement survey (Plan).
- Provide storage bins for recyclable materials (Do).
- Provide sufficient receptacles for waste and refuse (Do).
- Provide receptacles with lids or devices to contain the contents (Do).
- Provide the correct type and size of receptacles (Do).
- Demarcate container positions (Do).
- Schedule removal periods (Do).

- Recycling of materials (Do).
- Monitor the system (Check).
- Rectify nonconformances (Act).

SCRAP, WASTE, AND REFUSE BIN REQUIREMENT SURVEY

All areas should be surveyed to determine what types of receptacles are required and where they should be positioned. Canteens, ablution blocks, and offices should be included in this survey.

PROVIDE STORAGE BINS FOR RECYCLABLE MATERIALS

Storage bins for recyclable materials should be provided based on the type and quantity of material generated and the frequency of the removal schedule. Recyclable material such as wood, certain plastics, and aluminum should also have separate bins clearly indicated for their purpose.

PROVIDE SUFFICIENT RECEPTACLES FOR WASTE AND REFUSE

Based on the survey, an adequate number of receptacles are to be supplied to ensure adequate coverage of the workplace, office buildings, and other areas.

PROVIDE RECEPTACLES WITH LIDS OR DEVICES TO CONTAIN THE CONTENTS

Wherever possible, lids or some form of containment should form part of the receptacle. Lids or other containing devices, such as nylon nets, will prevent refuse being blown out of the container or being removed by unauthorized people. Refuse bins should be lined with a plastic liner which should be removed on a regular basis.

PROVIDE THE CORRECT TYPE AND SIZE OF RECEPTACLES

Certain hazardous waste is collected in special receptacles provided by the approved contractor. The entire bin is removed on a predetermined basis by the contractor and handled according to accepted international norms.

There are a number of different types of receptacles for recyclable material, scrap, waste, or refuse. Depending on the application and the particular work environment, trash cans, rubbish bins, scrap drums, dumpsters, and other receptacles may be used. Where possible, separate bins should be supplied for separate material and different applications. Separate metal containers with tight-fitting lids should be provided for the storage of oil-impregnated rags or cloths.

Hygiene Waste

Hygiene waste is also handled separately. Special containers are provided, and contractors remove this waste and dispose of it according to accepted standards. These bins should be clearly labelled and identified so that proper control is exercised over their use, removal, and replacement.

Demarcate Container Positions

An initial survey of the scrap, waste, and refuse bin requirements in a work area will also determine the correct positioning thereof. Once the correct positioning has been determined, the position of the bins should be demarcated.

Demarcation can be done by means of a pictogram or symbolic sign erected on the wall in front of the bin's position, or a yellow circle or square could be painted on the floor to denote the bin's designated position.

Color Code

Scrap, waste, and refuse bins should be color coded in the same color for easy and speedy recognition. Color coding of scrap bins would form part of the organization's color coding program. Where possible, the type of scrap, recyclable material, or refuse should be indicated on the container.

In most instances, bins that contain flammable material, or material that is likely to ignite spontaneously, are color coded red to denote a fire hazard.

Schedule a Removal System

A structured, scheduled system should be introduced for the regular removal of all scrap, waste, and refuse bins. This system will ensure that the bins are emptied on a regular basis and do not overflow, causing a hazardous, untidy, and unhygienic situation. The method of removal is to be determined by the organization itself. In the case of hazardous waste, contractors normally call on a regular basis and remove the containers long before they are full or overflowing. Should more frequent removal periods be required, the contractors should be informed accordingly.

Recycling of Materials

Scrap recycling containers can be removed by contractors or emptied at the recycling dump and sold to scrap-metal or other dealers. In the case of nonrecyclable refuse such as old food, hygiene refuse, and certain plastics, these should be removed from the premises on a regular basis. Often the local authority, municipality, or waste removal contractor carries out this function.

Monitor the System

Regular inspections of the provision, positioning, and demarcation of the receptacles should be done. Overflowing receptacles would indicate that a change in the removal schedule is required or that more receptacles are needed.

Rectification of Nonconformances

Deviations, inadequacies, and nonconformances to the standard should be rectified and changes and improvements made to the system.

AUDIT OF A SCRAP, WASTE, AND REFUSE REMOVAL SYSTEM

The physical appearance of the workplace should indicate if a working scrap, waste, and refuse removal system is in place. Bins should be evident and their locations marked. They should be labeled as to their contents and not be overflowing. Good housekeeping should be evident as a result of no superfluous material or scrap being present in the workplace (Figure 38.1).

ELEMENT/PROGRAM/PROCESS	POINTS	QUESTIONS THAT COULD BE ASKED	VERIFICATION	WHAT TO LOOK FOR
SCRAP, WASTEAND REFUSE REMOVAL SYSTEM				
SCRAP, WASTE, REFUSE, BINS PROVIDED				
Sufficient bins provided	5	How was this determined?		Number of bins, lids on bins in certain applications, bins, adequate
Bins of the right type/size	5		Visual	
Lids where provided kept in place	5			Are they the same color (where possible?)
Color coded	5	How are bins identified?		
REGULAR CONTROLLED REMOVAL				
Bins removed as per schedule	5	How often are the bins emptied?	Removal schedule, high lighting different refuse removal systems where applicable	Are the bins emptied regularly?
Bins overflowing	5		Visual.	
REMOVAL OF HAZARDOUS WASTE				
Risk assessment done	5	Has a risk assessment been done?	List of identified hazardous waste.	Are the receptacles marked?
Approved contractors	5	What hazardous waste is removed and by who?	Appointment letters.	
Regular removal	5	How often is this done?	Copy of schedule.	Check for regular removal of hazardous waste
RECEPTICAL LOCATIONS MARKED				
Locations marked in a suitable way?.	5	What standard of demarcation is followed?	Demarcation standard.	All bin areas marked. Is the marking standard? Are all bins in the demarcated areas?
SEPARATE BINS FOR SEPARATE MATERIAL				
Materials separated	5	How are materials separated?	Visual	Separate bins for different materials
TOTAL	55			

FIGURE 38.1 Audit Protocol for the Element – Scrap, Waste, and Refuse Removal System.

39 Hearing Conservation Program

DESIGN OF A HEARING CONSERVATION PROGRAM

OBJECTIVE

The objective of a hearing conservation program is to identify and remove sources of noise (*unwanted sound or undesirable sound*) in an effort to prevent permanent loss of hearing caused by working in noise zones where the equivalent noise level is in excess of 85dB (A). (This figure may differ from country to country.)

SOUND

Sound consists of small pressure variations in the air. These pressure variations radiate from a source at a speed of approximately 350 m per second. Sound waves have two main properties: the frequency and the intensity. Sound may be defined as any pressure variation in air, water, or other medium that can be detected by the human ear. These pressure variations travel through any elastic medium from the source of the sound to the listener's ear.

INTENSITY

If a noise is made, the surrounding air particles are set into motion, each particle passing on the vibration to the next in diminishing vibrations. (This effect is similar to dropping a stone into a pond.) The concentric rings caused by the stone will grow larger but less turbulent as each successive vibration is passed on. Eventually the vibrations will smoothen out. The extent to which the air particle vibrates is called *sound pressure* and is observed as loudness by the human perception mechanism. The sound intensity is measured in decibels (dB) and frequencies on the (A) scale, which is the range of frequencies closest to that of humans.

FREQUENCY

The sound waves in the air cause a continuous variation in the sound pressure. This variation can be fast or slow. The frequency of sound is heard as being a pitch; in other words, a high pitch sound means that the variation in sound pressure is fast, which means the wavelength is short. A low-pitched sound will indicate that the wavelength is long.

This frequency is measured in Hertz (Hz). The normal range of hearing for a healthy young person extends from approximately 20 Hz up to 20,000 Hz.

DANGER OF NOISE

The outer ear concentrates sound waves and channels them via the eardrum to the middle ear. Tiny bones within the middle ear convert the waves to mechanical vibrations, and thousands of hair cells (sensory cells) in the inner ear convert these vibrations into electrical impulses that are transmitted to the brain for interpretation.

Healthy hair cells are the key to good hearing, but because they are fragile, they can be damaged by infection and some drugs, and others can be lost as a result of exposure to excessive noise.

DEAFNESS

The type of deafness which results from exposure to excessive noise is termed *perceptive deafness*. This means that little benefit can be derived from hearing aids, which are designed to overcome *conductive* deafness. Perceptive deafness is irreversible and does not respond to any type of medical treatment.

DISADVANTAGE

The main disadvantage of noise induced hearing loss is that the victim is not aware that they are becoming deaf. Employees working in noise zones merely state that they "Have become accustomed to the noise." This in fact means that they are slowly becoming deaf. Deafness normally occurs over a considerable period of time and lulls one into a false sense of security, so the wearing of hearing protection is not seen as being important.

NOISE LEVELS

Most experts agree that noise levels exposure to 85dB (A) or more over a 40-hour working week could result in permanent noise induced hearing loss.

HEARING LOSS

To determine hearing loss, a hearing test or audiogram is conducted. The person being tested is seated in an almost sound-proof booth and the audiometer feeds a tone through a set of earphones. As soon as the patient hears the signal, he or she pushes a button and a point is plotted on the audiogram. An audiogram tests the hearing level at different frequencies and plots a graph. Any perceivable reduction in the hearing ability of the patient is clearly indicated when the patient's current tests are compared with an original base line test.

IMPLEMENTATION OF A HEARING CONSERVATION PROGRAM

A comprehensive hearing conservation program consists of the following steps:

- Identification of the source of noise or vibration
- Reduction of noise at source

- Demarcation of noise zones
- Training of employees in the techniques of hearing conservation
- Selection, issue, and wearing of personal protective equipment
- The conducting of pre-employment and ongoing six-monthly audiograms
- Taking the necessary actions should hearing loss be noticed amongst employees

IDENTIFY

An occupational hygienist or person qualified in noise measurement and reduction will assist in identifying potential noise sources. These could be electrically driven machines, vibrators, rotating shafts, conveyor belts, or any other device that creates noise. Once the sources of the noise have been identified, attempts can then be made to reduce the noise levels.

REDUCE

The next step is to reduce the noise level at the source. This can be done by the following methods:

- Isolation
- Enclosure
- Modification
- Baffling
- Lubricating and maintaining
- Separating

These examples are actions which can be taken to reduce the noise at the point where it is generated.

NOISE ZONES DEMARCATED

Once all efforts have been made at noise reduction, then the particular noise zones must be demarcated and signposted. Ideally, the demarcation should be via means of physical barriers or some other clearly understood demarcation method. For example, if a machine is the source of noise within a room 10 feet × 20 feet (3 m × 6 m) in size, then the entire room will be demarcated as a noise zone.

Even though only the immediate vicinity of a machine may be in excess of 85dB (A), a physical area around the machine (the entire room or division) may have to be declared a noise zone. Correct signs should be erected at both the entrances and exits to the area instructing workers who enter into, or work in, the area to wear suitable hearing protectors.

TRAINING

All employees participating in the program must now be trained in the dangers of exposure to noise, as well as the wearing of protective equipment. Visiting contractors and suppliers should also be required to wear hearing protectors when entering into or passing through a noise zone. Workers should be made aware of the dangers of noise induced hearing loss and should be fully informed as to the purpose of the six-monthly hearing acuity tests.

Personal Protective Equipment (PPE)

Issuing of earmuffs and earplugs should now take place and workers should have a choice of the type of PPE that they wish to wear. Correct training in the use of hearing protectors should be given, and spare earplugs and muffs must be made available.

Depending on the type and brand selected, the noise reduction rating of the equipment must be considered. Hearing protectors normally reduce the noise by between 20 and 30 decibels, and in high noise level areas, it is crucial that they be worn correctly. Workers may need a period of adjustment to become accustomed to wearing them.

There are basically five classes of hearing protection devices:

- Earplug (aural insert) disposable and reusable type
- Headband earplug type (aural insert)
- Headband partial-insert type (super-aural)
- Earmuff (circum-aural)
- Helmet type (enclosure)

Specialists will advise what particular type is best for each application.

Hearing Acuity Testing Program

To ensure that employees who frequent noise zones are not suffering hearing loss, their hearing acuity should be tested at least every six months. A qualified person should do this testing. The audiometer must be correctly calibrated. Audiograms should be taken and compared with previous tests to identify any deterioration of the employee's hearing. The tests should also be conducted on all new employees and on employees leaving the service of the company.

Action

Should there be hearing threshold shifts noted on audiograms of employees, immediate action must be taken. Ideally, they should be removed from the noise zones, and further tests should be carried out after a period. A doctor should be consulted, as the hearing loss may be as a result of infection or other medical problems.

Should an employee suffer permanent hearing loss, then that employee should be removed from noise zones completely and placed in a different work position, away from noise zones. Relying on employees to wear hearing protection is not always foolproof, and therefore noise reduction at the source is the ideal in all situations.

A temporary threshold shift in hearing may be as a result of an acute exposure to noise such as spending a day on the rifle range or being exposed to a loud explosion. Temporary threshold shifts are indications that the work area noise zones may be causing the damage.

AUDIT OF A HEARING CONSERVATION PROGRAM

The organization should have conducted a survey of sources of noise and attempted to reduce the noise levels. If the organization has noise zones, they should be clearly marked. Employees entering into or working in those areas should have correct hearing protectors. Training should be conducted and six-monthly audiometric testing carried out. Any hearing loss detected in employees should result in corrective action (Figure 39.1).

ELEMENT/PROGRAM/PROCESS	POINTS	QUESTIONS THAT COULD BE ASKED	VERIFICATION	WHAT TO LOOK FOR
HEARING CONSERVATION PROGRAM				
NOISE SURVEY DONE				
Noise survey been conducted of all work areas	5	Has a noise survey been conducted?	Plan or map of zoning and readings	Noise zone signs, demarcation and pictograms
NOISE ZONES DEMARCATED				
Noise zones identified and indicated	5	Was this conducted by a qualified person?	Map or plan of noise zones	During the inspection, were employees wearing ear-plugs or ear-muffs?
Attempts been made to reduce the noise levels at source	5	Have all areas been zoned? What effort has been made to reduce noise?	Proof of noise reduction attempts	Check noise sources for noise reduction efforts
Hearing acuity testing being done according to legal and company standards	5	Has the zone been determined on the equivalent level?	Legal or company standards	
Records of hearing tests kept up-to-date	5	Are contractors who work in noise zones also tested?	Example	
Approved hearing protectors provided and worn where required	5	Do employees who work in noise zones have their hearing tested?	Audiogram schedule	
HEARING ACUITY TESTING				
Testing done	5	At what intervals are employees tested?	Audiograms/records	
TOTAL	35			

FIGURE 39.1 Audit Protocol for the Element – Hearing Conservation Program.

40 Occupational Stress Management Program

DESIGN OF AN OCCUPATIONAL STRESS MANAGEMENT PROGRAM

OCCUPATIONAL STRESS

Occupational stress is slight, temporary physical and/or mental overload caused by overwork, fatigue, depression, worry, and other factors. It normally arises out of and during the course of employment, and can be partially caused by external factors such as family life. This stress puts the victim in a position where their full concentration is not always on the job, and this in turn leads them to commit high risk acts or create high risk conditions, which could lead to accidents.

DESCRIPTION

There are numerous ways to describe occupational stress. One of the most prominent signs is that the person feels extremely tense and anxious. The individual does a great deal of worrying, and excessive work pressure increases this anxiety. People suffering from occupational stress are often termed "short tempered," as they are often inclined to fly off at the deep end or lose their temper very quickly, and become aggressive and emotionally upset. This stressful state of mind is not conducive to safe working habits.

TYPES OF STRESS

Although there are many types of stress, two basic types are discussed here: the stress that works *for* a person, and the stress that works *against* a person. A certain amount of positive stress is necessary and assists in helping one meet objectives. The stress that works against a person can create emotional upset, aggression, and forgetfulness, and this in turn has an effect on the individual's health.

THE EFFECTS OF OCCUPATIONAL STRESS

The effects of occupational stress can be devastating if the stress is not identified and treated as soon as possible, as stress is one of the root causes of accidents. These root causes lead to the committing of high risk acts or the creation of high risk conditions, which are the immediate causes of accidents.

Severely Stressed

As a result of tremendous work pressure and maintaining a high standard of living, emotional stress can build up within a person. A number of factors contribute to this emotional stress. Individuals are in daily contact with managers, peers, fellow workers, spouses, friends, and children, and this interaction could cause emotional stress. People lose faith in themselves; they lose confidence and worry about it. This constant worrying then builds up more stress and leads to a situation where the person becomes severely stressed.

Driving Skills

The driving skills of employees can be effected by their stressed state. Their aggression could be displayed in their driving habits. Lack of concentration could lead them to skip stop signs and traffic lights. The courtesy, patience, and self-discipline needed to drive motor vehicles may be hampered by the stress. Stress could lead to the person taking chances and not following the laid down safety procedures.

It must be remembered that everybody lives with a certain amount of stress, both from the home and the work environment. A certain level of stress is therefore always going to be present, but it is when this stress starts to cause an overload that we should show concern and take action.

IMPLEMENTATION OF AN OCCUPATIONAL STRESS MANAGEMENT PROGRAM

A simple approach to the implementation of a basic stress management program is given here, but this may need to be expanded and managed by specialists, depending on the specific situation.

STEP 1 – RECOGNIZING THE CAUSES OF OCCUPATIONAL STRESS

No single cause is responsible for creating an excessive amount of stress within a person. Regular personal contacts with employees by supervision and managers would identify those individuals suffering from certain level of stress, and counselling could then be arranged.

Some possible causes that could contribute to increasing stress levels which should be recognized are the following:

- The political climate
- Internal politics
- Fear of being fired
- Pending divorce action
- A family accident
- Work pressure
- Financial problems
- Not sharing anxiety and worries with family
- Children's academic achievements at school
- Relationships with fellow workers

Making employees aware of the causes and symptoms of stress via talks, meetings, and discussions will help them recognize the symptoms of stress.

STEP 2 – REDUCING THE LEVELS OF OCCUPATIONAL STRESS

Fortunately, there are remedies for both mental and physical stress. A qualified counselor will be able to advise specific changes to lessen the stress load. The four main remedies are:

Relaxation

To relieve the amount of stress being experienced, a change of environment and activity is necessary. A hobby or part time activity which takes the mind off of the stress-causing factors is a good outlet and can relieve stress.

Getting Out of the Rut

Getting out of the rut is important to help reduce stress. We all get into certain routines, and these routines become monotonous. Changing the routine wherever possible should break the monotony.

Changing Work Habits

Long hours on one's feet or behind a desk can also lead to physical stress, which is why it is so important to change work habits and take regular walks through the plant. Walking through the work area and speaking to people about their problems and their interests gives one both a mental and physical break. All these breaks refresh and rejuvenate, and are similar to a battery receiving a boost charge.

Looking After the Body and Mind

Where possible, the body should be exercised regularly. Having a hobby or sport is always a good idea. Two or three games of tennis played over a weekend is sufficient to get the heart rate up and to work up a sweat. Doctors often recommend that a person should sweat at least once a day as a result of physical activities, as this exercise does the body and mind good.

STEP 3 – COUNSELLING

One of the best ways to eliminate stress is to share anxieties, aspirations, and worries with a loved one or a trained counselor. The people closest to us are normally the most helpful. Together the causes of the stress can be identified. Once the causes are listed and identified, the best way to tackle them is head on. If money is owed, then a new budget must be compiled. If there is stress between individuals, this should be brought out into the open, and both sides of the story should be heard before some form of compromise is made.

Alcohol, pills, drugs, and stimulants do not relieve stress at all but only hide the symptoms temporarily, and they never treat the basic cause. Alcohol, pills, and any medication should be taken in moderation. A doctor should be consulted concerning the use of tranquilizers. Counselling may include counselling for alcohol or drug-related stress issues as well. Identifying and eliminating the basic cause of stress is the best method of dealing with it.

AUDIT OF AN OCCUPATIONAL STRESS MANAGEMENT PROGRAM

If an occupational stress management program is in place, it can best be audited during the documentation review session. A documented program should be in place and procedures established for dealing with employees suffering from stress (Figure 40.1).

ELEMENT/PROGRAM/PROCESS	POINTS	QUESTIONS THAT COULD BE ASKED	VERIFICATION	WHAT TO LOOK FOR
OOCUPATIONAL STRESS MANAGEMENT PROGRAM				
PROGRAM IN PLACE				
Program in place to manage stress.	5	Is there a stress program in place?	Copy of standard or program	
STRESSORS IDENTIFIED				
Stress factors been identified	5	How were these factors identified?	Identification method	
COUNCELLING				
Counselling available	5	Is counselling made available?		
PROGRAMS				
Other stress management programs	5	What other stress management programs are offered?		
TOTAL	20			

FIGURE 40.1   Audit Protocol for the Element – Occupational Stress Management Program.

41 Pollution Control Program

DESIGN OF A POLLUTION CONTROL PROGRAM

INTRODUCTION

Pollution is any substance introduced into the environment that is dirty or unclean or has a harmful or poisonous effect. It is the contamination of the environment caused by the dumping of toxic and poisonous waste and other contaminants into the air, water, or soil, thus rendering the environment unattractive, unhygienic, and spoilt.

TYPES OF POLLUTION

The main types of pollution are:

- Water pollution
- Air pollution
- Soil pollution
- Thermal pollution
- Radioactive pollution
- Noise pollution
- Light pollution

STATISTICS

It is estimated that in the United States, approximately 60% of air pollution is caused by motor vehicles. Seventeen percent of the total air pollution is as a result of industry and heating gasses, 14% as a result of power generating plant, and 9% as a result of incineration.

MAIN SOURCES OF POLLUTION

Some of the main sources of pollution are:

- Emissions from vehicles
- Combustion of fossil fuels
- Pollution from air conditioners
- Dust and dirt
- Household pollution
- Pollution from natural events

- Deforestation
- Pollution from industry
- End products of manufacturing, such as carbon monoxide and nitrogen oxide.

Air pollution affects the health of the people living in the environment and has more effect on people suffering from diseases such as asthma, chronic bronchitis, or emphysema.

PREVENTION

Pollution can be prevented, but at a cost. Most countries of the world have united in an effort to reduce pollution, and the move away from chlorofluorocarbons (CFCs) as aerosol can propellants is an example of this worldwide drive. It was generally believed that CFCs were responsible for damaging the ozone layer protecting the earth. Recycling of materials such as paper, steel, aluminum, and plastic is now part of day-to-day living in a number of countries. Recycling also conserves the dwindling natural resources of these substances. A move to solar energy sources is a great contributor to the reduction of pollution.

IMPLEMENTATION OF A POLLUTION CONTROL PROGRAM

A pollution control action plan consists of the following five steps:

Step 1 – Pollution survey
Step 2 – Identifying sources of pollution
Step 3 – Reducing and monitoring of the sources and assigning responsibility
Step 4 – Improvement of existing control methods
Step 5 – Training of employees and affected persons.

POLLUTION SURVEY

A thorough inspection should be carried out to determine what pollution problems exist concerning air, water, ground, landfill, and other types of pollution.

IDENTIFY SOURCES

Once the sources are identified, then the extent of the pollution problem should be measured and quantified by the necessary experts using the correct equipment and methods. Hazardous waste should receive special attention concerning its management and disposal and the training of employees working with this waste.

REDUCE AND MONITOR SOURCES

Once corrective steps to eliminate or reduce the sources of pollution are taken, responsible people should be appointed for ongoing monitoring and control of the pollution sources.

IMPROVE CONTROL MEASURES

An ongoing program should be set up to ensure that the control methods are constantly improved. The objective of the control measures is to protect the environment against any industrial related pollution.

TRAINING

The training of employees and affected parties should now take place. They should be trained in the methods used to prevent pollution and should also to be able to identify breakdowns in the pollution control systems.

AUDIT OF A POLLUTION CONTROL PROGRAM

The auditors need to consider the plant inputs in the form of materials and sources of energy and the final product produced. All form of pollution created during the processes should be controlled by the pollution control program. Has the organization identified all pollution sources and has an effort been made to reduce them? (Figure 41.1)

ELEMENT/PROGRAM/PROCESS	POINTS	QUESTIONS THAT COULD BE ASKED	VERIFICATION	WHAT TO LOOK FOR
POLLUTION CONTROL PROGRAM				
STUDY MADE TO DETERMINE POLLUTION PROBLEMS				
Air pollution	5	Has a study been conducted to determine if a pollution problem exists?	A copy of the report or the study. Copy of legal permits	Oil on the floor. Water pollution, air pollution, chemical discharges
Water pollution	5	Was the entire site covered or was it only a specific problem?		Environment clean?
Ground pollution	5	What specific problem was identified?		Dust, leaks, smells, odors, storm water and sewer drains
ACCUMILATION AREAS				
Areas compliant with standards	5	Is the area compliant?	Copy of standards	
MONITORING OF EXISTING PREVENTION MEASURES				
Responsibility for monitoring the pollution control measures at the location	5	What was the specific pollution problem identified?	Letters of appointment	Is there evidence of pollution control?
Existing methods adequate	5	What positive steps have been taken to deal with the problem?	Quotes	Does the pollution still persists?
Supervisors monitoring control measures	5	Is the situation monitored on an ongoing basis?	Reports	Employee awareness e.g.. paint in drains
Corrective actions taken	5			
Are employees aware of the pollution hazards on site?	5	What bodies or outside authorities do you liaise with in this regard? How are employees made aware of pollution hazards?	Reports	
DECONTAMINATION/DISPOSAL OF HAZARDOUS WASTE				
List of all hazardous waste being disposed of?	5	(What, how and who) hazardous chemicals are disposed of here?	A list of hazardous wastes	Old chemical, and oil tins, empty poison containers.
Treatment Storage Disposal Facility site comply with permit requirements	5	Is there such a site?	Contract with the removal firm. Letters from local authority/professional bodies	Thinners, old paint, asbestos waste, syringes, old transformer oil
Handlers of hazardous waste properly trained	5	How often is training given?	Procedures	Sharps containers
Adequate PPE provided and worn	5	Is training in PPE usage given?	Training certificates	
Manifests and clearance certificates received from waste removal contractors.	5	Have these been received?	Copies	
TOTAL	70			

FIGURE 41.1   Audit Protocol for the Element – Pollution Control Program.

Part 4

Design, Implementation, and Audit of Occupational Health and Safety Management System, Accident and Near Miss Incident Reporting and Investigation Elements and Processes

42 Recording System for Injuries, Illnesses, and Diseases

DESIGN OF A RECORDING SYSTEM FOR INJURIES, ILLNESSES, AND DISEASES

OBJECTIVE

The objective of this health and safety management system (SMS) element is to ensure that all occupational injuries and diseases are recorded and reported in terms of legislative and company requirements, and to maintain registers and records of such events.

The official recording of occupational injuries and diseases can be regarded as one of the most important aspects of the safety process, and it is also a legal requirement. When it comes to recording injuries, the severity of such injuries should never be the sole criteria, as any injury reflects the existence of SMS failures. Therefore, all occupational injuries and/or diseases, including those of a minor nature, should be recorded for future analysis. This will assist in determining trends and problem areas.

PROPERTY DAMAGE, NEAR-MISS INCIDENTS, AND DANGEROUS OCCURRENCES REGISTER

Property damage accidents, near-miss incidents, and dangerous occurrences are equally important when it comes to recording and reporting, and they should therefore also be recorded and treated with the same importance as occupational injuries and diseases. It is recommended that for these purposes two registers be kept:

- Injury registers for all injuries (excluding first-aid cases)
- Property damage, near-miss incidents, and dangerous occurrence register

IMPLEMENTATION OF A RECORDING SYSTEM FOR INJURIES, ILLNESSES, AND DISEASES

To implement this record keeping element, a standard should be set and written which could include the following:

RESPONSIBILITY AND ACCOUNTABILITY

Managers, supervisors, and contractors (Responsible persons) are responsible for the reporting of all reportable occupational injuries, illness or disease-related accidents, near-miss incidents, and other reportable events, including dangerous occurrences, to their superiors and other relevant authorities where applicable.

They are further responsible for the keeping of the official injury and disease register for these occurrences. A brief description of the event must be also be included in the register or record.

MEDICAL CENTER/FIRST AID STATION

The medical center or first aid station (where applicable) are responsible for keeping the official work-related injury and disease register for work-related reportable, lost-time injuries and diseases affecting company employees and contractors.

Responsible persons should obtain a copy of this information related to their area of responsibility on a monthly basis, for information purposes.

Where there is no medical center and another medical facility is used to treat the accident victims, the responsible persons should retain a record of all work-related injuries and illnesses, and maintain all official records or registers of occupational injuries, illnesses, or diseases and have these documents and records readily available for audit purposes.

The health and safety department are to:

- Ensure periodic internal audits of the injury/disease register
- Ensure periodic internal audits of the damage dangerous occurrence register
- Provide training workshops on what events employees must report, and how they should report them

EMPLOYEES AND CONTRACTORS

Injured employees and contractors shall immediately report the accident and subsequent injury or illness to their supervisor, and they are encouraged to report all other events that result in, or have potential to cause, harm to employees or damage to equipment, such as near-miss incidents.

AUDIT OF A RECORDING SYSTEM FOR INJURIES, ILLNESSES, AND DISEASES

During the audit, these two registers should be scrutinized to ensure they are being correctly kept and that the correct information is recorded. The legal requirements should be ascertained and the registers examined for compliance. Another question to be asked is whether the record keeping is in line with the requirements of workers' compensation insurance guidelines (Figure 42.1).

ELEMENT/PROGRAM/PROCESS	POINTS	QUESTIONS THAT COULD BE ASKED	VERIFICATION	WHAT TO LOOK FOR
RECORDING SYSTEM/INJURY/OCCUPATIONAL DISEASE/ILLNESS /OCCURRENCE				
OFFICIAL RECORD/REGISTER				
Reportable injuries/occupational diseases recorded on the official record as required by regulations	5	Is an injury/occupational disease register kept?	Look at the register or similar	
Compensation forms correctly filled in	5	What is the claim methodology? Has the proper claims methodology been followed?	Compensation forms	Is the legal system being followed?
First-aid treatments recorded in first aid locations	5	Where are these kept?	See an example	
REGISTER CORRECTLY FILLED IN				
Correct description of event given	5	Are correct descriptions of accidents given in the record/register (i.e. not only type and extend of injury but of the event that caused the injury)?	Read through a representative sample of injuries. Is the accident described? (Not only description of the injury)	Description of accident in record/register
AUTHORITIES INFORMED				
Reportable accidents reported to the relevant authorities in the prescribed manner and within the prescribed period	5	What reportable injuries/diseases have you had during the last 12 months?	Copies of the report or a list of reportables or are they marked in the register?	Reportable accidents are reported to authorities as above
DAMAGE, NEAR MISS INCIDENT, DANGEROUS OCCURRENCE REGISTER	5			
Reportable occurrences	5	What reportable events occurred during the last 12 months?	Copies of the report or a list of reportable events or are they marked in the register?	Reportable events are reported to authorities as above
Register kept	5	What is recorded in this register?	Check entries	Is this a good record of these events?
TOTAL	40			

FIGURE 42.1 Audit Protocol for the Element – Recording System for Injuries, Illnesses, and Diseases.

43 Accident and Near Miss Incident Reporting and Investigation Process

DESIGN OF AN ACCIDENT AND NEAR MISS INCIDENT REPORTING AND INVESTIGATION PROCESS

OBJECTIVE

The objective of this safety management system (SMS) element is to define the methodology for reporting and investigating injury-causing accidents and near miss incidents so that the immediate and root causes of the event are identified and recommendations to prevent a recurrence are proposed and implemented. A further objective is to ensure that the company carries out its obligations under the health and safety law.

DEFINITIONS

The organization must clearly define what events must be reported, and how. The following is an example of reportable event definitions:

Accident – An undesired event which causes harm (injury or ill health) to people, damage to property, or loss to the process (production or business interruption). This includes fires s there is a lost incurred.

Near Miss Incident – An undesired event which, under slightly different circumstances, could have caused harm (injury or ill health) to people, damage to property, or loss to the process. (There is no loss.)

Major Loss Event – All major loss events such as fatal accidents, major fires, explosions, or multiple injury scenarios should be classified as major loss events.

Injury – An injury is physical harm to a person's body as a result of an accidental contact with a source of energy.

First Aid Injury – A first aid injury is the treatment of minor scratches, cuts, burns, splinters, and other injuries where treatment is not normally required by a doctor, nurse, or other medical professional.

Medical Treatment Cases – An injury which requires treatment by a doctor or nurse or other medical professional. These injuries are more serious than those requiring simple first aid treatment.

Restricted Work Cases – Injuries which result in the injured person being assigned to another job, usually of a less demanding physical nature (light or restricted duty), until recovery allows return to normal activity, that is, the work they normally do. These are recorded as lost time injuries (LTIs).

Lost Time Injury (LTI) – An injury which results in the injured person being absent for one or more scheduled workdays, beyond the day of the accident.

Disabling Injury – A disabling injury is the same as a LTI.

Fatality – A fatality is a fatal injury as a result of a work related accident. (A fatality is regarded as a lost time (+1 day) injury for recording purposes.)

IMPLEMENTATION OF AN ACCIDENT AND NEAR MISS INCIDENT REPORTING AND INVESTIGATION PROCESS

REPORTING AND INVESTIGATION PROCESS

A standard should be written for this SMS element process, and responsibilities should be assigned. An example follows:

Responsibility and Accountability

Any employee involved in an accident, or who witnesses a near miss incident, or who suffers injury or illness, however trivial, shall:

- Notify their supervisor immediately (but do not delay getting treatment)
- Arrange to make the scene of the accident safe and ensure that site evidence is not destroyed unless unavoidable to prevent further injury or damage
- If injured, attend the medical center/hospital for treatment
- If an ambulance or emergency services have been summoned, the employee should not be moved if likely to cause further injury. (Moving an injured person could aggravate the injury.)
- When possible, co-operate with the investigation

The manager/supervisor/contractor (Responsible person) of the injured employee, upon being notified of the near miss incident or injury, shall (where applicable):

- Arrange medical attention for the injured person
- Visit the scene of the accident
- Arrange to make the scene of the accident safe and ensure that site evidence is not destroyed unless unavoidable to prevent further injury
- Nominate an Accident Investigator (NAI) to assist in the investigation
- Publish the near miss incident/accident initial report form for all injuries and high potential near miss incidents and send a copy to the health and safety department
- Should the injury result in a lost time injury (+1 day), or more serious injury, notify their one-up-manager and the health and safety department
- Commence the accident investigation process and head the investigation meeting
- Complete the front page of the investigation form within 24 hours and submit to the health and safety department
- When convenient, visit the injured employee at the medical center/hospital to ascertain their condition

- Finalize the investigation as soon as possible (maximum 72 hours) and implement the remedial measures immediately
- Circulate the investigation findings to all sections within the department and send a copy to the health and safety department for their information
- Ensure that both the immediate and root causes of the event are identified
- Follow up to ensure that the remedial measures have been implemented as soon as is practicable after the event
- Ensure that the investigation form is completed correctly and submitted to the next level of authority (one-up-manager) for signature
- The manager of that division will then sign off on the form and submit it to the health and safety department for signature and submission to management

Investigation Process

All high potential near miss incidents and injury or damage-causing accidents involving company employees, contractors, and visitors or others on site shall be investigated as follows:

High potential near misses and accidents causing injury shall be reported and thoroughly investigated using the near miss/accident investigation (NMAI) form.

The supervisor/manager or contractor (Responsible person) will nominate an accident investigator (NAI) for the particular event, and commence the investigation with them. The NAI should not always be the health and safety personnel. The NAI may be a special committee established for the purpose of investigating the event.

The NAI should be a company qualified investigator who has passed the company accident/near miss incident investigation training program.

The responsible person (or nominated NAI) will initiate and circulate the initial report form within the same shift. The front page of the investigation form is to be completed and a copy sent to health and safety within 24 hours by the responsible person or nominated investigator.

The health and safety department will record the event in the register and allocate a tracking number for follow-up purposes.

During normal working hours, the investigation shall be started as soon as possible after the occurrence and completed within 72 consecutive hours. If more time is required, the health and safety department should be notified. Outside of normal working hours, the investigation shall be initiated by the responsible person in whose area of responsibility the accident occurred, and a NAI shall be nominated.

The NAI shall record investigation findings on the investigation form, and both the immediate as well as the root causes of the event must be determined.

The investigation shall include recommendations for actions to prevent recurrence by listing:

- WHAT should be done to prevent a recurrence
- WHO is responsible for doing the work or taking action
- By WHEN the actions are to be completed

Only once these actions have been implemented should the NAI and responsible person and the health and safety representative (if applicable) sign the form.

The signed form must now be circulated to the one-up-manager (next level of supervision) for comments and signature. All high potential near misses and lost time injury investigations are to be circulated to the vice president concerned for comments and signature. Once signed by the executive, the form is returned to the health and safety department for filing and sign-off in the register.

The completed investigation report shall be issued to the health and safety department within 72 hours of the event. Advice and assistance in investigation of high potential near misses and serious injury cases can be obtained from the local health and safety coordinator.

AUDIT OF AN ACCIDENT AND NEAR MISS INCIDENT REPORTING AND INVESTIGATION PROCESS

A written process for the reporting and investigation of undesired events should be available for examination, as well as copies of completed initial report forms and investigation forms. The auditors should select three forms for scrutiny: one from the top of the pile of forms, one from the bottom, and one from the middle. A list of trained accident investigators must be presented as well as a training syllabus. The auditor should follow the three selected investigated accidents through the system to ascertain if they were reported, investigated, and closed off correctly. Several questions are to be answered: Is there an effective accident reporting and investigation process in place? Does it determine the root accident cause? Does it pose solutions that will fix the problem? (Figure 43.1)

ELEMENT/PROGRAM/PROCESS	POINTS	QUESTIONS THAT COULD BE ASKED	VERIFICATION	WHAT TO LOOK FOR
ACCIDENT AND NEAR MISS REPORTING AND INVESTIGATION PROCESS				
INJURY/ILLNESS REPORTING				
Reporting of injuries	5	How are injuries reported?		
Reporting and investigation form	5	What forms are used?	Copy of completed forms	
INTERNAL REPORTING OF NEAR MISS INCIDENTS, PROPERTY DAMAGE AND OTHER				
Property damage accidents recorded on an internal report form	5	Are all damage accidents investigated?	Accident investigation forms for accidental damage	
Near miss incidents reported and investigated	5	How many near miss incidents were reported?		
Details required on the form accurately and completely filled in	5	What is the cut-off figure for damage investigation?		
INVESTIGATIONS BY NOMINATED INVESTIGATOR				
Investigators been nominated	5	Who is the designated investigator?	Appointed in writing?	
Investigators trained in the techniques of investigation	5	How are they trained?	Copies of training certificates	
Health and safety representatives involved in investigations?	5	How are they involved?		
CAUSES IDENTIFIED				
Root causes identified and documented for every investigation	5	How are investigators trained to identify root causes?	Check representative sample of investigations	
Immediate causes identified	5		Follow an investigation through the system	
Root causes conform to the accepted format	5	Are these root causes?	Follow an investigation through the system	
ACTION TAKEN				
Positive recommendations for minimization or elimination of possible recurrence	5	See an example of positive remedial measures taken	Were recommendations made?	
Recommendations practical in terms of feasibility and cost consideration	5	Can we see an example?	Check whether all the actions are consistent with the basic causes	
FOLLOW-UP				
Recommended action taken within a reasonable time?	5	How long does it take to close off an investigation?	Check whether action was taken within reasonable time and followed up	
Follow-up carried out after the action has been taken to determine if the action was effective and practical	5		Action lists/Meeting minutes, form signed off/loop closed?	Was the problem solved?
TOTAL	**75**			

FIGURE 43.1 Audit Protocol for the Element – Accident and Near Miss Incident Reporting and Investigation Process.

44 Near Miss Incident Reporting and Tracking System

DESIGN OF A NEAR MISS INCIDENT REPORTING AND TRACKING SYSTEM

NEAR MISS INCIDENT

A near miss incident is an undesired event which, under slightly different circumstances, could have led to injury, property damage, or business interruption. Near miss incidents can also be defined as *close calls that have the potential for injury or property loss.*

RECOGNITION

Most organizations do not encourage employees to report near miss incidents. Since there has been no injury, little importance is placed on the seemingly trivial event. Most near miss incidents have some form of potential for injury and loss – no matter how trivial they may seem. Although there may not have been a serious outcome, near miss incidents could result in future accidents.

BENEFITS

The main benefit of a near miss recognition, reporting, investigation, and remedy system is that by recognizing near miss incidents and taking action to correct the underlying problems, an organization will not only reduce the number of near miss incidents but also, more importantly, reduce the number of actual accidents in the future. Reducing the number of near miss incidents will fix the problems before they can cause accidents.

PREDICTIVE TOOL

Many accidents are predicted by close calls. These are accidents that almost happened or possibly did happen, but simply didn't result in an injury this time around. In fact, all the stages of the accident were present, in the correct sequence, except for the exchange of energy segment that would have caused injury, damage, loss, or a combination thereof.

ACCIDENT RATIO

The accident ratio shows that for every serious or disabling injury an organization experiences, it could be experiencing some minor injuries, more property damage accidents, and plenty of near miss incidents.

Studies show the futility of investigating only the few serious injuries when there are hundreds of near miss incidents which, if investigated and their causes corrected, would have prevented the occurrence of the more serious injury-causing accidents.

IMPLEMENTATION OF A NEAR MISS INCIDENT REPORTING AND TRACKING SYSTEM

STANDARD

A standard should be written for this element of the safety management system (SMS). This standard should explain all aspects of the system, including how to report, what actions to take, how to risk rank the event, and other information.

TRAINING

Before implementing the system, a series of training sessions should be held with all employees, contractors, and interested and affected parties. The training should inform participants how to recognize a near miss incident, how to report it, and how to do the risk assessment.

REPORTING SYSTEMS

A system that allows for reporting of near miss incidents needs to be developed. This could involve reporting booklets, reporting stations, or electronic reporting methods. The reporting and recording form or method should be as simple as possible, portable, and always available. Bulky reporting sheets that cannot be carried by the employees will not work. A small pocket-size card or booklet is ideal and has proved to be very successful in a number of instances.

FORMAL REPORTING

A formal reporting system is where the observer fills in the report form and posts it in the near miss incident box or hands it in to the supervisor, who then enters it into the system. Many modern systems use cell phones to report near miss incidents. The formal system is the main reporting method.

INFORMAL REPORTING

Informal reporting is when near miss incidents are reported verbally without filling in the form or online report. This could be an employee who tells his supervisor about a safety deviation. It could involve an employee telling another employee about a certain situation. Observations discussed at safety meetings and tailgate safety sessions would fall into the informal category.

All safety meetings and pre-task talks should begin with an incident recall session as part of the informal reporting process. The discussions from incident and accident recall sessions are informal reports and form an invaluable part of the near miss incident reporting system.

RISK RANKING

Depending on the sophistication of the workforce, a risk matrix should be incorporated into the reporting form or booklet, so that once trained, employees can do a risk ranking of the near miss incident as it is reported.

Risk ranking of the event reported may deter reporters from reporting and participating in the system if the procedure is too complex and they do not understand it fully. The best advice is to keep it very simple. During the training session, the attendees should go through the motions of actually ranking near miss incident examples so that they are familiar with the process. They should be taught how to use the simple risk matrix. There should be no concern if different attendees give different rankings for the same hazard. People see things differently and have different perceptions of risk.

INVESTIGATION

The risk ranking will indicate whether or not the event warrants a full investigation, as would an injury-producing accident. This aspect of the system is crucial, as all near miss incidents with high loss potential and high probability of recurrence are the events that may have ended up as loss-producing accidents, had it not been for slightly difference circumstances. This means that the safety efforts can now be leveled at those near miss events that had a high likelihood of being serious accidents. Events reported that have lower risk rankings will be items that the reporter rectified themselves, or near miss incidents that warrant attention but not necessarily a full blown investigation.

COLLECTION

A central collection area should be established where all reports are collected. This is normally an administrative function. In some organizations, a safety coordinator is allocated the responsibility of administrating the collection, analysis, and submission of near miss incident summaries. Both formal and informal incident reports should be collected and tabulated on a simple spreadsheet. Each report should be allocated a tracking number. This database should be tabled at health and safety committee meetings for discussion.

The spreadsheet should list the report number, the area concerned, a description of the situation, the risk ranking of the event, and corrective action required. If action has already been taken, this should also be listed. Pending actions should be time-based.

REMEDIAL ACTION

Immediate action should be taken on all high potential near miss incidents. In many instances, these should be investigated with the same vigor as injury-producing accidents. Some remedial action may be long term. Employees need to be informed of the progress of each near miss incident reported as well as the progress of the implementation of remedial actions.

FOLLOW UP

A follow up is done after the remedial measures have been implemented. This is essential before the report is closed. This may entail an inspection to ensure that the actions have been taken and the risk has been mitigated. Generally, a monthly list of all the items reported is circulated to all via the intranet, or it is posted on the notice boards or featured in the newsletter. Employees want to see what they have reported and want to see some action being taken on their report. In most instances, the reports will be of high risk acts or high risk conditions and safe work observations, and few may be true near miss incidents. What is important is the feedback and action instigated by management to rectify the hazard.

CLOSE OUT

Once the actions are completed, the near miss report should be closed out. This means that the necessary steps have been taken to prevent a recurrence of a near miss incident.

AMNESTY

If an organization wants this system to work and contribute to the reduction of risk and consequent losses to the organization, a decision to declare amnesty must be made. The reporting mechanism should allow for anonymity of reporting, but also allow for the reporter to volunteer their name if they feel comfortable to do so, such as in the case of reporting safe work or deeds. Blame-fixing and punitive actions based on reports where the employee was obviously at fault must be avoided. The employee grapevine works well, and the first time there is punishment leveled at an employee who reports a high risk act of another employee, or themselves, the reporting will dry up.

AUDIT OF A NEAR MISS INCIDENT REPORTING AND TRACKING SYSTEM

It must be established if employees and others are aware of what a near miss incident is, how to report it, and how to risk rank it using a simple risk matrix. More near miss incidents should be reported than injuries. Are employees kept informed of the progress of their report, and are high potential events investigated thoroughly?

The system must be consistent, and there must be follow up action on reports. This element is audited in parallel with injury and property damage investigation.

During the employee interview session, the employee's knowledge of and participation in the near miss incident reporting system can be tested. There should be more near miss incident reports than injury reports reported during the audit period (Figure 44.1).

ELEMENT/PROGRAM/PROCESS	POINTS	QUESTIONS THAT COULD BE ASKED	VERIFICATION	WHAT TO LOOK FOR
NEAR MISS INCIDENT REPORTING AND TRACKING SYSTEM				
Near miss incident report form/method	5	How are near miss incidents reported? How many during the last 12 months?	Does the number of near miss incidents give an accident ratio?	
Risk matrix incorporated	5	How are they risk ranked?	Examples of ranked reports	
Reporting methods	5	What other reporting avenues are there?	Examples	
No name reporting option	5	Must reporters disclose their names?	Examples	
RECORDS				
Central records of reports	5	Centralized reports	Example of recording system	
Feedback system	5	Progress report to employees	Is this done?	
CLOSED OUT				
Action taken	5	Is positive action taken on reports?	Example-follow through the system.	
Feedback given	5	Is feedback given to employees?	Proof of this	
TRAINING/AWARENESS				
Employee training	5	What awareness training is given to employees?	Copy of attendance registers?	
Incident recall sessions held	5	Are near miss incidents reported via incident recall sessions?	Examples of this	
TOTAL	**50**			

FIGURE 44.1   Audit Protocol for the Element – Near Miss Incident Reporting and Tracking System.

45 Injury, Damage, and Loss Statistics Recording System

DESIGN OF AN INJURY, DAMAGE, AND LOSS STATISTICS RECORDING SYSTEM

Loss statistics are a vital part of any health and safety management system (SMS). Compiling of injury and loss statistics and the accompanying costs is a reactive activity, but it nevertheless serves its purpose in identifying past history and helping to predict future experience. Injury statistics give us a picture of the losses experienced in relation to the exposure to risk measured in work hours.

Statistics do not necessarily indicate what level of control is present, nor where the SMS end results are headed, but rather show consequences of system failures. Statistics can be used to compare with past experience, so that any improvement or worsening of the injury trends can be highlighted.

Statistics can be analyzed to indicate what energy exchange (contact) types are most prominent. The numbers and types of unsafe acts being committed and unsafe conditions identified can also be tabled and presented in statistical form.

Sophisticated statistics could also analyzed during which work-hour period the most lost time injuries, minor injuries, and near miss incidents take place. They can pinpoint which groups or departments are experiencing injuries. Statistics are helpful in determining certain trends.

IMPLEMENTATION OF AN INJURY, DAMAGE, AND LOSS STATISTICS RECORDING SYSTEM

INJURY STATISTICS

There are numerous ways to record, measure, and present injury statistics, and the following are a few of the most widely used:

Lost Time Injury A *lost time injury* (LTI) is defined as an injury which results in the injured person being absent for one (1) or more scheduled workdays beyond the day (shift) of the accident. This includes industrial diseases and illnesses.

Disabling Injury A *disabling injury* is defined as the same as a LTI.

LOST TIME INJURY FREQUENCY RATE

The *lost time injury frequency rate* (LTIFR) records the number of lost time injuries experienced per one million work hours. One million work hours are used as this equates to approximately 500 employees working for one year. The total injury frequency rate is calculated on the same basis, except all injuries are used for the calculation.

LOST TIME INJURY INCIDENCE RATE

The *lost time injury incidence rate* (LTIIR) is the number of disabling injuries experienced per 200,000 workhours. The LTIIR equates to 100 workers working for approximately 1 year, giving an exposure of 200,000 work hours. This also represents the percentage (%) of workers injured during the period.

LOST TIME INJURY SEVERITY RATE

The *lost time injury severity rate* (LTISR) is a term for measuring the actual number of days, or shifts, lost as a result of injury per million workhours worked, or per 500 workers working for a year.

Although the severity of an injury is fortuitous, and therefore not an accurate or meaningful measurement of safety performance, it is nevertheless essential for costing actual costs.

FATALITY RATE

The *fatality rate* is the number of fatal injuries as a result of accidents per 1,000 workers per annum.

MILLION WORKHOUR PERIODS

The periods between LTIs can also be statistically calculated in workhour exposures as "workhours worked without a LTI." A most common objective is to work at least 1,000,000 work hours without a LTI.

BODY PARTS INJURED

The parts of the body being injured as a result of an accidents should also be compiled and tabulated. This could include the number of head injuries, chest injuries, arm injuries, finger injuries, and so on, and will provide valuable information to management.

An analysis of the body parts that are being injured more frequently will then indicate a problem area and help direct the safety effort. A pictorial representation allows for immediate recognition and identification of the problem areas. This information can be circulated, posted, or displayed on a safety promotion board in the plant.

ACCIDENT RATIO

The accident ratio is a triangular model depicting the ratio between the LTIs, minor injuries, property damage accidents, and near miss incidents (with no visible sign of loss) and unsafe acts and conditions. The philosophy behind the accident ratio is that had circumstances been slightly different, each one of the numerous near misses *could have* resulted in either a property damage or an injury-causing accident.

This ratio is one of the most important statistics in any SMS. It indicates whether or not most injuries are being reported. The ratio also indicates the effectiveness of the near miss incident reporting system, as the number of near misses reported should be higher than the injury and damage accidents.

The reduction of the base of this triangle would be the objective of the SMS. If the unsafe conditions/behaviors and near miss incidents are reported, investigated, and remedied, the loss-producing accidents should be reduced significantly.

WHERE STATISTICS SHOULD BE PRESENTED

Statistics should be presented and circulated at the executive health and safety committee meetings and other health and safety meetings. These statistics can then be summarized at the end of the quarter and tabled at the board of directors' meeting.

A brief discussion and explanation should follow the presentation of the statistics, and actions needed should be discussed. The safety newsletter could contain the main statistics, such as the number of LTIs per month and the body part most often injured.

Health and safety coordinators should provide graphs for departments in their area of responsibility and should be responsible for reporting of the following information:

- Disabling injury (LTIIR) incidence rate
- Disabling injury severity (LTISR) rate
- Accident ratio
- Property damages
- Near miss incident reports and follow-up actions

NON-INJURY STATISTICS

The objective of this record is to keep up-to-date statistics of non-injury accidental losses for future analysis and to ensure that this management information is available.

Most organizations keep statistics of injuries and diseases caused by accidental events but tend to ignore the losses incurred by non-injury accidents. For every serious injury incurred, there are many accidents that result in property damage or business interruption. These losses should be tracked and a record of them kept in the form of non-injury statistics.

OTHER ACCIDENTAL LOSSES

Statistics should be kept of all non-injury accidental losses. These can include:

- Property damage
- Business interruption events
- Damage to machinery, tools, equipment, vehicles, structures, buildings, or floors
- Fires
- Environmental incidents
- Spoilage
- Losses to raw materials or damage to finished products

Figures should be calculated on a monthly and annual accumulative basis. Trends can be plotted graphically and tabled at committee meetings for discussion. The costs of the damage or loss should be calculated and kept as a separate statistic, and plotted on a monthly and annual progressive basis. These trends should be reviewed monthly to monitor improvements or increasing trends. Every property damage accident should be analyzed in terms of cost of the damage, interruption, or fire, and this cost should be produced monthly and on an annual progressive basis.

AUDIT OF AN INJURY, DAMAGE, AND LOSS STATISTICS RECORDING SYSTEM

Injury statistics should be tabulated for all injuries as well as damage and other losses caused by accidents. The auditors should confirm that these figures are tracked on a progressive basis and are presented to the health and safety committees for review and discussion. Graphical displays should be used where possible, and this information should be shared with all employees (Figure 45.1).

ELEMENT/PROGRAM/PROCESS	POINTS	QUESTIONS THAT COULD BE ASKED	VERIFICATION	WHAT TO LOOK FOR
INJURY/DAMAGE AND LOSS STATISTICS RECORDING SYSTEM				
PROGRESSIVE STATISTICAL DATA				
Injury, occupational disease, near miss incidents statistics kept for the month and past 12 months.	5	What is the DIIR of this division? Is the severity rate recorded? Are near miss incidents recorded? Property damage?	Injury/occupational disease statistics: monthly, 12 monthly NDI and DI statistics. Breakdown of monthly and 12-monthly actual workhours, injury, diseases and incidence rates. Near miss incidents, property damage	
Property Damage/Fires/Other	5	What property damage events were reported?	Check the statistics and costing	
GRAPHIC DISPLAY				Check safety boards. Are current statistics displayed?
Are statistics displayed in graphic form?	5	Are the statistics displayed on the notice boards? At how many places? How are they made know to workforce?	Graph of monthly and 12 monthly, DIIR	
ANALYSIS OF STATISTICS				
Injuries and disease statistics analyzed by section or department and used to identify certain trends	5	What part of body was injured most last year?	Matrix of department and body part	
Injury and disease statistics analyzed by part of body, department, process, etc.	5	What section/division or team was responsible for most of the injuries?		
STATISTICS PUBLISHED AND CIRCULATED				
All statistics circulated to management and published for information to the workforce	5	How are these statistics circulated to top management?	See a copy of the report or check to see if it is displayed or circulated on a circulation list	
Statistics discussed at health and safety committee meetings	5	Are they discussed at healthand safety committee meetings?	Check minutes of the meeting for discussion in minutes. Copy of latest statistics. Are the employeesand managers aware of these figures?	
Statistics updated.	5	Are these statistics updated regularly?		
TOTAL	40			

FIGURE 45.1 Audit Protocol for the Element – Injury, Damage, Loss Statistics, Recording System.

46 Accident and Near Miss Incident Recall Program

DESIGN OF AN ACCIDENT AND NEAR MISS INCIDENT RECALL PROGRAM

The objective of an accident and near miss incident recall program is to implement near miss incident and accident recall, which is a method of recalling unreported events (near miss incidents) that did not result in any visible injury, damage, or production loss, but which may have done if circumstances had been different, so as to learn from these events. It can also be uses to review and discuss past accidents.

A further goal is to systematically gather information and learn from near miss incidents and accidents that may not have been reported, so that the information can be shared and future events prevented.

DEFINITION OF AN ACCIDENT

An accident is an undesired event which results in harm to people and/or property damage and/or process interruption.

DEFINITION OF A NEAR MISS INCIDENT (CLOSE CALL)

A near miss incident is an undesired event which, under slightly different circumstances, may have caused harm to people and/or property damage and/or process loss.

The difference between an accident and a near miss incident is purely a matter of chance, as the outcome of an undesired event cannot be determined and is very difficult to predict.

ACCIDENT AND NEAR MISS INCIDENT RECALL

Accident recall is a technique of recalling past injury or damage-causing accidents. It is a way of reminding employees by bringing about an awareness of the accident causes, to ensure that steps are in place so that a recurrence does not happen.

Near miss incident recall is a method of recalling unreported near miss incidents (near misses) that did *not* result in any visible injury, damage, or production loss, but which may have done if circumstances had been different.

Recalling the past to improve the future is of vital importance in a safety management system, and the reason that most systems sometimes fail is that the underlying near miss incidents (near misses) are never reported, investigated, and eradicated.

Numerous health and safety management systems (SMS) are injury prevention programs and only concentrate on serious and minor injuries. The accident ratio studies conducted by Frank E. Bird Jr. in 1966 and published in *Practical Loss Control Leadership* have a clear message: For every 641 undesired occurrences, 1 will result in serious injury, 10 will result in minor injury, 30 will end up causing property and equipment damage, and some 600 (near miss incidents) will have no visible outcome or consequence. Proactive safety focuses on the near miss incidents which are accident precursors (p.21).

Near miss incident and accident recall are ideal methods for recalling the various accidents and near miss incidents that have occurred, so as to remind employees of what happened and also to highlight near miss incidents that were not reported.

IMPLEMENTATION OF AN ACCIDENT AND NEAR MISS INCIDENT RECALL PROGRAM

Near miss incident/accident recall sessions can be held during:

- Discussion of near miss incidents and accident reports (as they occur)
- Health and safety committee meetings
- Five-minute safety talks
- Formal near miss incident and accident recall sessions
- Safety training courses and workshops

An SMS standard for this element is as follows:

PROCEDURE

Accidents and near miss incidents can be recalled on the initial accident report that is circulated immediately after each event. Near miss incident recall should also be a fixed item on the agenda of the health and safety committees, and all attendees should be encouraged to recall unreported events that could have resulted in losses.

Five-minute safety talks should be used to disseminate information about accidents and near miss incidents experienced in other departments. Formal accident and near miss incident recall sessions should be planned and held on a regular basis, as well as during all safety training courses and workshops.

FORMAL RECALL

Formal recall can be tabled as an agenda item at health and safety committee meetings. During training sessions, a five-minute recall session should be held. The students attending the training session should be encouraged to recall incidents. These events recalled could be home, road, or workplace incidents.

INFORMAL RECALL

Informal recall sessions can be held on a person-to-person basis during the normal workday. The near miss reporting form could also be available and employees could then fill in the form and report a near miss incident. This report could remain anonymous, and the person reporting the near miss incident need not name the people involved.

RESPONSIBILITY AND ACCOUNTABILITY

Managers/supervisors/contractors (Responsible persons) should be responsible for fully supporting the formulation, administration, implementation, and performance of this standard. The health and safety department is responsible for administration and support of this standard. They should coordinate revisions and be responsible for record keeping of documentation and distribution of safety reports and statistics concerning near miss incident and accident recall.

AUDIT OF AN ACCIDENT AND NEAR MISS INCIDENT RECALL PROGRAM

The auditors should examine the incident recall system to establish if employees are recalling events that slipped past the normal reporting systems. Is this an agenda item for health and safety committees? Do the five-minute toolbox talks encourage the recalling of past happenings such as similar accidents or near miss incidents that happened? Is recall encouraged at training sessions? Do employees participate and share their knowledge with others? Proof of incidents recalled should be examined to confirm that the incident recall system is functioning. (Figure 46.1).

ELEMENT/PROGRAM/PROCESS	POINTS	QUESTIONS THAT COULD BE ASKED	VERIFICATION	WHAT TO LOOK FOR
ACCIDENT AND NEAR MISS INCIDENT RECALL				
ACCIDENT RECALL				
Is accident recall carried out by supervisors?	5	Accident recall sessions held?	List of sessions or people attending, highlighting accident reviewed and accident recall used.	Used in conjunction with safety talks by foreman/supervisor
Are safety talks used to stimulate discussion?	5	How many were held last year?		Review of previous accidents
Item on safety committee agenda	5	Is incident recall a fixed item on the committee agenda?		
Are previous accidents/near misses reviewed?	5	What events were recalled? How is this done?	Call for an example	Case study being used
Previous accident record used?	5	Who leads these sessions?	List of topics and dates	Are employees participating in incident recall?
Case studies used	5	Is a case study book used?	Case study book or similar	
NEAR MISS INCIDENT RECALL				
Incident recall done	5	Are previous near misses reviewed? How?	Review minute of committee or 5-minute talks	Are near miss incidents being recalled?
Formal recall system in place	5	What is the formal system?	Examples	
Informal system used	5	What informal methods are used?	Examples	
TOTAL	45			

FIGURE 46.1 Audit Protocol for the Element – Accident and Near Miss Incident Recall Program.

47 Risk Financing and Cost of Risk

DESIGN OF A SYSTEM TO REPORT THE COST OF RISK AND RISK FINANCING

The total cost of risk to a company includes costs of losses such as death and injuries caused by accidents, equipment damage, vehicle damage, product losses, and the cost of insuring residual risks and penalty costs.

The cost of risk can be determined through an analysis of the cost of all accidental losses. An analysis of insurance claims and accident costing will allow for the measurement of the effectiveness (or ineffectiveness) of the health and safety management system (SMS). Possible rebates or reduction in insurance premiums and elimination of high risk penalties could justify the costs of risk mitigation and of maintaining an SMS.

IMPLEMENTATION OF A SYSTEM TO REPORT THE COST OF RISK AND RISK FINANCING

The details of the annual assessment payable to the local workers' compensation insurer should be available. A graph could be tabulated comparing the claims against the assessment paid to the insurance carrier. This should be updated and presented to management on a monthly basis.

The worker's compensation claim details should also be circulated to management, the executive, and health and safety committees for their information.

Details of other insurance costs should be compiled in graphic format, showing the annual premium paid and the progressive claims made. These claims will include motor vehicle losses, fire, theft, and property damage accidents.

An appointed person should produce a table with all the loss costs for the month and progressive for the year to date. This should include all costs related to unintended loss events that occurred on the premises, for example, theft, fires, vehicle accidents, production losses as a result of damage accidents, medical claims, liability claims, and fines for nonconformances.

The following could be tabulated and presented on a monthly basis:

- Insurance costs
- Cost of occupational injuries and diseases
- Cost of accidental property damage
- Cost of accidental business interruption
- Vehicle damage costs
- Cost of fire damage
- Other unintentional losses

AUDIT OF A SYSTEM TO REPORT THE COST
OF RISK AND RISK FINANCING

The organization should keep a record of the expenses incurred as a result of accidental injury, disease, property damage, and other unintended losses, which should be presented to the auditors. All insurance cost and claims should be included. These should be tabulated for the current month and progressively for a 12-month period to indicate trends. This information should be made available, circulated, and discussed at health and safety committee meetings. The auditors should confirm this by reviewing the applicable documentation during the audit (Figure 47.1).

ELEMENT/PROGRAM/PROCESS	POINTS	QUESTIONS THAT COULD BE ASKED	VERIFICATION	WHAT TO LOOK FOR
RISK FINANCING AND COST OF RISK :				
RISK FINANCING: INSURANCE COSTS				
Details of worker's compensation assessments and annual returns available	5	How much was the compensation fund contributions last year?	Graph of approx. payment	Insurance (current year)
Details of the claims made on the compensation fund	5	What was claimed as a result of work injuries?	Graph showing claims against payments	Assessment paid/payable Claims on insurance. Expected rebate if applicable
Details of the estimated rebate/discount available	5	Are the figures circulated to all managers and committees, and employees? How?	Document listing claims against insurance	Graph circulated to managers
Compensation details circulated to management and health and safety committee in graph form (i.e. assessment vs. claims)?	5	How is this done?	Copies of verification documentation	Other insurance claims compared to premiums
Details of other insurances available (i.e. motor, fire, theft, etc., premiums)	5	Is the accident experience schedule available?	List of claims or costing	
Injury/disease claims	5	Is the accident experience schedule available from the compensation insurer?	List of claims	Is this information being circulated to management and committees?
COST OF RISK				
Cost of damage, fire, vehicle accidents	5	What was the cost of other accidents for last 12 months, e.g. vehicles, fires, contractors? Are these costs tabulated and presented monthly?	Documented costs	
TOTAL	**35**			

FIGURE 47.1 Audit Protocol for the Element – Risk Financing and Cost of Risk.

Part 5

Design, Implementation, and Audit of Occupational Health and Safety Management System, Emergency Preparedness and Fire Prevention and Protection Elements

48 Fire Risk Assessment

DESIGN OF A FIRE RISK ASSESSMENT SURVEY

It is essential that the fire risks of an organization are correctly identified and assessed to ensure that the appropriate fire detection, protection, and extinguishing equipment is provided at the appropriate locations. This includes fixed fire systems and passive protection as well as firefighting and rescue equipment. A fire risk assessment survey should be conducted by qualified and experienced inspectors to determine the total fire risk and what fire prevention and protection equipment and systems are required.

IMPLEMENTATION OF A FIRE RISK ASSESSMENT SURVEY

A fire risk assessment consists of five basic steps:

Step 1 – Identify any fire hazards
Step 2 – Evaluate the hazards
Step 3 – Eliminate the hazards, or reduce the risk to as low a level as reasonably practicable
Step 4 – Decide what physical fire precautions and management arrangements are necessary to ensure the safety of people in the building if a fire does start
Step 5 – Implement the control measures and monitor

The fire risk assessment survey should at least cover the following points:

- Description of the fire hazard
- Hazard priority ranking (High, Medium, Low)
- Details of the precautionary measures taken
- The procedure to be followed in case of a fire occurring
- The health, safety, and environmental risks associated with fires

EMERGENCY COORDINATOR

The appointed fire or emergency coordinator should ensure that the total fire risk readiness is appropriate to the risk and in line with the organization's insurance risk tolerance. The appointee should advise management on the appropriate cost effective level of fire readiness and should ensure that the fire risks are identified and assessed. The local fire services department could be invited to visit the premises and be requested to issue a report stating that all its requirements have been met with regard to fire prevention and protection procedures, equipment, and escape routes.

The monthly inspection checklist completed by health and safety representatives should include checking that fire equipment is available and in a good state of repair.

AUDIT OF A FIRE RISK ASSESSMENT SURVEY

Fire prevention and protection equipment and installations should be inspected during the audit inspection. Random sampling techniques should be used. Adequacy and accessibility of equipment should be noted during the inspection. The fire risk assessment requirements should have been implemented, and this should be confirmed during the inspection (Figure 48.1).

ELEMENT/PROGRAM/PROCESS	POINTS	QUESTIONS THAT COULD BE ASKED	VERIFICATION	WHAT TO LOOK FOR
FIRE RISK ASSESSMENT				
RISK ASSESSMENT SURVEY				
Risk assessment carried out	5	Has a fire risk assessment been done? Who did this assessment?	Copy of risk assessment	
Fire hazards identified	5	Were fire hazards identified?	Copy of assessment	
Fire hazards evaluated	5	Were the risks evaluated and prioritized?	Evaluation method used	
Elimination efforts	5	What was done to eliminate the risks?	Documented risk reduction actions	Visual.
Precautions implemented	5	What precautions have been implemented?	List of fire prevention/protection actions.	Visual.
Control measures in place	5	What other controls are in place?	List	
FIRE/EMERGENCY COORDINATOR				
Emergency coordinator appointed	5	Has a coordinator been appointed?	Copy of appointment	
Duties and functions explained	5	Are the duties and functions documented?	Copy of job description	
TOTAL	40			

FIGURE 48.1 Audit Protocol for the Element – Fire Risk Assessment.

49 Fire Prevention and Protection Equipment

DESIGN FOR THE PROVISION OF FIRE PREVENTION AND PROTECTION EQUIPMENT

Being a specialized and critical area, specialist consultation should be considered when designing a system of fire prevention and protection and the ancillary installations and equipment required. World class standards and codes are available from the National Fire Protection Association (NFPA), which can be followed to ensure requirements are adequate and that the correct equipment is installed and maintained.

NATIONAL FIRE PROTECTION ASSOCIATION (NFPA)

One of the best standards available for fire prevention and protection standards and information are the NFPA standards, the NFPA 101®: *Life Safety Code®*, and the NFPA 1, *Fire Code.*

DOCUMENT SCOPE OF NFPA 101®

The NFPA 101®, *Life Safety Code®* is the most widely used source for strategies to protect people based on building construction, protection, and occupancy features that minimize the effects of fire and related hazards. Unique in the field, it is the only document that covers life safety in both new and existing structures.

NFPA 1, FIRE CODE

NFPA 1 advances fire and life safety for the public and first responders as well as property protection by providing a comprehensive, integrated approach to fire code regulation and hazard management. It addresses all the bases with extracts from and references to more than 130 NFPA® codes and standards including such industry benchmarks as NFPA 101®, NFPA 54, NFPA 58, NFPA 30, NFPA 13, NFPA 25, and NFPA 72®.

(Reproduced with permission of NFPA from NFPA website. Copyright© 2017, National Fire Protection Association. For a full copy of NFPA 1 or NFPA 101®, please go to www.nfpa.org)

Any organization wishing to maintain a best-in-practice safety management system should ensure that the requirements and recommendations of this code are incorporated into the health and safety management system's (SMS) standards and practices.

PROVISION OF FIRE PREVENTION AND PROTECTION EQUIPMENT

It is essential that the fire risks of the organization are correctly identified and assessed to ensure that the appropriate fire detection, protection, and extinguishing equipment is provided at the appropriate locations, according to NFPA guidelines and codes. Local fire codes should also be incorporated. This includes fixed fire systems and passive protection, as well as firefighting and rescue equipment.

The provided equipment should be strategically placed, well signposted, and easily accessible at all times. Personnel should be trained in the use of fire prevention and firefighting equipment and must be shown how to operate fire alarms when necessary. Specialized fire systems should be planned, installed, and maintained by specialists according to the NFPA recommended codes.

AUDIT OF FIRE PREVENTION AND PROTECTION EQUIPMENT

The initial fire risk assessment survey should be examined. The audit inspection should include inspecting fire prevention and protection equipment and installations. These should show evidence of maintenance and should be clearly marked and demarcated for accessibility. Records of maintenance and testing should be reviewed during the document review session (Figure 49.1).

ELEMENT/PROGRAM/PROCESS	POINTS	QUESTIONS THAT COULD BE ASKED	VERIFICATION	WHAT TO LOOK FOR
FIRE PREVENTION AND PROTECTION EQUIPMENT				
RISK ASSESSMENT				
Risk assessment done	5	Has a fire risk assessment been done to determine what equipment and systems are needed?		
NFPA STANDARD OR SIMILAR				
NFPA code or similar followed	5	Is the NFPA Code or similar followed?	Is the code similar to NFPA?	
PROVISION OF EQUIPMENT				
Equipment provided	5	Has equipment and systems been provided according to the code?		Fire protection installations
MAINTENANCE OF EQUIPMENT				
Equipment and installations maintained	5	Are these systems on planned maintenance?	Copy of maintenance schedule	
EQUIPMENT ACCESSABLE				
Equipment accessible where necessary	5	What equipment needs to be accessible?		Visual
TOTAL	25			

FIGURE 49.1 Audit Protocol for the Element – Fire Prevention and Protection Equipment.

50 Alarm Systems

DESIGN OF ALARM SYSTEMS

Alarms are audible or visual messages that indicate certain problems or situations. The objective of this health and safety management system (SMS) element is to ensure that alarm systems are adequate, in working condition, and can be effectively activated in an emergency situation, and that all persons on site are familiar with the alarms.

The effective communication of imminent danger to all parties on site during emergency situations will facilitate appropriate response and ensure that exposure to danger is limited to those dealing with the emergency situation.

Appropriate alarms with back-up systems in case of a power failure should be installed in locations where there is a need to warn employees of certain situations. There are a number of alarms that could be in operation in a workplace. The following are some examples:

- A carbon monoxide detector, which uses electrochemical sensing technology, sounds an alarm if carbon monoxide is detected. Many carbon monoxide alarms are combined with smoke alarms in one device.
- A deterrence alarm is a high-pitched sound which can be used to warn intruders to keep away.
- Fire and emergency evacuation alarms give early warning of developing fires or other emergencies to enable timeous evacuation.
- Flood alarms sense the presence of water and can provide early warning of leaks in pipework or boilers.
- A proximity alarm is triggered by a proximity sensor, which is a sensor able to detect the presence of nearby objects without any physical contact. A proximity sensor often emits an electromagnetic field or a beam of electromagnetic radiation (e.g., infrared) and looks for changes in the field or return signal.
- Intruder alarms detect attempted intrusion or unauthorized entry into a building, room, site, or secure installation and trigger a response. Some burglar alarms are simple auditory warnings, while others are linked to surveillance cameras, light systems, and remote monitoring by security companies.
- Heat alarms have fixed-temperature elements and respond to the temperature of the fire gases in the immediate vicinity of the alarm.
- Multi-sensor alarms detect more than one fire phenomena, for example, optical and heat detection.
- Smoke alarms can be optical in that they detect the scattering or absorption of light within the detector chamber, or ionization; this makes them more

sensitive to smoke containing small particles such as rapidly burning flaming fires, but they are less sensitive to steam.
- Elevator emergency alarms sound an alarm in the event of a passenger lift breakdown to alert personnel.
- Stench alarms are used to warn underground miners to evacuate the mine. A foul-smelling gas is introduced into the mine ventilation system which ventilates all underground areas, warning miners that they must evacuate.
- Back-up warning alarms warn when heavy vehicles are reversing.

IMPLEMENTATION OF ALARM SYSTEMS

ALARM SURVEY

An alarm survey will help to determine what alarms are required and where they should be installed. New alarms may be required with the modification of processes or implementation of new methods. Each alarm must be unique, and if one alarm is used for different signals, employees must understand the different meanings. The meaning of different alarms and the action to be taken should form part of the induction and annual safety refresher training.

BACKUP

Where practicable, alarms should have a back-up in case of a failure of the main source of power. The person responsible for fire coordination should ensure that all the fire and evacuation alarm activating points are indicated on a layout plan of the premises.

TESTING OF ALARMS

Arrangements should be made to test the fixed fire and evacuation alarm, and other critical alarms, at least once every three months. A record of these tests should be kept and made available for inspection. Fixed alarm systems should be included on planned maintenance. Any isolation of any alarm system due to maintenance or malfunction should be backed up by a manual alarm system, and the employees in the area should be informed.

AUDIT OF ALARM SYSTEMS

Alarms are critical to warn employees of certain hazards and must be clear, be audible, and have a back-up in case of a power source failure. All employees must be familiar with the alarms and their meaning. Drills should be activated by the alarm so that all become familiar with the routine. The alarm system should not create confusion by having the same alarm for different emergencies. The auditors could ask an employee the meaning of the different alarms during employee interviews (Figure 50.1).

ELEMENT / PROGRAM / PROCESS	POINTS	QUESTIONS THAT COULD BE ASKED	VERIFICATION	WHAT TO LOOK FOR
ALARM SYSTEMS				
INDEPENDENT ALARM				
Alarms unique	5	What major alarms are used here?	Study of alarm systems	Review documents of testing scheduled, drill critiques
Heard or seen in all areas	5	Can the alarm requiring evacuation of a facility can be heard everywhere?		
Alarms tested	5	What actions should be taken by persons when an alarm sounds?	Plan of site with alarm stations indicated	
BACK-UP ALARM				
Back-up alarm independent of electricity supply	5	The fire alarm should always have a back-up alarm in case of electrical failure. Is there a back-up alarm?		Proof of annual inspections
Tested at regular intervals (Both alarms and back-up)	5	What is the alarm and how often is it tested?	Copy of test runs	
EMPLOYEES IDENTIFY ALARMS		Do employees know what the different alarms signal?	Induction training syllabus, 5-minute talk	
Alarm system discussed with employees and contractors	5	How are they informed of the different alarms?	Training records of local new employee Orientation, Hazard Communication	
Employees know the alarm and what to do	5	Do employees know what the fire or evacuation alarm is?	Interview: During the audit, ask any employee what the alarms is	
TOTAL	35			

FIGURE 50.1 Audit Protocol for the Element – Alarm Systems.

51 Emergency Plans

DESIGN OF EMERGENCY PLANS

An emergency plan is a written set of instructions that outlines what management, employees, and others at the workplace should do in an emergency.

An emergency plan must provide for the following:

- Emergency procedures
- Effective communication
- Informing affected parties of the procedures
- Training in the procedures
- Testing of the procedures

EMERGENCY SITUATIONS

No matter how good or efficient an organization's safety management system, the possibility still exists for the company to experience a natural or man-made emergency situation. It is through good planning and experience that the severity of the situation can be limited and the effects reduced. Emergency plans should also include business continuity plans to enable the business to continue to function during and after the emergency.

TYPES OF EMERGENCIES

Emergencies that disrupt the normal operation of the organization could include:

- Vehicle accident
- On-the-job injury, fatality, or multiple fatalities
- Fire in the vicinity or in the workplace
- Bomb threat
- Act of terrorism
- Strike action or demonstration
- Power outage

Natural disasters could include:

- Hurricane
- Earthquake
- Mudslide
- Tsunami
- Flood
- Threatening weather

IMPLEMENTATION OF EMERGENCY PLANS

The first step in compiling and implementing emergency plans is to list the possible emergencies that the organization may experience. A simple risk ranking should be done to determine the probability of the emergency occurring and the resultant severity.

RISK RANKING

Figure 51.1 is an example of a simple method of risk ranking the disaster scenario. The probability (what could happen), the severity (how bad could it be), and the frequency (how often the organization is exposed to the threat) are ranked on a scale of 1 to 10, where 10 is the highest and 1 the lowest. The ranking must take into account the amount of disruption and resultant costs of the disruption.

RESPONSIBILITY AND ACCOUNTABILITY

Each site or divisional manager, supervisor, and contractor should ensure that a written detailed emergency plan is available for their respective facility, work area, or building. The emergency plan should address all types of expected events. It should include actions to be taken before, during, and after the event, and the roles of all participants. The plans should be discussed with all affected parties and be made available in strategic positions. Where possible, the organization should ensure the periodic testing of the emergency plan, during which likely scenarios should be practiced.

CREDIBLE SCENARIOS INCLUDED

The appropriate managers should ensure that the credible scenarios are covered in the emergency plans. The environmental department should utilize the environmental aspect register and significance rating process to identify environmental emergency scenarios and should notify the coordinator for inclusion in the emergency drills and training. The appointed fire coordinator should ensure that the emergency

DISASTER	DESCRIPTION	PROBABILITY	SEVERITY	FREQUENCY	RISK
1	Vehicle Accident	2	5	4	40
2	Employee Injury	4	4	3	48
3	Employee fatality	1	9	2	18
4	Bomb Threat	1	6	2	12
5	Act of Terrorism	3	8	1	24
6	Strike	2	6	2	24
7	Power Outage	4	8	2	64

FIGURE 51.1   Disaster Risk Ranking.

teams are trained in emergency situations and that they participate in emergency drills. The organization could liaise with the local fire authority regarding assistance to supplement the onsite teams, where the situation may be beyond their capabilities or control.

The responsible persons should advise senior management on the appropriate systems and facilities required for effective emergency response, and the management should provide the necessary resources and infrastructure for this response.

INCIDENT COMMANDER

A responsible person should be appointed to act as the incident commander to coordinate all emergency procedures. The incident commander can use the emergency plan to anticipate likely scenarios and develop tactical operations. He or she should obtain and post floor plans with evacuation routes and other information as specified in the emergency plan, schedule fire drills and emergency evacuations, and determine and supervise the roles of outside service entities participating in the drills. During exercises, the incident commander should wear a reflective vest, suitably labeled, for easy identification.

EMERGENCY TEAMS

Depending on the nature of the emergency that the organization could face, specific emergency teams should be appointed and trained. These could include firefighting, first aid, rescue, or maintenance teams. A list of teams and members should be available in the emergency plan, along with their contact numbers.

AUDIT OF EMERGENCY PLANS

The auditors should ascertain if the organization has identified possible disaster threats, and if these have been ranked in terms of risk. Have emergency plans been compiled for these threats? Have employees been trained in the actions to take? Has an incident commander been appointed? Regular drills should be carried out where practicable, and a record of these exercises should be kept and made available during the audit (Figure 51.2).

ELEMENT/PROGRAM/PROCESS	POINTS	QUESTIONS THAT COULD BE ASKED	VERIFICATION	WHAT TO LOOK FOR
EMERGENCY PLANS				
EMERGENCIES IDENTIFIED				
Possible emergencies identified	5	Have all possible disasters been identified?	List of scenarios	
Written emergency plans available	5	Is the emergency plan current? What emergency plans are in place?	Ask to see the emergency plan	
Plans to cover all calculated emergencies from both natural and man-caused sources	5	Is top management aware of the plan?		
Emergency scenarios risk ranked	5	What is the greatest threat to this organization?	List of risk ranking	
Copies of the plan or parts thereof available to all employees? (need to know basis)	5	Is it part of safety induction training?		
SEPARATE FIRST-AID AND SERVICES TEAMS TRAINED AND INCLUDED IN EMERGENCY DRILLS				
First-aid, fire, maintenance and/or environmental teams for emergencies	5	Are there separate first aid teams? If so, how many first aid teams are there? What services teams are there (e.g. rescue team, teams to maintain production, etc.?) Are these teams included in the emergency drills?	See a report of the emergency drill where the teams are included	Is there a first-aid team for emergencies?
List of teams available	5	Where are the lists of these teams kept?	Appointments of first-aiders. Appointment of services team	Notice boards. Location of emergency plans.
Drills held	5	How often are drills held?	Copy of report.	
INCIDENT COORDINATOR TRAINED TO TAKE CONTROL				
Coordinator appointed to control the emergency action plans	5	Is a coordinator appointed to take control?	Review the appointment document	
TOTAL	**45**			

FIGURE 51.2 Audit Protocol for the Element – Emergency Plans.

52 Flammable Substance Storage

DESIGN FOR THE STORAGE AND USE OF FLAMMABLE SUBSTANCES

Flammable, explosive, and otherwise hazardous materials not only pose a fire, injury, and health hazard but also a hazard to facilities and personnel in the proximity. These materials are inherently hazardous, and this needs to be considered when planning for the storage and use thereof.

This health and safety management system (SMS) element summary offers basic guidelines for the use and storage of flammable substances. In designing for the storage and use of flammable substances, a complete inventory needs to be compiled. Where possible, the elimination or substitution of flammable substances should be considered, and a risk assessment would be a good guide in this regard. Fire specialists should be consulted concerning the correct use and storage of these substances.

IMPLEMENTATION OF STANDARDS FOR THE STORAGE AND USE OF FLAMMABLE SUBSTANCES

The use and storage of flammable liquids and substances varies from workplace to workplace. A basic SMS standard for storage and use of flammable substances is as follows:

FLAMMABLE SUBSTANCE STORAGE AND USE STANDARD

Responsibility and Accountability

Each area, site manager, supervisor, and contractor should be responsible for the application of this standard in their work area and will be accountable for compliance with this standard. They should ensure that flammable and explosive materials are stored in a manner which meets the legal requirements as well as the nature of the risk that they pose. The site fire coordinator will advise management on the appropriate, cost effective level of fire readiness and will ensure that the fire risks are identified and assessed.

Requirements

One of the primary methods of reducing the risk posed by flammables is to restrict the quantities to acceptable levels during storage and use. A risk assessment should be carried out to determine if the quantity of flammable liquid kept on site warrants the building of one or more flammable substance stores.

The warehousing department should, where necessary, obtain formal approval for a flammable substance store from the relevant authority. A copy of the certificate should be displayed at the store. The site fire coordinator is to consider the chemical compatibility of the various chemicals and provide advice on segregation where necessary.

Competent Person

Each department using flammable and explosive materials should appoint a competent person (supervisor or line manager) to take responsibility for the storage of all flammable material in their area. The storage and issue of chemicals must comply with local legal requirements, this standard, and other company standards and procedures.

Containment

Storage areas should have containment facilities. Containment of flammable liquids shall be determined at 110% of the capacity of the store. All electrical equipment used within the unsafe zone of a flammable substance should be intrinsically safe and have explosion-proof enclosures. Intrinsically safe electrical installations should be placed on a planned maintenance schedule and inspected as to the integrity of the seals on an annual basis. All intrinsic electrical equipment should be inspected annually. These inspections are to be documented.

Signage

Each flammable store or cupboard should have a clear indication on the outside of the entrance door. Where there is no need for a flammable liquid store, flammable liquids can be stored in an approved flammable liquid cabinet. All items in flammable stores and cabinets should be properly and clearly labeled as to the content and volume and arranged neatly on racks and shelves. No combustible material such as wood, rags, and carton boxes should be kept in a flammable liquid store or cabinet.

"No open flames" and "No smoking" symbolic signs should be displayed in the vicinity of the flammable liquid store or, where applicable, on the doors of the flammable liquid cabinets.

The use of mobile phones and radios and any similar potential source of sparks is prohibited in flammable liquid storage areas and fuel bays.

Hazardous Atmosphere

Flammable liquids should be issued only on a need-to-use volume basis, and strict control is to be exercised to ensure that personnel do not draw more than what is needed for the specific job.

Bonding cables or chains should be provided to bond containers of highly volatile liquids when decanting takes place, and drip trays should be provided wherever there is transfer of flammable liquid. Drip trays should be emptied so as to ensure that a hazardous atmosphere is not created by evaporating liquids from drip trays.

Spill Control

Spill-absorbent material should be available where there is a risk of spills. Sufficient numbers of the correct fire-fighting equipment should be made available in close vicinity of the flammable liquid store. Sawdust or rags may not be used to absorb flammable liquids. Only approved spill kit absorbent materials should be used for spill control. Old and used chemicals, as well as those in damaged containers, should be disposed of in a manner prescribed by the local environmental regulations.

Information

Material safety data sheets (MSDS) information, including handling, storage, emergency, and first aid instructions, is to be available at all areas where flammable materials are stored. All employees using flammable materials should be trained and informed about the hazards and emergency procedures related to the chemical they are using.

Explosives

The use and storage of explosives is a specialized area and is controlled by local health and safety regulations. The storage and use of explosives should be under the strict supervision of a well-qualified person, experienced in the handling and storage of explosives. Storage magazines must conform to the local legal requirements concerning design, construction, and maintenance.

AUDIT OF THE STORAGE AND USE OF FLAMMABLE SUBSTANCES

During the audit inspection, the auditors should visit an area where flammables or explosives are stored and inspect the facility thoroughly. The storage method should be scrutinized as well as the applicable signage. The facility should be allocated to an appointed person who is responsible for ensuring that the storage and distribution is within standards. No combustibles should be stored in the storage facility, and the electrical installation must be intrinsic. Records of the electrical installation inspections should be examined during the documentation review session (Figure 52.1).

ELEMENT/PROGRAM/PROCESS	POINTS	QUESTIONS THAT COULD BE ASKED	VERIFICATION	WHAT TO LOOK FOR
STORAGE AND USE OF FLAMMABLE SUBSTANCES AND EXPLOSIVE MATERIAL				
STORAGE PROVIDED WITH SUITABLE DOORS, WINDOWS (IF ANY), VENTILATION				Inspect at leas one storage area. Signs erected?
Responsibilities allocated for flammable stores	5	Have responsibilities been allocated?	Copy of standard or appointment letter	
Risk Assessment done	5	Has a risk assessment been done concerning flammable materials?	Copy of risk assessment or survey	
Does the flammable storage comply with regulatory requirements?	5	Are flammable cabinets equipped with self closing doors? Does the storage meet local requirements?	Visual Inspection	During the inspection, inspect the flammable liquid storage and look for ventilation, housekeeping, electrical installations, etc. Is the cabinet bonded?
Are ventilation systems, drainage, etc. regularly checked for efficiency?	5	Does storage rooms meet fire code requirements?	Inspection.	Are there flammable materials such as oily rags, bits of paper and wood stored with flammable liquids?
Correct usage	5	Are compressed gases, combustibles or incompatibles stored in flammable cabinets. Is a standard available?	Cross refer to electrical machinery in hazardous locations	The ventilation should be adequate and light fittings and other electrical equipment in the flammable liquid storage area should be explosion-proof. (Please note that oils stored in a storage area do not constitute a F.L. store)
Standard available.				
STORAGE AREA NEAT, TIDY AND CLEAN				
Are all items in store neatly arranged on racks or shelving?	5	What are products are incompatibles with the products stored?	Visual	There should be no spilling of liquid on the floor, no impregnated sawdust or wood or other combustibles. The stacking should be neat, and the store should be clean and tidy and housekeeping should be excellent
Are all containers in store kept closed?	5	How are storage cabinets with non automatic doors identified	Inspection	
EXPLOSIVES				
Storage and handling (If applicable)	5	Is this done under the supervision of an qualified person?	Standard	Inspect a magazine and ask if it complies with legal requirements
TOTAL	40			

FIGURE 52.1 Audit Protocol for the Element – Flammable Substance Storage.

53 First Aid and First Responder Program

DESIGN OF A FIRST AID AND FIRST RESPONDER PROGRAM

INTRODUCTION

It is the legal and moral duty of an employer to provide first aid facilities for the treatment of injured employees or contractors. A workplace should have a standard to provide guidelines for the training of first aiders, the provision of medical treatment, and the transportation of injured employees, contractors, or site visitors to a medical facility in case of injury.

In the event of an accident, the organization should ensure that all injuries are treated promptly. The provision of adequate first aid facilities, such as a first aid center and trained personnel, to provide first aid medical treatment is an essential factor in ensuring that competent persons treat injuries and occupational diseases promptly.

IMPLEMENTATION OF A FIRST AID AND FIRST RESPONDER PROGRAM

FIRST AID FACILITIES

The organization should nominate an external medical treatment facility, such as a hospital or clinic, and all injuries and diseases, beyond first aid injuries, should be treated at this facility. If the organization has remote sites, medical facilities in those areas should be nominated.

Where 100 or more employees are employed in a workplace, a first aid room under the control of a qualified first aider should be provided. The contents of the first aid room must comply with the local legal requirements.

There should be a qualified first aider for every 50 employees. In remote areas and work sites, a qualified first aider should be a part of every work team, even if the team has less than 50 employees. For every 50 employees, a fully equipped and maintained first aid box should be available, and in remote areas or other outside workplaces, first aid boxes should be made available.

Automatic electric defibrillators (AEDs) should be available in all first aid rooms and in other high risk areas that may require such a device, or as prescribed by local regulations.

FIRST AID TRAINING

The objective of a first aid training program is to ensure that effective emergency medical response is available, and that sufficient personnel are trained in first aid to render emergency treatment to injured persons awaiting transportation to the nominated medical facility.

Example Standard for First Aid training:

- First aiders should receive first aid training from an accredited body and should be familiar with the applicable work site's specific hazards.
- Appointed first responders may need to attend advanced first aid training.
- At least 5% of the workforce should hold first aid certificates, and 5% should be trained or retrained annually.
- In workplaces, first aiders will be identified by a high visibility vest (or similar), where practicable.
- The training department should maintain a register of qualified first aiders.
- Only employees who have the necessary physical and mental attributes necessary should be nominated as candidates for first aid training.

Responsibility and Accountability

Managers, supervisors, and contractors (Responsible persons) should take suitable precautions to ensure that injured employees, contractors, and visitors receive immediate and correct first aid medical treatment without delay. They should ensure that all employees, contractors, and visitors follow the procedure for the reporting of accidental injuries and diseases and make sure that such injuries and occupational diseases are treated at the company first aid center as soon as possible.

Employees and Visitors

It is the responsibility of all employees to report injuries or occupational diseases to their immediate supervisors as soon as possible, and to attend the first aid center for immediate treatment. All company employees hosting visitors are responsible for seeing that their visitor(s), if injured, receive immediate and correct first aid treatment at the company first aid center.

First Aiders (First Responders)

First responders are responsible for the immediate and correct first aid treatment of injured workers at the first aid center and during their transportation to the nearest medical facility. They are also to assist supervision by encouraging employees to report all injuries and occupational diseases to their supervisor, and to have the condition attended to at the nominated first aid center.

Procedure in Case of Injury
- All injuries and occupational diseases must be reported to the local first aider and supervisor immediately.
- The injured person must be transported to the first aid center
- Employees that suffer injury or occupational diseases more severe than a first aid injury should be transported by ambulance to the nearest medical facility.
- All employees treated at the medical facility must follow the doctor's treatment orders concerning additional visits, medication, and so on.

Transport

Suitable transport shall be:

- A well-equipped ambulance or any other suitable vehicle
- Provided to convey injured or sick workers to the nominated medical facility
- Readily available for use on all shifts
- Maintained in good working order at all times

AUDIT OF A FIRST AID AND FIRST RESPONDER PROGRAM

The auditor should be satisfied that enough first aiders are available and that the required number have been trained or retrained according to the standard. First aid facilities should be inspected, as well as the contents of the first aid cabinets, to ensure correct and sufficient supplies. Arrangements with local medical facilities should be reviewed. The position, condition, and control over first aid cabinets and AEDs need to be checked. The auditor must be convinced that the organization is in a position to render effective first aid medical aid to an injured employee, and that suitable and reliable transportation is available, should the injured person need to be transported to a medical facility (Figure 53.1).

ELEMENT/PROGRAM/PROCESS	POINTS	QUESTIONS THAT COULD BE ASKED	VERIFICATION	WHAT TO LOOK FOR
FIRST AID AND FIRST RESPONDER PROGRAM				
APPOINTMENTS				
First Aides appointed.	5	Have first aides been appointed?	Appointment letters.	
First Responders appointed.	5	Have first responders been appointed?	Appointment letters.	
FIRST AIDE ROOM/FACITILY				
First aid room available.	5	Is there a first aid room or facility available?	Visual inspection.	Inspect the first aid facility during the inspection.
FUST AID BOXES				
First aid boxes/cabinets available	5	How many are there?	Visual.	Check random cabinets for content and control.
Control over and condition of cabinets.	5	Under whose control are they?	Visual.	
AEDs available as required.	5	Where are AEDS situated?	Visual.	Check positions during in section.
NOMINATED MEDICAL FACILITY				
Hospital/Clinic nominated.	5	Has a medical facility been nominated? Are supervisors aware of this?	Confirmation of this.	
FIRST AID TRAINING				
Employees trained.	5	What percentage of employees trained/retrained annually?	Copy of training records. At least 5% per annum.	
TOTAL	40			

FIGURE 53.1 Audit Protocol for the Element – First Aid and First Responder Program.

54 Firefighting and Evacuation Drills

DESIGN OF FIREFIGHTING AND EVACUATION DRILLS

INTRODUCTION

Every building, facility, and workplace should have its own documented emergency plan and should conduct a fire drill and emergency evacuation for their respective area. These areas should include buildings, general offices, warehouses, workshops, and other occupied structures.

An evacuation drill should be conducted at least once a year for each occupied building and, dependent on the fire risk, periodic fire drills should also be held.

OBJECTIVES

The main objectives of firefighting and evacuation drills are as follows:

- To provide an orderly emergency evacuation plan for all employees
- To ensure all exit routes, emergency staircases, and fire doors are not obstructed and can be used during emergencies
- To familiarize building occupants with the means of escape routes from the building
- To identify any weakness in the evacuation plan
- To ensure fast, organized, and smooth evacuation of buildings during emergencies
- To test the working conditions and effectiveness of all fire and emergency equipment and systems for all buildings
- To offer the firefighting teams an opportunity to practice their skills

PLANNING

When planning and organizing a fire drill and emergency evacuation, the following points should be considered:

Buildings
- Is the building occupied by one or multiple departments?
- Is the building single story or multistory?
- Are fire extinguishers, hose reels, and other fire equipment available?
- Are firefighting teams available?
- Is there a safe and accessible emergency assembly area?

Occupants of the Building
- Number of occupants
- Location of occupants in the building
- Physical condition of occupants in the building (will some need assistance to evacuate?)
- Activities of occupants
- Emergency lights and other emergency equipment
- Escape routes

IMPLEMENTING FIREFIGHTING AND EVACUATION DRILLS

When implementing a system of firefighting and evacuation drills, emergency plans need to be compiled and responsibility for the execution of these plans should be allocated.

EXAMPLE OF RESPONSIBILITIES FOR FIREFIGHTING AND EVACUATION DRILLS

Responsible Persons

Each site manager, supervisor, and contractor (Responsible person) should ensure a written detailed emergency plan is available for his or her respective facility or building. The emergency plan should address all types of expected events. It should include actions to be taken before, during, and after the event. The roles of all participants must be defined.

The responsible person should ensure the test and practice of the emergency plan periodically. They should appoint fire and emergency teams, an incident commander, emergency evacuation officers, and building and floor wardens to coordinate fire drills and emergency evacuations. The responsible person should arrange for the training of these appointees and ensure that the emergency plan is updated as needed.

Fire and Emergency Teams

The firefighting team, under the guidance of the incident commander, responds to fire scenarios and endeavors to extinguish the fire or contain it until external assistance arrives on the scene. They should be trained in basic firefighting methods and practice regularly by holding fire drills. The emergency teams could include maintenance team members who are familiar with emergency shut-off valves, water supplies, and electrical systems. A team consisting of trained first aiders could be used to provide first aid medical assistance during emergencies.

Incident Commander

The incident commander should use the emergency plan to anticipate likely scenarios and develop tactical operations. He or she should obtain and post floor plans in strategic places showing evacuation routes and other information as specified in the emergency plan. The incident commander schedules fire drills and emergency evacuations and supervises and determine the roles of outside service entities participating in the drills.

Emergency Evacuation Officer

The emergency evacuation officer is responsible for the occupants' safety during evacuation and to ensure first aid is given to evacuees if needed. He or she cooperates with other officers during the evacuation and advises the building and floor wardens if needed. The officer should wear a reflective vest for easy identification.

Building and Floor Wardens

These wardens ensure all occupants have evacuated the respective floors, including people in the toilet, meeting room, and so on, during evacuations by doing a floor sweep. The wardens ensure that evacuees use the correct evacuation route to leave the floor or building, and informs the emergency evacuation officer of disabled occupants in their respective buildings or floors.

AUDITING OF FIREFIGHTING AND EVACUATION DRILLS

The organization should conduct a survey of the types of emergencies it could be faced with, and it should have appropriate emergency plans in place. Regular drills should be held to check the efficiency of the plan, and appointed emergency personnel should be trained and participate in the drills. Emergency assembly areas should be clearly marked, and employees should know where they are. Dependent on the organization, appropriate emergency equipment should be available. Drills should be documented and changes to the emergency plan made where necessary (Figure 54.1).

ELEMENT/PROGRAM/PROCESS	POINTS	QUESTIONS THAT COULD BE ASKED	VERIFICATION	WHAT TO LOOK FOR
FIREFIGHTING AND EVACUATION DRILLS				
DRILLS HELD				
Evacuation drills	5	How often are these held?	Copy of report	
Firefighting drills	5	How often are these held?	Copy of report	
APPOINTMENTS				
Emergency teams	5	Have teams been appointed?	List of teams	
Incident commander	5	Incident commander appointed? How recognized?	Appointment	
Emergency evacuation officer	5	Emergency evacuation officer appointed? How recognized?	Appointment	
Building and floor wardens	5	Building and floor wardens appointed. How recognized?	Appointment	
EMERGENCY PLAN				
Emergency plan followed	5	Is there an emergency plan, is it followed	Copy of plan and modifications	
Emergency plan updated	5	Is it updated after drills?	Changes to plan	
ASSEMBLY AREAS				
Areas designated	5	Where are these?	Map or plan	Visual during inspection
TOTAL	45			

FIGURE 54.1 Audit Protocol for the Element – Firefighting and Evacuation Drills.

55 Fire Prevention and Emergency Coordinator

DESIGN OF THE ROLE OF A FIRE PREVENTION AND EMERGENCY COORDINATOR

The objective of this element of the health and safety management system (SMS) element is to ensure the appointment of an employee with appropriate knowledge and practical experience to perform the overall coordination of fire prevention tasks and emergency response coordination, in accordance with the fire risks of the organization.

Such a person should be appointed at each site to coordinate and control the company's overall fire prevention tasks and emergency response initiative. Fire risks vary from company to company, and in some instances a full-time fire coordinator is appointed in this role.

IMPLEMENTING THE ROLE OF A FIRE PREVENTION AND EMERGENCY COORDINATOR

The site manager, supervisor, or contractor (Responsible person) should appoint one of his or her employees with the overall responsibility for coordination of the fire prevention tasks and emergency response program. This appointment will be supplementary to the appointee's scope of employment and job description, unless a full-time appointment is called for.

The responsible person will determine the necessary competencies of the coordinator and ensure that the person is suitably trained and is appointed in writing. The responsible person may appoint other employees to perform fire prevention tasks and emergency related tasks, supplementary to the overall coordination of the program, as required.

Examples of the duties of the fire prevention and emergency coordinator are as follows:

- To draw up an emergency plan for the premises to cater for any foreseeable natural or man-made emergency, disaster, or production interruption
- To identify and appoint suitable persons to take control of certain functions during an emergency to minimize the effect of the emergency situation, for example, fire teams, first-aid teams, and evacuation marshals
- To liaise with government agencies such as the local law enforcement agencies, local civil defense, fire department, and neighboring industries to coordinate those aspects of the emergency plan which are of concern or benefit to both parties

- To revise the laid-down emergency procedures at least once every six months and ensure that they are practical and current in terms of the prevailing conditions
- Ensure that parts of the plan are available to all employees on a need-to-know basis, and that emergency escape routes and assembly points are displayed prominently on a layout plan of the premises
- When required, assume the duties of the incident commander

AUDIT OF THE ROLE OF A FIRE PREVENTION AND EMERGENCY COORDINATOR

A fire risk assessment should have been conducted to determine if a fire coordinator is needed or if a full-time coordinator is required. In many industries and mines, full-time coordinators are appointed. The appointment must be in writing and the duties and functions must be spelt out in the appointment letter. The coordinator and his or her teams must receive periodic training to enable them to carry out their duties successfully, and regular drills should be held (Figure 55.1).

ELEMENT/PROGRAM/PROCESS	POINTS	QUESTIONS THAT COULD BE ASKED	VERIFICATION	WHAT TO LOOK FOR
FIRE PREVENTION AND EMERGENCY COORDINATOR				
APPOINTMENT IN WRITING - DUTIES DEFINED				
Fire risk assessment done	5	Has a fire risk assessment been done?	Copy of the fire risk assessment	
Coordinator appointed according to the fire risk assessment	5	Who is the fire/emergency coordinator?	Copy of letter of appointment	
Duties been defined in writing - duties and functions stipulated	5	Has he been appointed in writing? Are the duties and functions been spelt out?	Are the duties defined in the letter of appointment? Is it his or her duty to train people, to do fire inspection, to organize the maintenance of fire equipment, train teams and so on?	Notice boards indicating fire team members
MINIMUM TRAINING				
Appointed person trained to an acceptable standard	5	Has this person completed fire training course, or equivalent or is he an ex-fireman or has he received some refresher training?	See copies of training certificate / qualifications	
Training or refresher training done within the last five years	5	When last was training done?	Copy of training certificate or report of practical training	
DATE OF LAST DRILL OR EXERCISE				
Drill/exercise held	5	When was the last drill held?	Report from the last drill or emergency exercise	
TOTAL	30			

FIGURE 55.1   Audit Protocol for the Element – Fire Prevention and Emergency Coordinator.

Part 6

Design, Implementation, and Audit of Occupational Health and Safety Management System, Electrical, Mechanical, and Personal Safeguarding Elements

56 Fall Protection System

DESIGN OF A FALL PROTECTION SYSTEM

For a number of years, fall protection has been rated as one of the most citable of the Occupational Safety and Health Administration (OSHA) regulations, and in many instances, it has been cited more than any other safety regulation.

Fall protection is a vital component of any health and safety management system (SMS) as the potential for falls is high, as is the consequence of a fall from height. Being such a high risk element that is often not fully complied with, it should receive the utmost attention.

To eliminate injuries caused by falls where a fall hazard is present, a safety harness should be used as a component of a personal fall arrest system. If an employee is exposed to falling 6 feet (2 m) or more from an unprotected side or edge, he or she must wear a personal fall arrest system to protect themselves.

DESCRIPTION AND USE OF PERSONAL FALL ARREST SYSTEMS

Each department should conduct a survey or risk assessment to determine where personal fall arrest systems are required. The list of jobs or tasks and areas which require personal fall arrest systems must be identified and listed and be available upon request.

A personal fall arrest system means a system used to arrest an employee in a fall from a working level. It consists of an anchorage, connectors, and body harness and includes a deceleration device (shock-absorbing lanyard), lifeline, or suitable combination of these.

Only safety harnesses and shock-absorbing lanyards should be used as components of a fall arrest system. The use of body belts and web lanyards for fall arrest should be prohibited.

Personal fall arrest systems should, when stopping a fall,

- Limit maximum arresting force on an employee to 1,800 lbs (800 kg) when used with a body harness
- Bring an employee to a complete stop, and limit maximum deceleration distance an employee travels to 3.5 feet (1.1 m)
- Have sufficient strength to withstand twice the potential impact energy of an employee free-falling a distance of 6 feet (2 m), or the free-fall distance permitted by the system, whichever is less

GENERAL REQUIREMENTS

- Personal fall arrest systems shall be rigged such that an employee can neither free-fall more than 6 feet (2 m) nor contact any lower level.
- Ropes and straps used in lanyards, lifelines, and strength components of body harnesses should be made of synthetic fibers.
- Anchorages should be designed, installed, and used under the supervision of a qualified person as part of a complete personal fall arrest system that maintains a safety factor of at least two, that is, capable of supporting at least twice the weight expected to be imposed upon it
- Anchorages used to attach personal fall arrest systems shall be independent of any anchorage being used to support or suspend platforms, and must be capable of supporting at least 5,000 lbs (2,267 kg) per person attached.
- Snap-hooks, D-rings, and connectors shall be capable of sustaining a minimum tensile load of 5,000 lbs (2,267 kg).
- Snap-hooks shall be a locking type designed and used to prevent disengagement of the snap-hook by the contact of the snap-hook keeper by the connected person.

POSITIONING DEVICE SYSTEMS

- Positioning device systems are primarily used for safe positioning.
- Safety belts and web lanyards can be used as a positioning devise system.
- This system should be set up so that workers can free-fall no farther than 6 feet (1.8 m).
- They should be secured to an anchorage capable of supporting at least twice the potential impact load of an employee's fall or 3,000 lbs (1,360 kg), whichever is greater.
- The requirements for snap-hooks, D-rings, and other connectors used with positioning device systems must meet the same criteria as those for personal fall arrest systems.

IMPLEMENTATION OF A FALL PROTECTION SYSTEM

RESPONSIBILITY AND ACCOUNTABILITY

Managers, supervisors, and contractors (Responsible persons) are responsible for the identification of areas, jobs, or tasks which require the use of personal fall arrest systems, and are accountable for ensuring that conformity is maintained regarding the fall protection standard. The occupational health and safety department is responsible for coordination and update of this standard.

Responsible persons are responsible for ensuring that employees (and contractors in their area) use personal fall arrest systems when required, and each employee will be accountable for the wearing of fall protection in required areas and during specified tasks.

Inspection of Personal Fall Arrest Systems

All personal fall arrest systems should be inspected and recorded monthly by the responsible persons or their deputies. Personal fall arrest systems should be inspected prior to each use for mildew, wear, damage, and other deterioration. Defective components should be removed from service if their strength or function may be adversely affected. These records should be filed and made available upon request.

Training in the Use of Personal Fall Arrest Systems

Employees who are required to wear personal fall arrest or positioning device systems should be suitably trained in the safe use of these systems. This should include the following: application limits; proper anchoring and tie-off techniques; estimation of free fall distance, including determination of deceleration distance and total fall distance to prevent striking a lower level; methods of use; and inspection and storage of the systems. Names of all employees who have received training should be recorded on a register which should be signed by the instructor and employees.

AUDIT OF A FALL PROTECTION SYSTEM

The organization should have conducted a fall risk assessment to determine what fall protection measures are required. The ideal method to audit a fall protection system is to inspect a site where fall protection is in use. This will answer a number of questions concerning the standard for fall protection and its application. Fall protection equipment inspection checks should be scrutinized, as well as the training records (Figure 56.1).

ELEMENT/PROGRAM/PROCESS	POINTS	QUESTIONS THAT COULD BE ASKED	VERIFICATION	WHAT TO LOOK FOR
FALL PROTECTION SYSTEM				
RISK ASSESSMENT				
Risk Assessment done	5	Has a risk assessment or critical task analysis been done to determine where fall protection is needed?	Copy of risk assessment, survey or critical task analysis	Are there tasks where fall protection is required?
TYPES REQUIRED AND USED				
Fall protection equipment used	5	What fall protection devices are used?	As indicated in the risk assessment	
Restraint systems	5	Are restraint systems used?	Full harness or lanyard used?	
TRAINING OF USERS				
Training conducted	5	Have employees who use fall protection been trained?	Copy of training records	
Refresher training	5	Is there a refresher training? What about new employees who are part of the program?	Copy of refresher training	
INSPECTION OF EQUIPMENT				
Inspection check list	5	Is an inspection check list used?	See a copy of a completed checklist	
Regular inspections	5	Who does the inspections? How often?	Copy of inspection schedule	Visual check of fall protection equipment
TOTAL	**35**			

FIGURE 56.1　Audit Protocol for the Element – Fall Protection Systems.

57 Hazardous Material Control Program

DESIGN OF A HAZARDOUS MATERIAL CONTROL PROGRAM

This chapter outlines basic controls for the purchasing, handling, use, distribution, and storage of any hazardous materials (hazardous substances) that are known to be present in the workplace. Hazardous material could be in liquid, gas, powder, radioactive, or other form. When hazardous materials are present, used, stored, or manufactured, employees may be exposed to them under normal conditions of use at workplaces. The Occupational Safety and Health Administration (OSHA) has found this standard to be one of the most cited standards over a period of years.

STANDARD

Where hazardous materials are stored, used, or may be handled, a company safety management system (SMS) standard should be drafted and applied to all company operations to ensure that employees are informed of workplace hazards associated with the use of hazardous materials. The standard should include compliance policies and guidelines from the regulatory agencies, training, and information programs, and should define the program for the safe use, storage, or manufacture of hazardous materials. This standard should be reviewed and updated no less than every year from the publication date, or more frequently as required.

IMPLEMENTATION OF A HAZARDOUS MATERIAL CONTROL PROGRAM

The regulatory requirements should be the minimum standard to strive for concerning hazardous materials, their safe use, and employee information and training. An example of a hazardous material program SMS standard is as follows:

RESPONSIBILITY AND ACCOUNTABILITY

As with most SMS programs and processes, responsibility and accountability must be allocated.

Purchasing Department

The purchasing department should ensure that the request for a material safety data sheet (MSDS) is described on each purchase order, and also ensure that an MSDS is requested for all emergency or rush orders placed by telephone, fax, or email. Further, they should ensure that initial purchase requests for new hazardous materials (those not on the hazardous materials inventory list) have been reviewed by the industrial hygienist (IH) prior to purchase.

Purchasing should ensure that the contractor(s) and/or individuals under contract with the company receive a list of the hazardous agents and potential physical hazards associated with their contracted work. A statement should be included in the contract documents stating that this information has been supplied, and that it is the responsibility of the contractor to evaluate the information and present it to their employees. Conversely, the contractor must inform the company in writing of any hazardous materials to be used in their work.

Warehouse, Shipping, and Receiving Department

This department should ensure that all incoming containers or shipments of hazardous materials are properly labeled and should immediately replace damaged, missing, or defaced labels. If the contents of a particular container are unknown, the employee working on the situation should contact the environmental department and the industrial hygienist (IH) for their assistance.

These departments should check that the original MSDS received with a hazardous material, and the name of the department that ordered the agent, are forwarded to the industrial hygienist. They should also ensure that an MSDS is maintained within the MSDS manual for each hazardous material stocked by the warehouse.

Company Departments

The managers of departments where hazardous material is used should ensure that employees who work with such materials have undergone the prescribed medical examinations, and should designate a responsible individual to implement the requirements of this SMS standard.

Departments must make sure that a MSDS is obtained for each hazardous material proposed for use, trial, or testing prior to its delivery. They should forward the MSDS to the IH for review and approvals and should confirm that employees are effectively informed of existing job-related hazards upon initial assignment and prior to beginning new procedures and jobs.

Training

The departments should provide employees with comprehensive and effective training prior to initial job assignment and material specific training any time a new hazardous agent is introduced into the work area. As a minimum, training shall be provided in accordance with the company hazard communication program. Training records, including training program outlines, attendance lists, and comprehension or proficiency tests, should be maintained and made accessible for inspection.

Department managers are responsible for establishing a specific location for the MSDS manual and ensuring that employee access to the MSDS manual is unrestricted throughout all work shifts.

Departments should also check that MSDSs received from industrial hygiene are placed in the MSDS manuals, that the old or obsolete MSDSs are destroyed, and that all original containers of hazardous materials are properly labeled. Where applicable, they should develop and implement a written job safe practice (JSP) for nonroutine tasks involving hazardous materials.

Occupational Health and Safety Department (Industrial Hygienist)

The IH should define and oversee the company hazard communication program and prepare and update it for distribution throughout the company. He or she maintains the master file system of MSDSs and approved chemicals inventory list for all company sites and determines the adequacy of MSDSs prior to distribution. The occupational health and safety department should review and approve new hazardous materials prior to use throughout the company, and should oversee the development of a MSDS for each hazardous material used by the company. They maintain and update this standard as necessary.

Environmental Department

The environmental department determines the adequacy of environmental information on MSDSs and provides information for the environmental sections of the company's MSDSs.

They review and approve new hazardous materials prior to use throughout company sites in conjunction with the IH.

Engineering/Maintenance Department

These departments ensure that the contractor and or individuals under contract with the company receives information, outlined in the contract proposal, concerning potential hazards associated with their contracted work. A statement shall be included in the contract documents stating that this information has been supplied and that it is the responsibility of the contractor to obtain the information and present it to their employees. Conversely, the contractor must inform the company of any hazardous materials to be used during the project.

Employees

All employees should review the MSDS for each hazardous agent in their work area and review the labels and other forms of warning for the hazardous materials. They should not remove any MSDS from the MSDS manual, and at all times they should wear the prescribed personal protective equipment (PPE) when working with hazardous materials.

MATERIAL SAFETY DATA SHEETS (MSDS)

An MSDS is required for each hazardous material located, used, or produced at company sites. A master file system of MSDSs for all hazardous materials used, stored, or produced at the company will be maintained by the IH. This may also be a contracted database website which gives access to the MSDs used at the company. Each department that utilizes hazardous material shall perform an annual inventory and verify the accuracy of the aforementioned inventory.

MSDS Manuals

Departmental locations shall be established for employee access to the MSDS manual. Each manual should contain a current copy of a MSDS for each hazardous material used or stored in the associated work area. The MSDS manual should contain a current hazardous material inventory list for the respective work area, compiled in alphabetical order, by product name.

Maintenance, updating, and replacement of damaged or missing MSDSs shall be performed by a designated individual in each department whose name and telephone extension will be printed on a label on the MSDS manual's cover. Supervisors shall ensure that employees can immediately obtain the required information in an emergency. A hazardous material inventory should be conducted annually in each department, and the completed inventory is to be delivered to industrial hygiene.

Labels and other Forms of Warning

Manufacturers' "original" labels must include the product name, the identity of the hazardous materials, the manufacturer's name and address, and hazard warnings. The labels on original containers of hazardous materials shall not be removed or defaced.

Hazard Information

All employees who may work with hazardous materials or who may accidentally have contact with hazardous materials in the course of their duties should receive appropriate hazard information under this standard, which includes the exact location of the MSDS manuals(s) for their area.

HAZARD COMMUNICATION PROGRAM

All employees should receive comprehensive hazard communication training and must be informed of the hazards which are unique to his or her job area prior to job assignment. All operations where hazardous materials are present shall be described. Employee should be informed of and must review the contents of the MSDSs applicable to their area, including the physical and health hazards of any new hazardous material introduced into the work area. Review of the MSDS and labeling associated with a new material shall be conducted. A written record of such training must be maintained.

Work Area Training Program

A foundation course in hazard communication compliance and basic chemical/physical agent safety shall be provided as outlined in the company hazard communication program. Outlines of the work area specific training programs shall be filed with the written hazard communication program in the MSDS master files system. Initial training should be followed by work area specific training. A refresher course for the comprehensive training should be conducted as needed.

Employees should be informed of emergency procedures, specific to the substance, to be followed in case of a spill, leak, release, or process upset, as well as in the proper use of personal protective equipment (PPE) during routine procedures and in the case of emergencies. Proper PPE donning techniques and post-use decontamination and storage shall be demonstrated.

AUDIT OF A HAZARDOUS MATERIAL CONTROL PROGRAM

The audit inspection should include a visit to areas where hazardous materials are stored, used, or manufactured to ensure adherence to the legal requirements and the SMS standard. MSDSs should be freely available, and all containers should be clearly labelled. The correct PPE should be worn by employees working with the substances, and emergency procedures should be in place. Emergency showers and eyewashes should be demarcated and accessible, and a visible record of inspections should be displayed. Consideration should be made for extreme weather conditions that could affect the temperature of the water in the shower and eyewash.

During employee interviews, the effectiveness of the hazard communication training should be tested by questioning the employee concerning their knowledge of hazardous materials (Figure 57.1).

ELEMENT / PROGRAM / PROCESS	POINTS	QUESTIONS THAT COULD BE ASKED	VERIFICATION	WHAT TO LOOK FOR
HAZARDOUS MATERIAL CONTROL PROGRAM				
ALPHABETICAL LIST OF ALL SUBSTANCES				
Hazardous substance risk analysis been conducted	5	Has the company compiled an alphabetical list of all chemical substances on the premises?	Check the list for those noted during physical inspection	Identify the storage and types of substances and make a note of one or more and follow through the system
Alphabetical list of all substances including products and by-products of the manufacturing process	5	Is the alphabetical list up-to-date?		Are substances labeled?
Products/substances clearly labeled as per the list	5	Are all containers correctly labeled?		Storage of chemicals in unlabeled bottles.
RISK ASSESSMENT				
Hazardous substance risk analysis conducted based on an alphabetical list of all substances including products and by-products of the manufacturing process	5	Has the company compiled an alphabetical list of all chemical substances on the premises?	Check the list for those noted during physical inspection	Identify the storage and types of substances and make a note of one or more
PERSON DESIGNATED TO CONTROL THE LIST				
Has a person been appointed to control all hazardous substances?	5	Has a person been appointed to co-ordinate the list?	Appointment of co-coordinator with duties defined	
MATERIAL SAFETY DATA SHEETS MSDSs AVAILABLE AND USED IN DEPARTMENT BY EMPLOYEES, BUYER AND FIRST-AIDER		Are MSDS available in all users departments, buying office, clinic or first-aid posts and stores?		
		Are MSDS available?		
Are MSDS in a uniform, easily readable format?	5	Have the buyers received copies of these sheets?	Do a random check on the MSDS for e.g. first-aid treatment, alphabetical order, etc.	During the inspection ensure that the MSDS are available to the first-aiders, user departments and buyers
HAZARD COMMUNICATION PROGRAM			Check for MSDS in departments	
Training provided	5	Has the regulatory training been provided? (HazCom)	Attendance registers	
Employees and contractors warned of hazards	5	How is this done?	Call for an example	
TOTAL	**45**			

FIGURE 57.1   Audit Protocol for the Element – Hazardous Material Control.

58 Scaffold Safety Program

DESIGN OF A SCAFFOLD SAFETY PROGRAM

The design of a scaffold safety program would include:

- Setting a health and safety management system (SMS) standard for scaffolds and their use
- Purchasing scaffolding structures
- Appointment of persons responsible for the erection and inspection of scaffolds
- Appointment of an approved scaffold erection contractor
- Training in the safe use of scaffolding
- Inspection schedules and criteria

IMPLEMENTATION OF A SCAFFOLD SAFETY PROGRAM

SCAFFOLDING STRUCTURES AND ACCESS PLATFORM

- Every scaffold and every part thereof should be of good construction; of suitable sound material which complies with the requirements of local safety regulations or applicable international standards; properly maintained; and of adequate strength for the purpose which it is used.
- Sited, where practicable, on adequate foundations capable of carrying and disposing the load imposed to carry the whole weight of the scaffold. The foundations shall also be adequate to support the scaffold when fully loaded. They should be erected, added to, altered or dismantled only by a suitably competent person or an approved scaffold contactor.
- Inspected every seven days by a competent person, who should record the details on a waterproof tag attached to the scaffold structure at every access point. The tag should state the date of erection, the duration the scaffold will be in place, and the name and contact number of the person responsible. Where any part of the scaffolding or access platform is incomplete or does not comply with company requirements, then access to that part shall as far as is practicable be prevented by a "Do Not Use" sign and a physical barrier.

WORKING PLATFORMS

Working platforms from which a person is likely to fall a distance of 6 ft (2 m) or more should be:

- Closely boarded and at least 2 ft 3 in (720 mm) wide if used as a footing only
- Provided with guardrails to a height of at least 3 ft (910 mm) above the platform or any elevated working place, and with toe boards at least 6 in

(150 mm) high. The distance between the lowest rail and the toe board shall not exceed 18 in (470 mm)

- Constructed so that the space between the edges of the platform and any building or structure be as small as practicable and in no case exceed 13 in (330 mm)
- Kept free of unnecessary obstructions, materials, and rubbish with a clear access way to the ladder maintained at all times

Working Platform Boards (Decking)

Scaffolding boards should be of the same length with all boards of the same thickness, and as a minimum they should be five boards or 3 ft 3 in (1 m) wide, where practicable, when used for workers and materials. Boards should overhang the scaffold structure by a minimum of four times their thickness and never less than 2 in (50 mm), and they should be secured to prevent movement by use of toe boards or fixings.

The gaps between the boards should be as small as is practicable. No gaps should have dimensions exceeding 2 in (50 mm). Holes covered by loose boards are not acceptable, and each board shall have sufficient supports to prevent undue sagging; precautions shall also be taken to hold down decking in high winds.

Toe Boards

Toe boards should be suitably fixed to working platforms where a person may fall more than 6 ft 6 in (2 m) and mounted at a height so that the gap between the top of the toe board and guard rail does not exceed 2 ft 5 in (750 mm). Wherever possible, toe boards should be attached to standards and should not cross access or egress points on the working scaffold.

Guard Rails

Guardrails should be fitted to working platforms where a person may fall more than 6 ft 6 in (2 m) and an end guard rail fixed inside the standards at a height of between 3 ft (910 mm) and 3 ft 7 in (1150 mm) above the decking, and not have an unprotected gap exceeding 1 ft 6 in (0.5 m) between any guard rail, toe board, barrier, or other similar means of protection.

ACCESS TO SCAFFOLDS

Every ladder used for access or as part of a scaffold should be properly secured or lashed (using proprietary clamping devices or good quality rope) to prevent slipping or sliding at the top or bottom and should rest on a secure, stable base. Ladders should not rest against or secured to any fragile surface or fittings such as gutters or drainpipes and extend at least 3 ft 6 in (1.150 m) above any landing or working point unless another handhold is provided. Ladders should not be used if the landing place or working point is more than 30 ft (9 m) above ground level unless an intermediate landing or platform is provided. The maximum rise of any one ladder should not exceed 20 ft (6.1 m).

Scaffold access ladders should be placed at an angle of 75 degrees (4:1 rule) out and rest on firm, even ground. They should be taken out of service if found to be defective or damaged and clearly marked "Do Not Use" until repaired or, if repair is not practical, destroyed.

SAFETY NETS

Where it is impractical to barrier the area off beneath scaffolding where employees are working, then the scaffold structure shall be fitted with a safety net projecting 3 ft 3 in (1 m) each side of the structure to prevent potential injuries from falling objects or tools.

AUDIT OF A SCAFFOLD SAFETY PROGRAM

The audit of a scaffold safety program should include a review of the scaffold standards and checklists. The standard should include the name of the persons or the contractor authorized to erect and inspect scaffolding, as well as the scaffold training program. A physical inspection of an erected scaffold will give the auditors an opportunity to compare actual scaffold standards with the written standards (Figure 58.1).

ELEMENT/PROGRAM/PROCESS	POINTS	QUESTIONS THAT COULD BE ASKED	VERIFICATION	WHAT TO LOOK FOR
SCAFFOLD SAFETY PROGRAM				
RISK ASSESSMENT				
Risk assessment to determine scaffold need and type	5	Has an assessment been done to ascertain what type of scaffolding is required?	List of types of scaffolding used and when	Inspection to check state of scaffold
Erectors.	5	Who erects the scaffold? Training and qualifications	Appointment of a scaffolding contractor or internal staff	Check requirements are fulfilled by onsite inspection
SCAFFOLDING STANDARD				
Standard written or legal standard	5	Is there a standard/ Are the legal requirement followed?	Copy of standard and legal requirements	
Responsible persons assigned	5	Has responsibility been assigned?	Appointment/training	
SCAFFOLD INSPECTIONS				
Inspection against the standard	5	How often, and who inspects erected scaffolds?	Copy of completed checklists	
LEGAL REQUIREMENTS				
Legal requirements met	5	Are the legal requirements for scaffolds followed?	Visual	
Training	5	Training for erectors, users and contractors?	Training program	
TOTAL	**35**			

FIGURE 58.1   Audit Protocol for the Element – Scaffold Safety Program.

59 Respiratory Protection Program

DESIGN OF A RESPIRATORY PROTECTION PROGRAM

Where applicable, an organization should administer a continuing, effective respiratory protection program and establish controls for the safe and effective use of respiratory protection devices for potentially hazardous occupations and tasks. This would ensure that employees do not experience occupationally related respiratory damage or disease. It should further establish medical surveillance requirements for the use of respiratory protection devices, as well as procurement standards for these devices and appropriate training programs.

ENGINEERING CONTROLS

The control of respiratory hazards should be accomplished as far as feasible through the implementation of accepted engineering control measures. Whenever engineering controls and/or substitution are deemed to be not feasible, or while they are being implemented, appropriate respiratory protection should be used.

QUALITY SPECIFICATIONS

Respiratory protection devices (RPDs) used should be certified by an international authorizing body such as British Standards Institute (BSI), the National Institute of Occupational Safety and Health (NIOSH), the Mine Safety and Health Agency (MSHA), or similar approval body.

RESPIRATORY PROTECTION PROGRAM

A risk assessment should be performed and work areas evaluated for potential respiratory hazards. Respirators should be provided when such equipment is necessary to protect the health of the employee, as determined by industrial hygiene air quality risk assessments. Employees who meet the following criteria should participate in the company respiratory protection program:

- Employees who wear or may wear a respirator
- Employees who supervise personnel who wear respirators
- Emergency response personnel
- Wearers of SCBA (self-contained breathing apparatus) sets

IMPLEMENTATION OF A RESPIRATORY PROTECTION PROGRAM

RPDs should be worn by personnel located within specified areas and operations where respiratory hazard exposure levels fluctuate significantly or where high worker mobility exists. These areas should be evaluated and designated individually by the industrial hygienist. RPDs shall not be physically modified, and RPD users shall remain clean-shaven on a daily basis.

HIGH HAZARD PARTICULATES

Respirators used to protect against high hazard particulates (i.e. dust, NO2, SO2, HF-AlF3) and VOCs (volatile organic compounds) which include carcinogenic PAHs (polycyclic aromatic hydrocarbons) should use respirator filters appropriate to the risk. Abrasive blasting operations should use airline respirators. SCBA respirators should be used for emergency response, firefighting, and rescue operations.

MEDICAL SURVEILLANCE

Employees should not be assigned to wear RPDs unless it has been medically determined that they are physically able to perform the work and wear RPDs and have been test fitted with the correct RPD.

INSPECTION AND MAINTENANCE OF RESPIRATORS

Respirators should be inspected prior to each use by the wearer. Emergency response respirators should be inspected for functionality on a monthly basis, and they should be cleaned after each use or should receive a complete system cleaning on an annual basis. Respirators should be maintained and repaired using only the manufacturer's approved parts and components. Emergency response respirators should receive an annual maintenance service.

STORAGE OF RESPIRATORS

Respirators should be stored in a clean location away from excess heat or moisture in either plastic bags or belt pouches designed for the class of respirator. Emergency response respirators should be stored within a dedicated housing unit specific for the class of respirator.

TRAINING AND INFORMATION

Employees who wear, or may wear, a respirator and who are, or may be, exposed to a respiratory hazard(s) and who may perform emergency response should receive respiratory protection training in the following:

- The basic selection criteria for RPDs
- The capabilities and limitations of each category of respiratory protection
- Instructions on determining failure of RPDs

- Training in the use of disposable respirators
- Access to information concerning RPDs

Information provided in the training program should be updated at least annually to reflect any changes in the equipment or processes.

RESPONSIBILITIES AND ACCOUNTABILITY

PURCHASING DEPARTMENT

The purchasing department should ensure that purchases of new respiratory protection equipment are from the approved equipment list as compiled by the PPE (personal protective equipment) selection committee in conjunction with the industrial hygienist, and that adequate supplies of the approved RPDs, parts, and replacement components are maintained in stock.

MANAGERS, SUPERVISORS, AND CONTRACTORS (RESPONSIBLE PERSONS)

The responsible persons should ensure that new equipment, plant designs, and purchases include an occupational health review for potential respiratory hazards. They should ensure and enforce the use of approved RPDs in designated respirator required areas. They should make sure that adequate supplies of approved RPDs are available for employees. They must further ensure that employees who work in designated respirator required areas participate in the company respiratory protection program.

EMPLOYEES

Employees should use approved RPDs in accordance with training and instructions, and should wear RPDs continuously when in a respirator-required area or when performing operations or tasks that pose a respiratory hazard. They should report changes in equipment, operations, or tasks that may result in a respiratory hazard, and should not modify respirators or fabricate devices, which defeat the operation and effectiveness of hazard controls.

AUDIT OF A RESPIRATORY PROTECTION PROGRAM

The audit criteria for this element are as follows:

- Has a respiratory hazard risk assessment been done?
- Have areas and tasks been designated for RPD use?
- Have employees who participate in the program been medically examined and fit tested?
- Have they received training in RPDs?

An inspection of work areas where RPDs are required to be worn will indicate conformance to this standard, and a review of the risk assessment, training, and medical records will indicate if the standard is being followed. The same criteria should be applied to contractors on site (Figure 59.1).

ELEMENT/PROGRAM/PROCESS	POINTS	QUESTIONS THAT COULD BE ASKED	VERIFICATION	WHAT TO LOOK FOR
RESPIRATORY PROTECTION PROGRAM				
RISK ASSESSMENT				
Areas and tasks defined	5	Have all situations been identified where RPDs are required?	Is there a list of these areas and the types of RPDs required?	During the inspection, look for areas where mists, sprays, fumes, gases, etc. are generated and ascertain whether RPDs should be worn
Standard available.	5	Is there an SMS standard for this element?	Company standard	
EMPLOYEES IDENTIFIED				
Medical examinations	5	Are all in the RPD program been medically examined?	Proof of medical examinations	
Fit testing	5	Have these employees all been fit tested for RPDs?	Example of fit test records	
TRAINING PROGRAM				
Employees trained in RPD use	5	What RPD training do these employees receive? How often?	Copy of training program	Signs erected?
STORAGE AND MAINTENANCE				
Correct storage	5	Are RPD stored correctly? Are regular checks carried out by supervisors?		
Correct maintenance	5	What is the maintenance program?		
SCBA SETS				
Used, storage, training	5	Are SCBA sets required?	Areas or tasks where required, proof of training and maintenance	Visual
TOTAL	**40**			

FIGURE 59.1 Audit Protocol for the Element – Respiratory Protection Program.

60 Energy Control Program

DESIGN OF AN ENERGY CONTROL PROGRAM

OBJECTIVE

Energy sources including electrical, mechanical, hydraulic, pneumatic, chemical, thermal, stored, or other sources of energy in machines and equipment can be hazardous to workers. During the servicing and maintenance of machines and equipment, the unexpected startup or release of stored energy can result in serious injury or death to workers.

The objective of this health and safety management system (SMS) element is to ensure the safety of personnel working on equipment in the workplace and other work areas by defining how isolations should be made and secured so as to protect persons from the risks associated with unexpected releases of energy sources.

The purpose of an effective lockout, tag-out procedure is to fully isolate an energy source by:

- Identifying the energy source
- Isolating the energy source
- Locking and tagging the energy source
- Proving that the equipment isolation is effective

DEFINITIONS

Equipment is mechanically or hydraulically operated machines, electrical equipment, or any other source of stored energy, such as pipelines or vessels, which contain hazardous material. Generally, all machinery, equipment, and controls that are operated, maintained, or serviced by employees should be covered by an energy control procedure.

An *energy source* is any source of electrical, mechanical, hydraulic, pneumatic, chemical, thermal, stored, or any other energy.

An *authorized person* is someone with sufficient theoretical knowledge and practical experience who, to the satisfaction of his or her manager, understands how to effectively isolate and lock out energy sources through the application of the energy control procedure.

A *lockout device* is a device that utilizes a positive physical means to hold an energy-isolating device in the safe position. The device prevents the energizing of the equipment, and cannot easily be removed unintentionally. Included are blind flanges and bolted slip blinds.

A *personal lock* is a nontransferable lock issued to an employee and which is permanently stamped with his, or her company number, or name. Additional locks issued (sometimes called *group* locks) should be of the same approved type, and must be identified and controlled by the site engineer or site manager.

Lockout point(s) are points identified on equipment that prevent operation, release, or energizing of equipment when a lockout device(s) is affixed.

A *lockout tag* is a prominent warning device and a means of attachment, which can be securely fastened to an energy isolating device in accordance with the established energy control procedure to indicate that the energy isolating device, and the equipment being controlled, may not be operated until the tag is removed. A tag shall always require a lockout device.

Tryout is the physical operation of all control devices after the lockout tag-out has been performed to ensure that all energy sources have been isolated and stored energy released (where appropriate). In electrical circuits, it shall include checking each phase-to-earth (ground) and each phase-to-phase.

IMPLEMENTATION OF AN ENERGY CONTROL PROGRAM

APPLICATION OF THE LOCKOUT AND TAG-OUT PROGRAM

All sources of energy that endanger the safety of persons working on or in equipment should be isolated, secured with a locking device, and tagged before work is done on or in that equipment. Where practical, engineering staff should ensure that all relevant equipment isolation points are clearly identified and adequately labeled. Individual diagrams or drawings should be made available to show relevant isolation points for each item of equipment. Reference to relevant equipment isolation points shall be included on preventative maintenance or shutdown schedules.

Each authorized person should be issued with locks and identification tags. The lock should be attached to a lockout point and the tag attached to the lock. Both lock and tag should remain in place until the job is completed. The authorized person is responsible for testing the effectiveness of isolation and tryout before allowing work to commence on locked out equipment. Multi-lockout devices must be used where more than one person is working on equipment to be locked out.

Prior to commencing work, each person who is to work on the job should satisfy him- or herself that all necessary isolations have been made and should check that the work area is safe. Where a single isolation provides safe working conditions for more than one job, then that isolation should be secured by a multi-lockout device, and each job or person, dependent on the isolation, should have his or her own personal lock and tag fitted to the multi-lockout device. Only when all of the work is complete will the locks be removed.

RESPONSIBILITIES

Site managers should:

- Ensure that employees involved in applying this procedure are familiar with the requirements
- Ensure that authorized persons are validated to ensure the requirements of this procedure are met

- Together with relevant manager(s) and engineers, review and update this procedure, as and when required
- Conduct random inspections to ensure compliance with this procedure
- Ensure isolation points are reviewed frequently with respect to adequacy and labeling
- Ensure drawings and diagrams are available which detail relevant isolation points for equipment
- Ensure all requirements of this procedure are complied with, and the effectiveness of all isolations is tested prior to allowing work to commence
- Where it is found that the source of energy cannot be physically locked out, report the situation to his or her immediate superior so that action can be taken and a device be fitted

AUDIT OF AN ENERGY CONTROL PROGRAM

During the audit inspection, the auditors should follow the energy control program through the system. Where possible, an energy isolation in progress should be inspected to see if the standard is being applied. Lockout sources, locks, and tags should be checked as well as the labeling accuracy of the isolation point. Authorized persons should receive training in isolation procedures, and where a permit is required, this should be posted at the isolation point. Locks must accompany lockout tags, and tags should not be used on their own as substitutes for lockout. Lockout tags should be correctly filled in with the employee's name, the date, and the reason for the isolation (Figure 60.1).

ELEMENT/PROGRAM/PROCESS	POINTS	QUESTIONS THAT COULD BE ASKED	VERIFICATION	WHAT TO LOOK FOR
ENERGY CONTROL PROGRAM				
Energy sources identified by risk assessment.	5	If other sources of energy, gravity, steam, air, chemical exist, is there a lock-out procedure? Was this determined by a risk assessment?	list of energy sources that must be locked. Lock out risk assessment report	Visual. Lockout stations available? Locks and tags being used
WRITTEN PROCEDURE AVAILABLE AND APPLIED				
Procedure available and updated	5	Is an energy control procedure available? ? Is the procedure valid? Is the procedure clear? When last was it updated?	Copy of the procedure	Are the standards being applied in the workplace?
LOCKOUT TAG-OUT TRY OUT				
Task specific procedures available?	5	Is there a written lock-out procedure for all energy sources. Is a lock required in conjunction with a tag – always?	Call for the procedure and check that it covers not only electricity but also pipelines, steam driven equipment and air equipment, and all sources of energy if applicable	Are the applicable work crews aware of the procedure? There MUST be a LOCK and a TAG always
Locks and tags used. Hardware meet the standard?	5	What hardware is used and available?	Lockout stations locations or personal locks	
Field activities match policy and procedure	5	Is lock out application in the field ever inspected by supervision?	Inspection reports. Permits issues if applicable	
Energy control training	5	Are all affected staff trained?	Proof of training. Training plan	
Tags and locks used correctly?	5	Are the locks identified or the user identified?		During the inspection the system should be tested by endeavoring to find maintenance crews at work and checking to see whether or not the energysourcehas been locked out
ALL SOURCES OF ENERGY CAN BE ISOLATED AND LOCKED				
Points of control identified and labelled.	5	How are these identified?	Visual.	Can all high voltage and low voltage circuits and critical valves, taps, andsources of stored energybe locked out? Do they have a lock out box with various attachments? Do a random test of any energy source and ask the same question during the inspection
Locks used in conjunction with tags	5	Are locks always used with tags. What information must be on the tag?	The ideal is for the source to be lockable at the point of control / operation. The minimum to strive for is that all equipment can be individually isolated and locked at some point in the energy circuit to render it inoperative	
MAIN SWITCH ACCESSIBLE				
Main switches accessible even when circuits are locked out?	5		Visual	If the doors to the distribution board are locked, can one still get access to the main switch?
TOTAL	50			

FIGURE 60.1 Audit Protocol for the Element – Energy Control Systems.

61 Machine Guarding Program

DESIGN OF A MACHINE GUARDING PROGRAM

INTRODUCTION

Unguarded or inadequately guarded machines cause a high percent of injuries which are normally serious, and many of them are permanent. Unguarded machines are also responsible for a number of accidental deaths each year.

It is often asked, "How do we know if the machine is sufficiently guarded?" A rule of thumb is that if a person should stumble and fall with outstretched hands, could they be injured in a machine or unguarded pinch point? Machine guards should be fitted wherever rotating or operating machinery is within normal reach.

DEFINITIONS

A *machine guard* is a device that prevents limbs and other body parts from contacting the dangerous moving parts of machinery.

Guarding means effectively preventing people from coming into contact with the moving parts of machinery or equipment that could injure them.

Enclosing means guarding by means of physical barriers which are mounted on a machine in an effort to prevent access to the hazardous parts.

Fencing means erecting a fence or rail which restricts access to a machine.

CLASSES OF MACHINE GUARDS

There are two basic classes of machine guards: transmission and point-of-operation guards. *Transmission guards* are guards which guard all mechanical components including gears, cams, shafts, pulleys, belts, and rods that transmit energy and motion from a source of power to a point of operation. *Point-of-operation guards* effectively shield the area on a machine where the material is positioned for processing and where an exchange of energy takes place.

TYPES OF MACHINE GUARDS

There are four main types of machine guards: fixed guards, interlocking guards, automatic guards, and point-of-operation guards.

A *fixed guard* is preferable and should be used in all cases where possible. It prevents access to the danger areas at all times and is normally a part of the machine.

Interlocking guards are either mechanical, electrical, or pneumatic and prevent the operation of the controls that set the machine in motion until the guard is in position. Removing or opening the guard locks the starting mechanism, and the machine cannot be operated. An interlocking guard must guard the nip point before the machine can be operated. It should stay closed until the dangerous part is at rest, and it should prevent the operation of the machine if the interlocking device fails.

An *automatic guard* functions independently of the operator, and its action is repeated as long as the machine is in operation. Automatic guards are fitted where neither a fixed nor interlocking guard is practical. Examples of automatic guards are two-handed push buttons, pull back devices, and photoelectric devices.

Point-of-operation guards prevent access to the nip or shear point. Point-of-operation guards are used extensively on guillotines, punch presses, and similar machines.

WHAT SHOULD BE GUARDED?

Things that must be guarded would include washing machines, projecting shaft ends, transmission belts, band saws and band knives, plaining machinery, woodworking machinery, rolls and calendars, or any moving, rotating, or vibrating part of any machine that could injure a person.

IMPLEMENTATION OF A MACHINE GUARDING PROGRAM

Here is an example of an SMS standard for the implementation of a machine guarding program:

APPLICATION

The following machine guarding standards and procedures will apply to all company (and affiliate companies) workplaces and sites and include all areas, equipment, and machinery within the company. This standard also applies to contractors and their employees.

OBJECTIVE

The objective of this program is to create standards and uniformity for machine guarding and to ensure that machinery is guarded in such a way that it provides operators and other employees protection from machine hazards such as those created by point-of-operation, in-running nip points, rotating parts, flying chips, and sparks.

RESPONSIBILITY AND ACCOUNTABILITY

In line with the single point safety accountabilities, the following applies:

- The engineering department must ensure that adequate machine guards are specified and fitted according to this standard for all new projects, design, modifications, and alteration work.

- The purchasing department are to ensure that equipment purchased or hired or replaced conforms to this machine guarding standard.
- Managers/supervisors/contractors (Responsible persons) are accountable for the education and training of their employees in this standard.
- Maintenance personnel are responsible for providing adequate machine guarding and for maintaining these in good condition.
- All employees are responsible for ensuring all guards are secured in place before operating machinery, equipment, or tools.
- Responsible persons, safety engineers, safety coordinators, and health and safety representatives are responsible for monthly inspections of machine guards and for recommending corrective actions.
- Responsible persons are responsible for ensuring that corrective actions are taken in providing and maintaining adequate machine guarding.
- Responsible persons who are responsible for the supply/installation/design/ specification of new/rented/modified plant, machinery, and equipment are responsible for ensuring that the plant, machinery, and equipment is guarded in line with this standard, legal requirements, and other company standards.

INSPECTIONS

Supervisors should ensure that monthly inspections are carried out in each area to inspect the condition of machine guarding. They should raise a work order to correct deviations to ensure appropriate guarding and prioritize the work request on the basis of the nature and extent of the risk of the hazard (Figure 61.1).

Point-of-operation guards should prevent entry of hands or fingers into the point of operation from reaching through, over, under, or around the guard. Guards should be constructed and maintained to withstand the vibration, shock, and wear to which they will be subjected during normal operations and not create a hazard by their use.

MACHINE GUARDING CHECKLIST	YES	NO
Are all machines that cannot be properly guarded, enclosed?		
Are all nip points guarded? (areas that could injure, crush, amputate or otherwise harm persons)		
Are all conveyor-rotating parts guarded?		
Are all V-drives and chain-drives guarded?		
Are all shaft ends and key ways guarded?		
Are all rotating or oscillating levers, cams, gears or shafts guarded?		
Are guards easily removable and just as easy to put back into position?		
Are guards robust and made of the correct material?		
Are moving parts within normal reach enclosed?		
Are heated / chilled structures and plant suitably barricaded?		

FIGURE 61.1 Machine Guarding Checklist.

Guards should be secured in place while machinery is operational, except when test-ing or making adjustments which cannot be performed without removal of the guard.

Testing or making adjustments while machines are operating should only be car-ried out by a competent person (a person qualified and authorized by his senior to do this task) or by following a Job Safe Practice (JSP) or work permit approved by a supervisor.

Moving Machine Parts

Moving machine parts should be guarded to protect persons from contacting gears, sprockets, chains, drives, heads, tails, and take-up pulleys, flywheels, couplings, shafts, fan blades, and other similar moving parts that can cause injury. Guards shall be required where the exposed moving parts are less than 6 ft (2 m) above a floor, platform, or catwalk.

Quality Specifications

All moving and rotating machinery guarding will provide maximum protection and remain in compliance with this standard as well as with legislation.

AUDIT OF A MACHINE GUARDING PROGRAM

A physical inspection of a random sample of guarded machines or items must be carried out to ascertain how efficient the guarding or barricading is. Interlocks on microwave ovens, paper guillotines, and washing or drying machines should be included under this element. The bypassing of guards should also be identified where covers are left open or guards have not been replaced. Guards should be closely scru-tinized to ensure that access to the danger area is fully blocked and that the guard conforms to the written standard for machine guarding (Figure 61.2).

ELEMENT/PROGRAM/PROCESS	POINTS	QUESTIONS THAT COULD BE ASKED	VERIFICATION	WHAT TO LOOK FOR
MACHINE GUARDING PROGRAM				
MACHINE GUARDING STANDARD				
Machine guarding standard available	5	Is a standard available?	Copy of the standard	
MACHINE GUARDING RISK ASSESSMENT				
Risk assessment done	5	Has a guarding risk assessment been done?	Copy of the risk assessment	
MACHINES AND HAZARDS GUARDED				
All nip-point/access points guarded	5	How often are machine guarding inspections done?	Inspection schedule	
Machines/electrical parts/conductors/panels enclosed	5		Visual	Auditors to check at least 5 machine guards to determine if the standard is being applied
Conveyors and switchgear guarded	5		Visual	
V-drives and chain drives/bus bars guarded	5		Visual	
Shaft ends and keyways guarded	5		Visual	
All rotating or oscillating levers, cams, gears or shafts guarded	5		Visual	
Guards/panel cover plates easily removed for maintenance	5		Visual	
Moving or energized parts within normal reach guarded	5		Visual	
Guards a part of the health and safety representative check list	5	Is guarding on the checklist?	Completed checklist	
Machines/electrical parts/conductors/panels that cannot be guarded, enclosed	5		Visual	
All nip points/access points guarded	5		Visual	
TOTAL	65			

FIGURE 61.2 Audit Protocol for the Element – Machine Guarding Program.

62 Motorized Equipment Safety Program

DESIGN OF A MOTORIZED EQUIPMENT SAFETY PROGRAM

Motorized equipment considered in this health and safety management system (SMS) element includes all self-propelled vehicles such as cars, pickups, forklift trucks, mobile cranes, and golf carts. Risks associated with motorized equipment should be identified, assessed, and managed as part of the SMS. This is a high risk area in most industries and mines, and consideration should be given to the type of motorized equipment in use, the training of drivers, the use of the equipment, checking of the vehicles, and general operating rules applicable to the type of equipment.

A basic motorized equipment safety program would cover at least the following aspects:

- Responsibility and accountability
- Training and driver authorization
- General rules
- Reporting of accidents
- Seat-belt use
- Driving of equipment
- Vehicle parking
- Reversing rules
- Loading and transporting materials
- Truck and trailer rules
- "How's my driving" campaign
- Forklift truck safety

IMPLEMENTATION OF A MOTORIZED EQUIPMENT SAFETY PROGRAM

RESPONSIBILITY AND ACCOUNTABILITY

Each area manager, supervisor, and contractor (Responsible person) should be responsible for the application of this standard in their work area and should be accountable for compliance to this standard. The transportation sector will be responsible for ensuring that all new vehicles purchased or leased meet minimum safety requirements, as well as for providing for the planned preventive maintenance of all vehicles.

TRAINING AND AUTHORIZATION

All drivers (including contractors) of company vehicles should be trained and tested and issued with a company driving license prior to operating any motorized equipment. A formal syllabus should be followed, tests written, and each operator issued with a company internal driving license for the specific category of vehicle or equipment that they may operate. Each operator is required to carry their license card whilst operating the vehicle or equipment. The operator's immediate superior shall nominate his or her employees to attend a defensive driving course once every three years. The official country or state driver's license of all company drivers who are driving company vehicles on public roads will be checked on an annual basis to ensure that they are valid.

CHECKLISTS

All motorized equipment should be inspected by the operator by completing an equipment specific checklist prior to start-up at the beginning of each shift. Deviations identified during the inspections are to be attended to as soon as possible. The manager in control of any motorized equipment may identify critical items for pre-start-up inspections which can be classified as "no-go" items. An operator shall not start a vehicle where a "no-go" item has been identified until the item has been repaired and a competent person has declared the vehicle fit for use and recorded so on the checklist. The direct supervisor should perform random checks on operators to ensure that the inspections are done correctly and that the checklists are being used.

HOUSEKEEPING

The operator of a vehicle is responsible for the housekeeping and cleanliness of the vehicle or equipment whilst it is under his or her control. This applies to the load area as well as the cabin. The driver is also responsible for ensuring that any load is secure and that any valves or hatches on the vehicle are closed and secure prior to departure.

USE OF SEAT BELTS

All operators and drivers (including contractors and visitors) must observe the rules of the road on site and off site. Any road marking or sign used on site will have the same meaning as the official country or state traffic law and will be considered as site safety rules. Seat belts will be used at all times by persons travelling in company vehicles. The general rule is that if there is a seat belt provided, it should be worn.

GENERAL RULES APPLICABLE TO ALL

Each employee should familiarize themselves with and obey traffic regulation and rules applied in the country or state. No employee shall operate or drive any of the company vehicle or equipment unless he or she holds a valid driving license for the category of respective vehicle or equipment, and he or she must be fully aware of the vehicle or equipment's proper operation.

Each vehicle or item of equipment must be in safe operating condition, and the respective employee should immediately inform and report in writing if the vehicle or equipment is deemed unsafe.

REPORTING OF ACCIDENTS

On occurrence of any accident involving motorized equipment, the operator should not discuss responsibility for the accident nor offer any form of settlement, but should report the accident to their immediate supervisor as soon as possible.

INSPECTION OF VEHICLES AND EQUIPMENT

Vehicle operators should monitor when the vehicle is due for maintenance by referring to the maintenance date tag or sticker in the vehicle. Vehicles should be inspected before use and at the beginning of every shift using the appropriate checklist.

HOW'S MY DRIVING CAMPAIGN

Many organizations maintain a "How's my driving" campaign. Vehicles have a phone number displayed on the rear of the vehicle for other road users to phone in comments, complaints, or suggestions concerning the vehicle's behavior on the road. Daily feedback is given to supervisors, which is then discussed with the drivers at the morning meeting at the beginning of the shift.

The system allows for the other road users to monitor the driver's performance, and this creates a constant awareness within the driver that he or she is been monitored. The phone number displayed on the vehicle should be large enough to allow it to be read at a safe distance. Many numbers are so small that it would be hazardous to read them, as one would have to be too close to the vehicle. This defeats the objective of this safety initiative.

FORKLIFT TRUCKS SAFETY PROGRAM

A basic safety program for forklift truck safety could include the following:

Step 1 – Understand the risk.
Forklift truck operators should understand the risks associated with forklift trucks. There are more than one million forklifts operating in the United States alone, and each year there are some 100,000 accidents involving forklift trucks.
Step 2 – Know the classes of forklift trucks
There are many different types of forklift trucks, and operators should understand the different types and specific safety rules applicable to different types.
Step 3 – Understand the hazards.
The hazards associated with for lift truck operation should be recognized. Some of the most common hazards are insecure and/or unbalanced loads, excessive speed, inexperienced operators, and employees riding on the forks.

Step 4 – Basic requirements.

The first requirement is that forklift truck drivers must be taught how to operate the equipment in accordance with Occupational Safety and Health Administration (OSHA) (or similar local) requirements. The employer must then certify the operators and ensure that periodic practical and theoretical training is ongoing. A formal training program should be in place to facilitate this. Driver performance should also be evaluated periodically.

Step 5 – Know what to watch for.

A daily check of each vehicle must be done before usage to check the brakes, horn, tires, oil, and any leaks. The work area is also checked for uneven surfaces and obstructions.

Step 6 – Basic safety rules.

- Seat belts must always be worn where provided
- The load must be correctly balanced
- The driver is to look in the direction of travel
- The load must be kept as low as possible
- The driver is to use the horn at intersections
- The driver is to keep away from areas where forklift trucks are not allowed

Step 7 – Demarcate walkways.

Walkways, aisles, and passageways should be clearly demarcated on the workplace floor. Normally this is done by means of yellow stripes laid down to mark the safe passage of employees, vehicles, and other items. Pedestrian walkways will ensure safe passageways away from forklift truck and other vehicle movements. Correct signage should also be displayed.

Step 8 – Vehicle visibility.

Forklift trucks and other heavy motorized equipment should have an orange flashing light mounted on the roof, which operates when the truck is in operation. This will give workers in the vicinity a warning of its presence.

AUDIT OF A MOTORIZED EQUIPMENT SAFETY PROGRAM

This element is one of the elements that pose the greatest threat to the safety of the drivers, other road users, and pedestrians, and the risk rating on this element would be high, perhaps (10) on a scale of (1–10).

The training program and internal licensing methods can be verified during the documentation verification session, but to see if there is compliance to the standards, the auditors should conduct an on-site observation of vehicles in action. The vehicle inspection log can then be checked and, with the auditee's permission, the driver questioned about the training program and his or her responsibilities as a driver. Internal licenses should be available with the driver. Random sampling of seat-belt use will give a good indicator of the effectiveness of the vehicle safety program (Figure 62.1).

ELEMENT/PROGRAM/PROCESS	POINTS	QUESTIONS THAT COULD BE ASKED	VERIFICATION	WHAT TO LOOK FOR
MOTORIZED EQUIPMENT SAFETY PROGRAM				
CONDITION OF VEHICLES/EQUIPMENT				
Condition of vehicles	5	What is the standard for the condition of vehicles?	Visual	During the inspection, inspect at least three vehicles or items of motorized equipment. Condition of vehicles/equipment i.e., tires, windows, brakes, lights, reflectors, mechanical operation.
Housekeeping of driving cab/load area.	5			Housekeeping in vehicles. What is the general condition like? Are there broken lights or seats, are the reflectors in order?
CHECKLISTS COMPLETED BY DRIVER/ OPERATOR				
Separate checklists for each type of vehicle/equipment	5	Are separate checklists used for different vehicles such as forklift trucks, utility vehicles	Call for a copy of the check list and correlate	During the inspection, test the driver's knowledge on the use of the checklist
Checklists correctly and regularly filled in by the operator/driver	5	Is a daily checklist completed by the operator?	Copy of a completed checklist	
DRIVER / OPERATOR TRAINING SYLLABUS				
Training syllabus to cover the types of vehicles/equipment used	5	Do drivers of motorized equipment/company vehicles receive specialized training?	Copy of the syllabus	Training records
All drivers/operators undergone training		Copy of training syllabus	Drivers of company cars should have some form of advanced driving license	
APPROPRIATE LICENSING				
Drivers/operators issued with a permit or license to drive the class of vehicles they are authorized to operate	5	For how long is the license valid? For what vehicles is this license issued?	Random check for license/list of authorized drivers. Training records for specialized equipment	
IDENTIFICATION OF DRIVERS				
All drivers/operators identified by some means	5	How are the drivers identified? How simple is it to operate without identification? Must the license be carried at all times?	Identification means	
VALIDITY OF DRIVER'S LICENSES				
Licenses checked within the last 12 months?	5	Is the validity of the license checked every 12 months?	List of license checked by authorities	
SAFETY TRAINING PROGRAM				
Ongoing training program for other drivers and employees in general	5	What about road safety publicity?	Copies of road safety campaign	Is an effort being made to promote general road safety?
TOTAL	50			

FIGURE 62.1 Audit Protocol for the Element – Motorized Equipment Safety Program.

63 Personal Protective Equipment Program

DESIGN OF A PERSONAL PROTECTIVE EQUIPMENT PROGRAM

PRE-CONTRACT, CONTACT, POST-CONTACT CONTROL

In the accident sequence, there are three main areas for control. They are the *pre-contact* stage (before the exchange of energy), the *contact stage* (during the exchange of energy), and the *post-contact* stage, which is after the energy has been exchanged.

Personal protective equipment (PPE) offers some form of control at the *contact* stage, as it reduces, or deflects, the exchange of energy. This helps prevent serious injury. PPE does not, however, prevent the accident. It merely reduces the impact of the contact with a substance or source of energy, thus reducing the consequence.

A safety belt in a motor vehicle does not prevent the accident but helps reduce the severity of injury by preventing the occupants from striking against the steering wheel or dashboard of the vehicle.

Failure to wear PPE is one of the basic high risk acts which lead to accidental injury. Another high risk act is wearing the improper attire or being incorrectly dressed for the job at hand. Injuries could be drastically reduced by correctly identifying, providing, and controlling the use of PPE. PPE is often essential and can be expensive; hence, strict control should be exercised over the selection, issue, usage, maintenance, and replacement thereof.

A PPE PROGRAM

A PPE program has four basic steps:

    Step 1 – Hazard elimination
    Step 2 – Selection and purchase
    Step 3 – Training in the use of PPE
    Step 4 – Monitoring

IMPLEMENTATION OF A PPE PROGRAM

OBJECTIVE

The objective of a personal protective equipment program is to ensure control of the purchase, issue, wearing, maintenance, repair, replacement and disposal of all PPE and personal protective clothing (PPC).

HAZARD ELIMINATION

The first steps in implementing a PPE program would be to identify and eliminate the workplace hazards by elimination, engineering revision, substitution, administrative controls and, as a final resort, the wearing of specific PPE, which includes PPC.

SELECTION AND PURCHASE

Once the remaining hazards have been identified, the next step is the selecting and purchasing of PPE. Dependent on the workplace and nature of the processes, PPE could include numerous items ranging from head protection to toe protection. PPE selection is often done by a committee consisting of different employees who wear PPE and who are in a position to advise on the best equipment to purchase.

TRAINING IN THE USE OF PPE

The third step is the training of employees in the correct use and maintenance of their PPE. A formal training program should be incorporated into the safety orientation program as well as the annual safety refresher training.

MONITORING

Ongoing monitoring should follow the issue of PPE to ensure that workers are wearing the correct PPE and that it is being stored and maintained correctly. The wearing of PPE should be emphasized during 5-minute toolbox talks and at other gatherings.

RESPONSIBILITIES

Employer and Employee

The employer must firstly ensure that the work environment is as safe as possible and that all hazards have been engineered out, enclosed, or protected. Once this is done, he or she must then provide and maintain suitable personal protective equipment for the employees. Employees have a role to play in that they must wear the PPE that has been issued and must not misuse, destroy, or discard any item that is supplied to them.

Managers, Supervisors, and Contractors (Responsible Persons)

Responsible persons are responsible for the issuing, wearing, usage, maintenance, replacement, recycling, and disposal of all PPE in their areas of responsibility, and they should ensure that:

- Adequate supplies of PPE are readily available and are provided for employee use
- They wear corrective PPE whenever they visit a work area or work site and set an example
- Employees attend the annual safety refresher training

- Contractors provide their own PPE
- They obtain the correct PPE for visitors to the company site

Users of PPE

Users of PPE should:

- Adhere to the rules referring to the wearing of PPE
- Acknowledge receipt of PPE issued to them
- Ensure that PPE issued to them is kept in good condition
- Ensure proper storage and timely exchange of equipment.

GENERAL REQUIREMENTS

PPE should be:

- Issued free of charge to employees
- Maintained in a good, clean order
- Stored in such a manner as to prevent equipment damage
- Recycled where possible
- Made readily available for use

A record of issuance of PPE to employees should be maintained, and areas requiring PPE should be clearly signposted.

AUDIT OF A PPE PROGRAM

The organization should have proof of the risk reduction efforts made before PPE was considered. A standard covering the issue, use, and training in the use of PPE should be available. Proof of training should also be available. During the audit inspection, the usage of PPE should be noted as well as the condition and storage of these items. Random checks during the inspection will indicate if employees are wearing PPE or not (Figure 63.1).

ELEMENT/PROGRAM/PROCESS	POINTS	QUESTIONS THAT COULD BE ASKED	VERIFICATION	WHAT TO LOOK FOR
PERSONAL PROTECTIVE EQUIPMENT PROGRAM				
RISKS IDENTIFIED				
Risk reduction efforts	5	What efforts were made to reduce the risks?	Examples	Visual
PPE SELECTION				
Selection criteria	5	How is PPE selected?	Committee, involvement of employees	
TRAINING PROGRAM			Copy of syllabus	
Training in PPE usage	5	Is there a PPE awareness training program?		
PPE USED ON SITE				
PPE is used on site	5	What items of PPE are used on site?		Visual during inspection
Contractors PPE	5	How are contractors managed with respect to PPE?	Contractors rules or similar	
PPE MONITORING				
Monitoring	5	How is the wearing of PPE monitored?	Examples of observations/ checklists	
USED PPE				
PPE recycling	5	Is PPE recycled where possible?	Example of recycle program	
PPE disposal	5	How is PPE disposed of?	PPE exposed to hazardous materials	
TOTAL	40			

FIGURE 63.1   Audit Protocol for the Element – Personal Protective Equipment Program.

64 An Ergonomic Safety Program

DESIGN OF AN ERGONOMIC SAFETY PROGRAM

Ergonomic related injuries include injuries related to lifting, pushing, pulling, holding, carrying, or throwing objects, and they recently accounted for nearly a quarter of all work injuries in the United States. An important step in the prevention of these types of injuries is to implement an ergonomic safety program, which is the science of adjusting the job to fit the body's needs. Ergonomics provides injury prevention solutions that are simple and relatively inexpensive. Some of these solutions include requiring frequent short breaks for workers assigned repetitive motion tasks, providing a manual for mechanical lifting equipment, and varying workers' tasks.

ERGONOMICS EXPLAINED

Ergonomics, or human factor engineering, concerns the interaction between the worker and machine and the work environment. The word ergonomics comes from the Greek words *ergo* meaning work and *nomus* meaning law. Ergonomics has also been called bio-mechanics, biotechnology, biophysics, human engineering, human factors, and engineering psychology. All the terms refer to the correct interaction between the person and their work environment.

ERGONOMICS DEFINED

Ergonomics is the general term used to identify the field of activity aimed at the matching of machines, equipment and the environment to humans in such a way that maximum performance can be achieved. The main goal of ergonomics is to reduce errors and injuries caused by repetitive or awkward motions and the incorrect matching of the worker to the job. Other goals are to improve the efficiency of the worker in the workplace and to reduce work fatigue, which can lead to accidents.

The comfort of the workplace is improved by applying ergonomics, and the reliability of humans as a sensor in the worker–machine cycle is improved. Improving ergonomics helps reduce the need for training as the relationship between the person and their work environment is improved. Applying ergonomics reduces errors and improves safety.

ERGONOMIC INSPECTION AND RISK ASSESSMENT

A specific planned inspection should be carried out using an ergonomic checklist. This inspection will be aimed at inspecting the availability and condition of seating, tables, and worktops as well as investigating the accessibility of tools, sample points, foot holes, platforms, and so on.

The ergonomic checklist should include all work situations and methods of handling materials and will also encompass inspection of gauges, signals and other warning devices that need counteractive action by a sensor. Once completed, the ergonomic risk identified should be assessed and prioritized for action.

IMPLEMENTATION OF AN ERGONOMIC SAFETY PROGRAM

An ergonomic safety program would cover three main areas: anatomy, physiology, and psychology.

ANATOMY

Anatomy is concerned with the dimensions of the human body and its variations, and it also includes bio-mechanics, or the forces which can be applied by the body under different conditions.

PHYSIOLOGY

Physiology includes both work physiology and environmental physiology. Environmental physiology is the effects of the physical environment on the workplace, and work physiology concerns the expenditure of energy.

PSYCHOLOGY

Psychology includes skill psychology and occupational psychology. Skill psychology is concerned with the mental activity of information receiving, information processing, and decision taking. Occupational psychology concerns individual differences, efforts required, and training. Humans interact with machines by reading gauges and controls; they process this information and give the machine further instructions. Psychological aspects of ergonomics include worker satisfaction and the comfort that the person feels in their job.

Anatomical Ergonomics

The first area of ergonomics, anatomy, concerns physical facilities such as seating, height of controls, body posture, and muscular strength and body movement. People have different body sizes and shapes, and ergonomics endeavors to accommodate the average person. The belief is that the work environment should fit people, not that people should fit the environment.

Bio-mechanics is to do with the forces that can be applied by a human body under certain circumstances. The main anatomical considerations in ergonomics are:

- Accessibility of valves, switches, and controls
- Size, shape, and comfort of seats and backrests
- Height and angle of tables and working countertops

An ergonomic checklist for seats would include the following:

- Availability of seats
- Condition of seats
- Height and tilt
- Backrest and lumbar support
- Foot and arm support
- General comfort and adjustment

A checklist for the accessibility of instruments and other equipment would include:

- Valves
- Switches
- Emergency controls
- Sample points
- Foot holes
- Platforms
- Fixed ladders

PHYSIOLOGICAL ERGONOMICS

The second main field of ergonomics is physiology, which concerns itself with the effects of the physical environment on the workplace as well as the expenditure of energy.

Various factors such as lighting, ventilation, and noise affect people in different ways. Ergonomics investigates and identifies the correct temperatures for work areas and also identifies where workers are exposed to vibration and other hazards. Work methods are studies in an effort to help prevent fatigue caused by monotonous tasks, and tasks that are too easy are also examined and modified.

A checklist for the physiological aspects of ergonomics would include the following:

- Machine vibration
- Lighting
- Fumes
- Gases
- Dust
- Noise

For the handling of material, the following factors would be considered:

- Mechanical aids
- Back support
- Reach distance
- Minimum carrying distance
- Use of mechanical loaders, and so on.

Psychological Ergonomics

Humans act as the sensor when they read instruments, check gauges, and react to warning systems. Because of this interaction, gauges must be easy to interpret and should indicate what they represent. Speedometers in motor vehicles move in a clockwise direction as the speed increases. Fuel gauges indicate high when full and low when empty. This interpretation of signals is an important part of ergonomics and ensures that the sensor reads instruments correctly and takes correct action.

The information given must be clear and unmistakable, and therefore the positioning, color, and indication on gauges and controls are important to prevent accidents. One normally expects to open a tap by turning it anti-clockwise and to close it by turning it clockwise. Electrical knobs are normally turned clockwise to increase the current and anti-clockwise to reduce the current.

Switching on a light in some countries means pushing the switch down, whereas in the United States, a switch is pushed up to switch the light on. These are classic example of poor psychological ergonomics.

A checklist for gauges and switches would be as follows:

- Are the gauges properly displayed?
- Is there any glare present?
- Are warning signals distinct and separate for separate messages?
- Do all the similar gauges read the same way?
- Can the dials and gauges be read quickly and accurately?
- Can any changes or differences on a gauge be easily spotted?
- Will the operator know when the gauge is malfunctioning?

AUDIT OF AN ERGONOMIC SAFETY PROGRAM

Auditors should ask the following questions:

- Has an ergonomic study been undertaken of all the workstations and situations throughout the workplace?
- Has the highest ergonomic risk been identified and assessed?
- Have improvements been implemented to make the work situations more worker friendly by changing work methods or providing mechanical aids?
- Are frequent and ongoing inspections carried out using checklists?
- Is there a positive reaction to reported ergonomic related injuries?

The answers to these questions will give the auditor a good idea as to the effectiveness of the program in place (Figure 64.1).

ELEMENT/PROGRAM/PROCESS	POINTS	QUESTIONS THAT COULD BE ASKED	VERIFICATION	WHAT TO LOOK FOR
ERGONOMIC SAFETY PROGRAM				
SURVEY CARRIED OUT USING A CHECKLIST				
Has an ergonomic risk assessment of the entire workplace been conducted?	5	Has a risk assessment been carried out with reference to ergonomics?	Copy of last survey	
Were contractor sites included	5		Copy of checklist	
Are appropriate checklists used?	5	How often is the survey carried out?	Field, office ergonomic surveys	
Were observations made with operators working?	5	Does the checklists cover body positions, seating, accessibility of valves, etc.		
OPERATORS COMFORTABLE				Body posture - seating, comfort, condition, back rests; foot supports, etc. Work stations - height, reach spaces, etc.
Posture	5	Is any manual handling done?		Accessibility - valves, switches, sample points, control levers, footholds, platforms and ladders.
Availability	5	What about disabled employees?	Job cards	During the inspection, were awkward body and working positions noted?
Ergonomic changes	5	What ergonomic changes have been made?	Checklist/report	Are valves, switches and levers easily accessible?
TOTAL	35			

FIGURE 64.1 Audit Protocol for the Element – Ergonomic Safety Program.

65 Electrical Safety Program

DESIGN OF AN ELECTRICAL SAFETY PROGRAM

Electrical safety is a very wide subject and its application will differ from site to site. Only a few basic guidelines are given in this chapter. The National Fire Protection Association (NFPA) 70E® standard focuses on the safety of workers exposed to electrical hazards, including electric shock, arc flash, and arc blast. This reference is an excellent guide to use to establish an electrical safety program.

ELECTRICAL SAFETY PROGRAM POLICIES AND PROCEDURES

An electrical safety program is an important part of the overall company health and safety management system (SMS), and NFPA 70E®'s policies and procedures are already written and available for use. Building upon those standards, the electrical safety program should act as a guideline for how to work safely around electrical parts and equipment.

An electrical safety program should include:

- A hazard identification and risk assessment and evaluation process to be undertaken before workers starting work on, or near, live parts
- Information and self-discipline. The electrical safety management program must provide information and awareness of electrical hazards, along with the required self-discipline so that employees can review the program and know what is required before proceeding with the work.
- Program practices and procedures. The electrical safety program should identify job safe practices (JSPs) for working on or near areas where an electrical hazard exists.
- Task risk assessment. Before the work is started, the supervisor in charge should perform a task risk assessment with the employees who will perform the work. This risk assessment will indicate the hazards associated with the task, any special precautions to be taken, and necessary personal protective equipment (PPE) to be worn.

ENERGIZED WORK PERMIT

In some cases, it is difficult or even impossible to de-energize systems. Life support equipment, ventilation equipment that controls a hazardous location, and emergency alarm systems are examples. In these cases, the organization's standards should include an energized work permit system. The permit should include work rules for the task and should be issued by an authorized issuer.

IMPLEMENTATION OF AN ELECTRICAL SAFETY PROGRAM

The electrical safety program standard should contain the basic rules and procedures to ensure that the electrical installation is safe and that work on or around it is carried out in a prescribed manner.

RULES FOR MAINTAINING A SAFE ELECTRICAL INSTALLATION

- Constantly inspect all aspects of the installation, and if any protruding wires, suspicious joints, broken fittings, or broken conduits are noted, ensure that they are reported. Follow up to see whether action has been taken to make the installation safe.
- Always regard the electrical installation as live (hot) at all times! Test, re-test, and re-check before working on any open wires or parts which could be energized. The correct testing equipment should be used for testing.
- Only authorized people should be allowed to work on fixed electrical installations.
- Any temporary wiring which has become part of the general installation should be removed, and the correct cables or conduits should be installed as necessary.
- The golden rule for working on any electrical equipment within the installation is to lock-out the circuit, test for energy, and tag. (*Tag* implies attaching a hold card or message to the lock indicating who locked out, at what time, and for what purpose.)
- Access to transformer rooms, high voltage transmission yards, and other distribution areas or switch stations must be kept locked at all times, and unauthorized people should be notified not to enter or tamper with the equipment therein. Adequate signage must be erected at the entrances.
- All distribution boards and transformers as well as multiphase sockets should be clearly labeled as to the type of voltage, AC or DC; the actual voltage, 220, 440, or other; what it feeds; and from which circuits it is fed.
- Educate employees in safety with electricity. Warn employees of the hazards and ensure good safety practices with electricity at all times.
- Where possible, only use double insulated equipment or equipment protected by ground fault interrupters (earth leakage devices). Ensure that the sockets being used are switched and that they have a ground receptacle.
- If in doubt, a qualified and authorized electrician should be consulted. Electricians have been appointed responsible for the safe maintenance and operation of electrical installations, and their advice should be followed at all times.
- Whenever working with items that have been connected to the electrical installation, wear the necessary PPE. Arc flash rules should be observed at all times.
- Joints in cables should not be allowed, unless they are properly made using the correct equipment, joint box resins, and so on. Merely taping the joints renders the electrical installation unsafe.

- Where possible, indicate the pathway and depth of all electrical cables that have been laid around the area. This will eliminate the problem of cables been accidentally dug up or damaged during excavation work or repairs or when contractors are seeking other items such as telephone cables and water pipes.
- The entire electrical installation, including distribution boards, switches, cables, and conduits, should be color coded according to the industry's color code.
- All electrical boards, boxes, isolators, switches, circuit breakers, cables, and conduits should be labeled at strategic positions indicating what they are, what they feed, where they originate, and what they contain (voltage and type of current).
- The entrances to all high voltage transformer yards should be locked at all times. Access to switch gear and other distribution centers must be either locked or restricted to authorized personnel only. The necessary signs must be posted as required by legislation.
- If flexible cables are rooted through walls and ceilings, then they start to become part of the fixed installation, whereas they are only meant for temporary use. Remove temporary electrical wiring and install the necessary permanent equipment.
- Regular polarity and phase checks should be carried out on any installation. To ensure that the single phase and neutral wires have not become accidentally reversed, annual checks on the polarity will give added safety to the installation.
- Where multiphase sockets are used and when any installation, maintenance, or additions have been carried out, or when suppliers have re-cabled, the phasing should be checked to ensure that the phases are correct.
- The ground continuity and the ground resistance from the main ground (earth) to the furthest electrical installation point should be measured regularly and compared with acceptable installation standards.
- The ground continuity will include an inspection of the earth mats, grounding cables, ground connections, ground spikes, straps, and all metal structures to ensure that they are grounded and that the resistance to ground is within acceptable standards.
- An annual inspection and test of the insulation resistance of certain circuits will also give an indication as to whether or not the insulation of the electrical conductors is as per accepted standards. Insulation may deteriorate with age, contact with corrosive substances, and exposure to heat or vibration, or the insulation may have been damaged during the initial installation of conductors.
- Electrical installations in hazardous atmospheres require specialized equipment installed by qualified people, and require annual checks to ensure the integrity of the installation. Records of these inspections should be retained for inspection.
- An arc flash risk assessment should be done, the necessary labelling and barriers erected, and the correct PPE provided, along with adequate training in arc flash safety methods.

AUDIT OF AN ELECTRICAL SAFETY PROGRAM

SMS STANDARD

The organization should have a SMS standard on the electrical safety program. This standard should be for the specific electrical installations and circumstances at that company. Within the standard, procedures for working on the installation must be clear and indicate the correct methods and steps for certain electrical tasks. This document should also form part of the training program for qualified employees who will do work on the installation.

WHAT TO CHECK

During the physical inspection, the auditors should check that the installation is safe and that no obvious hazards exist. Temporary wiring should not be allowed to become permanent. All warning and information signs and labels must be in place. No storage of goods should be allowed in switch rooms and substations. Regular checks on grounding and polarity should be done and recorded.

Since electrical requirements differ so vastly from workplace to workplace, the audit protocol will have to be modified to suit local conditions. The example below is a generalized audit protocol for an electrical safety program (Figure 65.1).

ELEMENT/PROGRAM/PROCESS	POINTS	QUESTIONS THAT COULD BE ASKED	VERIFICATION	WHAT TO LOOK FOR
ELECTRICAL SAFETY PROGRAM				
GENERAL ELECTRICAL INSTALLATIONS				
Risk assessment of total installation	5	Has a risk assessment been carried out?	Copy of document	
ELECTRICAL INSTALLATIONS SAFE		How often is the installation inspected?	Inspection report	Is all wiring safe?
Appointment of authorized persons	5	Who are authorized to work on the installation?	Appointments/lists	Is unauthorized access to switchgear and sub-stations restricted and locked? Panels and faceplates in position and locked/secured?
General checks	5	Is the electrical installation on a checklist used for inspections?	Copy of completed checklist	Are any flexible cords/cables routed through or along walls, floors or ceilings?
Temporary wiring	5		Visual	Is there any unsafe temporary wiring?
Unsafe wiring	5		Visual	Are there any damaged or faulty switches, plugs, joints, fuse boxes or distribution boards?
GFCI (Earth Leakage Device)	5	Where are GFCI's installed?	Visual	Is all wiring safe? GFCI's fitted in hazardous locations (sink/bathroom/near water/extension cords).
GROUNDING AND POLARITY CHECKS				
Installations been checked for grounding and polarity per NFPA regulation	5	Is a polarity check carried out? At what intervals? Is the grounding system checked? What items are checked and how often?	See a copy of the checks. Work orders and results of grounding tests	
ELECTRICAL EQUIPMENT IN HAZARDOUS LOCATIONS (Atmospheres)				
Hazardous locations identified	5	Are there any hazardous locations?	List of areas. Copies of installation checks done.	
Areas where found identified?	5	How often are inspections carried out?	Plan with classifications.	Condition of classified equipment.
Is all classified equipment on register?	5	Is a record kept of the inspections?	Copy of checklist.	Installation and maintained per applicable code.
Are the inspections up-to-date?	5	Who does these inspections?	Protocols for maintenance and inspections	
Has the person responsible for inspecting and maintaining equipment been trained?	5	What check-list is used or what standard is used?	Copy of training	
TOTAL	60			

FIGURE 65.1 Audit Protocol for the Element – Electrical Safety Program.

66 Electrical Arc Flash Safety Program

DESIGN OF AN ELECTRICAL ARC FLASH SAFETY PROGRAM

During an arc flash, electric current leaves its intended path and travels to the ground, or from one conductor to another, through the air. There are a number of factors that can cause an arc flash, including equipment failure, incorrect procedures, or corroded equipment. Injuries can be devastating, as arc flash temperatures can reach 35,000°F (19,426°C).

Numerous arc flash explosions occur daily across the United States, and it is estimated that arc flash accidents are responsible for roughly 7,000 injuries a year as well as a number of arc flash–related fatalities. Some 2,000 workers are treated in specialized burn trauma centers each year as a result of arc flash injuries. Electrocution is the fifth leading cause of workplace fatalities in the United States, and around 60% of these fatalities are caused by burn injuries.

Potential causes of an arc flash may include:

- Workers mistakenly dropping tools on live parts
- Pests entering switchgear through openings
- Faulty operation of a load break switch
- Dust or moisture accumulating to weaken air insulated bus bars
- Improper use of test equipment

OBJECTIVE OF AN ELECTRICAL ARC FLASH PROGRAM

The objective of an electrical arc flash safety program is to ensure that risks arising from electrical arc flashovers are identified and correctly labelled, that boundaries are defined, that the appropriate personal protective equipment (PPE) is specified and available, and that the necessary training has been done.

The arc flash protection program could consist of the following objectives:

- To complete an arc flash risk assessment throughout the company
- To endeavor to eliminate the risk of arc flash by incorporating alternate operating methods
- To label and identify arc flash risk equipment, switchgear, devices and circuits, and so on.
- To include in the label the flash hazard boundary, the flash hazard, the shock hazard, approach distances, and the level of arc flash personal protective equipment (AFPPE) needed for that particular situation

- To make appropriate AFPPE available to employees in respective areas
- To provide initial and ongoing arc flash awareness training for employees and affected contractors

The arc flash risk assessment process should consider the safety hierarchy of control, and consideration should be given to:

- The elimination of the arc flash hazard entirely
- The reduction of the arc flash hazard where possible
- The removal of the person from the arc flash hazard (mechanical or remote operation)
- Methods to contain the arc flash hazard
- The reduction of exposure to the arc flash hazard
- The system of work

IMPLEMENTATION OF AN ELECTRICAL ARC FLASH SAFETY PROGRAM

RESPONSIBILITY AND ACCOUNTABILITY

Each area manager, supervisor, and contractor (Responsible persons) should be responsible for the application of this standard in their work area where there is the possibility of electrical arc flash occurring.

PROTECTING WORKERS

To prevent arc flash incidents from occurring, equipment should be de-energized before beginning work. The industry standards are designed to protect workers and the workplace in the few instances where turning off the power could create a greater hazard to people or processes than leaving it on.

BOUNDARIES

Specific approach boundaries have been designed to protect employees while working on or near energized equipment. These boundaries are

Flash protection boundary: The outer boundary is the farthest established boundary from the energy source. If an arc flash occurred, this is where a worker would be exposed to a flash which could result in a curable second-degree burn. AFPPE should be worn to prevent second-degree or greater burns in the event of an arc flash.

Limited approach boundary: This is the distance from a live part where a shock hazard exists and where an unqualified person may safely stand. No untrained worker should approach any closer to the energized part than this boundary.

Restricted approach boundary: Only qualified workers who have completed required training and who wear appropriate AFPPE should cross this boundary. Ideally, the worker should have an approved work permit and written job safe procedure (JSP) for the job. The JSP should include shock-prevention procedures designed to keep all portions of the worker's body from crossing the prohibited approach boundary at any time.

LABELING

Each piece of equipment operating at 50 volts or more (and not put into a de-energized state) must be evaluated for arc flash protection. After the arc flash hazard analysis is completed, warning labels should be printed and affixed to the electrical equipment. The labels should include the level of AFPPE required, the flash hazard boundary, the flash hazard, the shock hazard, and approach distances.

ELECTRICAL ARC FLASH SAFETY PROGRAM TEAM

An arc flash team should be established to implement the initial arc flash safety program. The objective of the arc flash safety program would be to qualify and prepare the arc flash team to perform the following actions professionally and according to international standards and best practices:

- To predict the amount of available incident energy due to electric arc exposure on all electrical installations and distribution systems, via means of an arc flash risk assessment
- To perform an arc flash risk analysis using the short circuit current analysis, and overcurrent protective device, time current characteristic
- To develop and apply a proper labeling system for all situations where required, indicating the flash hazard boundary, the flash hazard, the shock hazard, approach distances, and the level of AFPPE to be worn
- To develop and present arc flash awareness and information workshops
- To select appropriate AFPPE and equipment, devices, and tools that reduce injury in the event of an arc exposure
- To develop JSPs for tasks involving arc flash hazards
- To train all affected employees and contractors in the JSP

ARC FLASH RISK ASSESSMENT (AFRA) INFORMATION COLLECTION

The AFRA is to be done by collecting information needed, such as diagrams, conductor specification, equipment in service, devices, and tools, and it should include tasks and processes that expose employees to arc flash hazards. Engineering analysis and fault analysis is to be done according to the latest methods. Arc flash hazard calculations needed for labeling, training, and the selection of the correct level of AFPPE shall be done on equipment/installations/switchgear that may pose a threat of arc flash injury. This shall include single and three-phase systems.

Training for the arc flash team should include practical exercises and learning forums which should cover the following:

- How to conduct an AFRA throughout selected sections of the company to identify equipment/installations/switchgear and so on that pose an arc flash potential according to the following standards: Arc flash requirements, National Electrical Code®, National Fire Protection Association 70E®, Occupational Safety and Health Administration (OSHA), and Institute of Electrical and Electronic Engineers (IEEE) Standard 1584a.
- How to explore means to reduce the exposure to arc flash hazards before considering AFPPE, which should be considered as the last level of defense.
- Use of special devices or tools used in the AFRA process.
- The method used to perform the needed calculation for each item, group of equipment, or installation to determine the risk, flash hazard boundary, flash hazard, shock hazard, approach distances, and proper level of AFPPE needed.
- How to select and apply the appropriate standardized labeling.
- Instruction on how to apply the arc flash JSP.
- How to conduct pre-work meetings to explain limits, safe work procedures, and use of proper AFPPE, equipment, devices, or tools.

AUDIT OF AN ELECTRICAL ARC FLASH SAFETY PROGRAM

The organization should have conducted an arc flash risk assessment on all electrical installations. If arc flash risks were identified, these should be listed and the appropriate calculations should have been done, and labeling must be in place. The AFPPE for each situation, as well as the hazards and boundaries, should be included in the labels. A formal training program should be in place, and workers should have attended this training. Written verification documents concerning the arc flash program must be scrutinized and rated during the audit (Figure 66.1).

ELEMENT/PROGRAM/PROCESS	POINTS	QUESTIONS THAT COULD BE ASKED	VERIFICATION	WHAT TO LOOK FOR
ELECRICAL ARC FLASH SAFETY PROGRAM				
Risk assessment done	5	Has an arc flash risk assessment been done?	Copy of the assessment	
AREAS EQUIPMENT IDENTIFIED				
All arc flash hazards identified	5	Have all the arc flash hazards been identified?	List of hazards	Visual
CONTROL MEASURES APPLIED				
Hierarchy of safety control	5	Were other control measures considered?	Documented efforts	
CALCULATIONS COMPLETED				
Flash hazard boundaries	5	Have the boundaries been identified?	Example of boundaries declared	Inspect electrical equipment where this has been done
Flash hazard	5	Has the flash hazard been calculated?	Example of calculations	
Shock hazard	5	Has the shock hazard been calculated?	Example of calculations	
Approach distances	5	Have approach distances been determined?	Example of calculations	Check visually
Arc flash PPE levels	5	Have the levels of AFPPE protection been determined?	Example of calculations	
LABELING DONE				
All labeling completed	5	Has all the labeling been completed	Labeling process timelines or similar	Visual
ARC FLASH PPE SUPPLIED				
Levels identified	5	What levels of AFPPE are used?	Example of levels approved	
Adequate AFPPE available	5	Is it available at all sites?		Inspect for storage and adequacy
ARC FLASH TRAINING				
Awareness training	5	Is there an awareness training program?		
AFPPE training	5	Is AFPPE training done?	Copy of syllabus	Employee interview
Refresher Training	5	Is there some follow up training?	Schedule/attendance register	
TOTAL	70			

FIGURE 66.1 Audit Protocol for the Element – Electrical Arc Flash Safety Program.

67 Contractor Health and Safety Management Program

DESIGN OF A CONTRACTOR HEALTH AND SAFETY MANAGEMENT PROGRAM

The purpose of a contractor health and safety management program (CHSMP) is to advise the prospective contractor of the health and safety requirements required by the hiring company before work is undertaken. This will help ensure that the necessary safety requirements will be in place on the contract site, and that the contractor will maintain a safe and clean worksite at all times.

The CHSMP has the following components:

1. The pre-contract document
2. The Contractor Health and Safety Management Program
3. Due diligence
4. Roles and Responsibilities
5. Hazard and Risk Assessment
6. Controls

THE PRE-CONTRACT DOCUMENT

When tenders are called for, this document, as well as the contractor safety rule book, should be sent to each contractor tendering (bidding) for the contract. Only bids that accompany the completed pre-contact safety requirement document will be considered for award. The contractor must be informed that any false information on the questionnaire will automatically disqualify them from obtaining the contract.

Example of a Contractor Pre-contact Document

The following document is sent to the bidding contractors:

The enclosed contractor safety rule book is included for your reference as it contains the health and safety standards to be implemented and maintained on the contract worksite at all times.

1. Please provide the following details about your company: name, company number, company size (turnover), and number of employees.
2. Attach details of your organization's experience in the area that you are tendering for, including details of previous contracts and references.

3. Attach a copy of your company's most recent health and safety policy, and list the qualifications and experience of persons appointed as onsite safety coordinators.

4. Please enclose copies of your safety arrangements relevant to this contract, to include:
   - Correct barricading of excavations
   - On-site safety talks
   - Safety inspections
   - On-site first aid facilities
   - Firefighting arrangement and equipment
   - Personal protective equipment (PPE) and clothing
   - Traffic signage
   - Emergency procedures
   - Fall protection plan
   - Lock-out, try out, and tag out

5. Provide the names and job titles of those people in your organization with the following responsibilities:
   - The person with ultimate responsibility for health and safety (managing director/CEO)
   - The person who would have responsibility for the day-to-day management of aspects of this contract
   - The person(s) appointed as health and safety coordinator(s) for the site.

6. Provide details of the experience and qualifications of the person who will have day-to-day responsibility for the safety of this contract.

7. Enclose any sample copies of any risk assessments undertaken relevant to this contract. Include:
   - General risk assessments
   - Material safety data sheets and assessments for all substances that you propose to use (if applicable)
   - Any other relevant assessments (e.g. working near energized lines, cables or equipment, manual handling, noise, etc.)

8. Provide details of health and safety training provided to all managers, staff, and sub-contractors (when used).

9. Include details of any future plans you have for future training if you win the contract.

10. Do you anticipate using sub-contractors on this contract? If yes, please provide details of the procedures you will use to ensure that they are competent and managed correctly.

11. Provide details of the accident near miss incident reporting and investigation procedures to be adopted for this contract. (The Contractor may agree to use the company accident/near miss incident reporting and investigation system).

12. Have any legal proceedings relating to health and safety been taken against your organization in the last three years? If so, please provide details.

13. Please provide details of any fatalities and accidents to employees or non-employees experienced by your organization during the last contract.

14. Please provide details of your emergency arrangements and procedures that you will use on this contract.
15. Please outline your health and safety plan for this contract.

IMPLEMENTATION OF A CONTRACTOR HEALTH AND SAFETY MANAGEMENT PROGRAM

THE CONTRACTOR HEALTH AND SAFETY MANAGEMENT PROGRAM (CHSMP)

The CHSMP outlines general health and safety requirements for the consistent management of risks associated with the contract work. A contractor performing the work for the company is to meet or exceed the company's health and safety requirements.

DUE DILIGENCE

Due diligence means that employers shall take all reasonable precautions to prevent injuries at a worksite. Due diligence is a legal concept, in that if a person is charged with a contravention of health and safety legislation, due diligence may be used as a defense if the person can establish that all reasonable precautions were taken to protect the health and safety of workers.

Due diligence be can demonstrated by:

- Performing hazard identification and risk assessments
- Orientating contractors
- Verifying qualifications, where required
- Performing start-up meetings
- Monitoring work (work observations)
- Involving senior management where problems arise.

ROLES AND RESPONSIBILITIES

On behalf of the company, the contract administrators are to orientate the contractor prior to work starting. They must verify that the contractor is informed of hazards and that they are aware of and abide by the applicable safety requirements included in the company health and safety management system; policies, standards and procedures; the company safety rulebook; the contract specifications; and the local health and safety legislation.

Contractors are to:

- Be aware of and abide by the applicable safety requirements included in local health and safety legislation.
- Understand the company CHSMP, company policies, standards, and the company safety rulebook.
- Ensure employees have the appropriate skills, ability, and qualifications to perform work.
- Ensure employees are fit for work and not under the influence of drugs or alcohol.

- Attend start-up meetings, where required, prior to starting work.
- Ensure activities under their control are adequately supervised.
- Perform regular hazard identification and risk assessment exercises.

HAZARD IDENTIFICATION AND RISK ASSESSMENT

The purpose of hazard identification and risk assessment is to identify hazards and evaluate the risk of injury or illness arising from exposure to a hazard, with the goal of eliminating the risk or using control measures to reduce the risk on the contract site.

The contractor shall perform ongoing documented hazard identification and risk assessments for the contracted work. The assessments shall identify competencies required of the contractor, as well as controls and barriers required to guard against identified hazards.

The assessments shall include identifying which company policies, standards, procedures, and processes apply to the situations. The company health and safety department may be consulted to establish a risk ranking of the work.

Hazard Identification and Risk Assessment Process

A hazard identification and risk assessment process includes:

- Identifying tasks done during and for completion of the work
- Identifying potential hazards for each task
- Determining level of risk, using probability and consequence on the risk matrix
- Identifying controls to put in place, with consideration given to how effective and adequate the proposed controls would be

Types of Controls

There should be multiple layers of controls protecting contract workers from hazards and associated risks.

The types of controls could include:

- Elimination – which would mean changing the way the work is to be done
- Engineering controls – such as re-design of a worksite, equipment re-design, and tool re-design
- Administrative controls – such as re-design of work methods and re-scheduling of work
- Health and safety system controls – such as safety policies and standards, work procedures, training, and PPE

AUDIT OF A CONTRACTOR HEALTH AND
SAFETY MANAGEMENT PROGRAM

The audit team should review the pre-audit documentation sent to the contractor to ascertain if it gathers enough information about the contractor and its commitment to safety on projects. The qualifications of the site safety coordinator should be examined as well as the contractor's past record concerning previous contracts. The site inspection should include the contract work area, and spot checks on items such as lifting gear, scaffolding, and other items should be carried out to ascertain if the contractor's health and safety management system is working. Site conditions should be compared with the required standards, and training records should indicate that the contractor and employees have received adequate safety orientation training from the hiring company. Safety department personnel should conduct regular inspections of the contractor's site and highlight any deficiencies to the contractor for rectification (Figure 67.1).

ELEMENT/PROGRAM/PROCESS	POINTS	QUESTIONS THAT COULD BE ASKED	VERIFICATION	WHAT TO LOOK FOR
CONTRACTOR HEALTH AND SAFETY MANAGEMENT PROGRAM				
PRE-BID DOCUMENT				
Pre bid document	5	Is a pre bid document sent to the bidding contractors?	Copy of document	
Pre-bid questionnaire	5	Is a pre-bid questionnaire submitted?	Copy of document	
HEALTH AND SAFETY MANAGEMENT PROGRAM				
Company contractor rule book	5	Is the rule book sent as part of the pre-bid documents?	Copy of rule book	
Safety orientation	5	Do contractors and employees attend orientation?	Training attendance sheets	
DUE DILIGENCE				
Due diligence conducted	5	Has a due diligence study been carried out for the work?	Example of what was done	
ROLES AND RESPONSIBILITIES				
Responsible person	5	Has the responsible person been identified?	Document	
On site Coordinator	5	Have onsite safety coordinators been appointed?	Appointment / qualifications	Site inspection
HAZARD IDENTIFICATION AND RISK ASSESSMENT				
Hazard identification	5	How are site hazard identifications done?	Copy of example	
Risk assessment	5	Have risk assessments been done on site?	Copy of some risk assessments	
CONTROLS				
Hazard elimination	5	What steps are taken to eliminate site hazards?	Proof of hazard reduction	Site inspection
Controls in place	5	What other safety controls are in place on site?	Examples in writing	Site inspection
ONGOING INSPECTIONS				
Follow up inspections	5	Are follow up inspections done?	Copy of site inspection sheet	
Action taken	5	Is action taken if hazards are identified?	Example of action taken	
TOTAL	**65**			

FIGURE 67.1   Audit Protocol for the Element – Contractor Health and Safety Management Program.

68 Summary

INTEGRATING HEALTH AND SAFETY MANAGEMENT SYSTEMS

The health and safety management system (SMS) in operation at an organization must be integrated with and operate alongside the day-to-day management of the operations. It is a major component of an organization's management system and should be based and run on the same principles as the organization's system.

ELEMENTS, SYSTEMS, PROCESSES, AND PROGRAMS

There are numerous elements, systems, processes, and programs that constitute a fully-fledged SMS. Not all could be included in this publication. This does not mean that they are not important, as some may be critical to specific workplaces. Rather than delve into the specifics of each element, it is hoped that the examples given can be used as models on which to design, implement, and audit those elements that are part of the organization's specific SMS.

Diverse workplaces have specific risks and need to implement the applicable SMS elements, processes, and programs. Based on sound risk management principles, the selection and application of those elements will lead to gaining control of potential areas of accidental loss.

EXAMPLES OF OTHER SMS ELEMENTS

Some of the SMS elements not covered in this publication, but which are just as important as the ones discussed, include:

- Portable electrical equipment control system
- Safety signage program
- Food safety program
- Welding safety program
- Blood-borne pathogens control program
- Ladder safety
- Illumination
- Ventilation systems
- Public safety
- Hand tool safety
- Safety checklists
- SMS documentation control system

Other elements may be local regulatory requirements specific to the type of industry. Applicable elements should be grouped into sections of a SMS and an element standard written to integrate it into the existing SMS. Ongoing audits should monitor the efficiency of the element's application and lead to a continual improvement process. All elements, programs, and processes of any SMS must be risk-based, management-led, and audit-driven.

References

ASK-EHS Engineering and Private Ltd. (2017). (Surat, India) Ask-ehs.com. *Types of Safety Audit and Effectively Conducting Them.* https://www.ask-ehs.com/blog/ehs-audit/types-of-safety-audit/

Bird, F. E. Jr. and Germain, G. L. (1996). *Practical Loss Control Leadership* (3rd ed.). Loganville, Georgia: Det Norske Veritas.

International Labor Organization (ILO). (2012). *Encyclopedia of Occupational Health and Safety* (4th ed.). Culture and Safety Policy. Copyright © International Labor Organization 2012. http://www.ilocis.org/documents/chpt59e.htm

McKinnon, Ron C. (2014). *Changing the Workplace Safety Culture*, Boca Raton, FL: CRC Press.

National Fire Protection Association. (NFPA). (2018a). *NFPA 101® Life Safety Code®.* https://www.nfpa.org/codes-and-standards/all-codes-and-standards/list-of-codes-and-standards/detail?code=101

National Fire Protection Association. (NFPA). (2018b). *NFPA 1 Fire Code.* https://www.nfpa.org/codes-and-standards/all-codes-and-standards/list-of-codes-and-standards/detail?code=1

Occupational Safety and Health Administration (OSHA). (2016). *Recommended Practices for Safety and Health.* https://www.osha.gov/shpguidelines/docs/OSHA_SHP_Recommended_Practices.pdf

Occupational Safety and Health Administration (OSHA). (2019). *Recommended Practices for Safety and Health Programs.* https://www.osha.gov/shpguidelines/hazard-Identification.html

Royal Society for the Prevention of Accidents (ROSPA). (2013a). *Health and Safety Audits e-Book.* http://safety.rospa.com/safetymatters/info/safety-audits-ebook.pdf

Royal Society for the Prevention of Accidents (ROSPA). (2013b). *The Five Step Guide to Risk Assessment.* https://rospaworkplacesafety.com/2013/01/21/what-is-a-risk-assessment/

Van Vliet, V. (2009). *14 Principles of Management (Fayol).* Retrieved (2019) from ToolsHero. https://www.toolshero.com/management/14-principles-of-management/

Index

For Product Safety Concerns and Information please contact our
EU representative GPSR@taylorandfrancis.com Taylor & Francis
Verlag GmbH, Kaufingerstraße 24, 80331 München, Germany